PRAISE FOR *A PRESCRIP*
CARING IN HEALTHCARE LEADERSHIP

A Prescription for Caring in Healthcare Leadership is a much needed, timely, and extraordinary work. The cost of leaders not caring is stunningly high and often harmful to caregivers, patients, and families. But it doesn't need to be that way. In this wonderful book, Dr. Josh Hartzell, offers engaging case examples, evidence from current research, and practical prescriptions showing how caring healthcare leaders can attain the highest levels of engagement and performance. And the most beneficial action you can take right now is to care for yourself by reading this book. I highly recommend you study it, take it to heart, and put its lessons into practice. You'll thank yourself, and so will your colleagues, team members, patients, clients, and family.

JIM KOUZES, coauthor of the bestselling
The Leadership Challenge, and a Fellow of the Doerr
Institute for New Leaders, Rice University

The concepts in this book create a bold new framework for how to approach leadership in the healthcare setting. Now, more than ever, healthcare professionals need a shared understanding of how caring as a leader can dramatically increase retention, lessen burnout and improve patient outcomes.

CHRIS BUSKY
CEO, Infectious Diseases Society of America

A Prescription for Caring in Healthcare Leadership is a vital roadmap for helping to heal our healthcare system. It is recommended reading for all who lead—or aspire to lead—in healthcare.

DR. PHILLIP M BOISELLE,
Medical School Dean

Dr. Hartzell led in military medicine for 25 years and based on his experience, as well as interviews with other leaders, has provided practical insights and actionable steps for leading with empathy and taking care of your people. This book emphasizes the importance of caring for caregivers, building resilient teams, and fostering a culture of well-being—all key to enhancing patient outcomes, reducing burnout, and ensuring organizational success.

> KIM "KC" CAMPBELL, Author of *Flying in the Face of Fear: A Fighter Pilot's Lessons on Leading with Courage*

Dr. Hartzell has reinforced how real physician leaders best care for the patients and families they serve! The book is packed with "prescriptions" for providers to bring caring and inspired leadership to life.

> LIEUTENANT GENERAL, US ARMY (RET.) MARK HERTLING Author of *Growing Physician Leaders: Empowering Doctors to Improve Our Healthcare*

"A Prescription for Caring in Healthcare Leadership: Building a Culture of Compassion and Excellence" is an essential guide for anyone who seeks to lead with both heart and purpose. Josh Hartzell's approach to leadership challenges the myth that caring is "soft" and instead shows how caring deeply for those we lead results in stronger teams, improved organizational outcomes, and personal transformation. Through tangible steps and insightful "prescriptions," this book provides practical tools that will help leaders cultivate compassion, foster excellence, and create brave spaces for innovation and ongoing learning.

In a world where healthcare demands more than ever, this book is a timely reminder that leading with care is not just a choice but a necessity. For those who are ready to embrace a new way of leading and inspire the next generation, *"A Prescription for Caring"* is a must-read. It's more than a book—it's a call to action. If you're committed to shaping the future of healthcare, Josh Hartzell's work will inspire you to lead with courage, compassion, and authenticity.

SARAH K. WOOD, MD
Director, Harvard Macy Institute

Page after page I found myself mentally circling, underlining, and staring at the guidance on becoming a great leader in this gem of a book, organized on sound educational principles to maximize impact. This is a must-read for leaders and future leaders in medicine!

COLLEEN CHRISTMAS, MD, FACP
Rosemarie Hope Reid, MD Professor
Director, Primary Care Leadership Track
Johns Hopkins School of Medicine

Dr. Josh Hartzell leans on his 20+ years in leadership roles in military and academic medicine as well as interviews with other leaders to encourage caring inspired leadership in healthcare. Given the high costs of training healthcare team members, rising rates of burnout in this group, and the challenge in replacing team members, a new approach focused on caring, team development, and investing in individuals makes intuitive sense. Dr. Hartzell advocates that healthcare workers who focus so much attention on patients and their needs also require real attention to their own needs. He presents the case that leaders should care deeply for their team members and should do everything possible to support them. As he states in the book, "Your number one priority should be taking care of your people in whatever arena you are leading."

TED O'CONNELL, MD, FAAFP
Director of Medical Education
Kaiser Permanente Northern California

There's no better way to describe leadership in healthcare than caring-inspired leadership. Written for leaders in healthcare, A Prescription for Caring in Healthcare Leadership, sets the bar high for leaders in any profession or industry who aspire to leading an organization founded on compassion and excellence. Hartzell's brilliant integration of examples and impact weaves a thought-provoking narrative of the traits, skills and behaviors that we should all expect in 21st century leaders.

DAVID SMITH, PHD & BRAD JOHNSON, PHD
Authors of *Good Guys and Athena Rising*

This book will supercharge your leadership skills, change how you care for yourself and your team, and optimize your performance. Dr. Hartzell distills his knowledge and experience from over 25 years as a leader in military medicine to bring readers practical tools, tips, and tactics to help reframe their mindset, rethink their leadership practices, and hopefully create joy for themselves and their teams.

MATTHEW WATTO MD, Cohost, *The Curbsiders*
Internal Medicine Podcast

Although Americans spend more to obtain healthcare any other citizens on earth, we fail too many of them too often. The U.S. currently ranks 57th in the world in adult life expectancy. Dr. Hartzell has a recipe for turning things around. If we want our healthcare teams to do a better job caring for patients, those who manage them must do a better job of caring for their teams. Having worked at every level of healthcare from "hospital orderly" to health system CEO, I can personally attest that Dr. Hartzell's approach works. This is a "must-read" book for all current and aspiring healthcare leaders. If you are on the front end of your career, it's not too early to start. And if you are responsible for thousands of employees and billions of dollars in annual revenue, it's not too late to learn.

ARTHUR L KELLERMANN, MD MPH

It was my privilege to practice and serve with Josh Hartzell in the Army Medical Corps, and I can attest from firsthand experience that he understands and lives out the caring leadership model he espouses. In this book, he provides a comprehensive perspective that both administrative and clinical leaders can apply in their own efforts to care for colleagues and drive improved performance in healthcare organizations.

WILLIAM JACKSON, MD, MBA

Healthcare is a dumpster fire right now. This timely and important book provides tangible ways to become a more effective leader.

ANDREA AUSTIN, MD, Author of *Revitalized: A Guidebook to Following Your Healing Heartline*

Dr. Hartzell expertly guides us down the path to caring-inspired leadership. Through interviews with top leaders and a masterful application of leadership science, we come to understand the caring approach and are prepared to apply it in a way which is both effective and genuine. His words will leave you with much to think about and even more to do, in the best possible way!

PATRICK E. YOUNG, MD, MACP, FACG, FASGE
Trustee, American College of Gastroenterology

A PRESCRIPTION FOR CARING IN HEALTHCARE LEADERSHIP

Building a Culture of Compassion and Excellence

JOSHUA D. HARTZELL, MD
COLONEL (RETIRED), U.S. ARMY

Foreword by

MARK C. CROWLEY
Author of *Lead From The Heart: Transformational Leadership For The 21st Century*

ISBN: 979-8-89316-344-5 Copyright © 2024 by Joshua Hartzell

A Prescription for Caring in Healthcare Leadership:
Building a Culture of Compassion and Excellence

ISBN: 979-8-89316-344-5 Hardcover
ISBN: 979-8-89316-475-6 Paperback
ISBN: 979-8-89316-474-9 eBook

Illustrations: Yeonsoo Sara Lee, MD

Dedication

To Grant and Emilia. You are the inspiration for everything I do. I love you both more than anything and am so proud of who you are. I love how you treat others and that you are already caring leaders! I look forward to seeing the amazing impact you will have on our world.

To my fellow healthcare providers. You deserve the best in leadership. My hope is that this book is a step in that direction so that all of us can raise our leadership game to support each other, our patients, and our trainees.

Contents

Foreword

SEVERAL YEARS AGO, I attended a funeral service for a family friend and ended up sitting next to a man named "John," who was later introduced to me as being a recent author.

As I'd just begun writing my own book, I was very interested in discovering what genre and topics John wrote in and to hear about his experience with agents and publishers.

As it turned out, my new acquaintance worked directly for Don Miguel Ruiz, author of the massive bestseller *The Four Agreements*. To reward John for all of his years of dedicated service, Miguel Ruiz gave him permission to write a sequel to *The Four Agreements*—this time applied to one specific industry of his choice.

At this point in his telling, John said he could have written *The Four Agreements For Architects* or *The Four Agreements For Teachers*. Miguel Ruiz simply asked him to choose an industry he believed was in the most need for leadership wisdom. He then asked me to guess which profession he picked.

I called out car salespeople, lobbyists, stockbrokers, politicians, and bankers. Each time he told me I was wrong. When I finally told him I'd given up, he said he chose *The Four Agreements For Healthcare*.

I thought he'd made a big mistake—I assumed that healthcare leaders (professional caregivers!) would naturally be more enlightened and informed—and I challenged him to explain his selection. I'll never forget the surprise I got when he told me that years of research had proven healthcare was one of the most toxic industries in existence.

Perhaps it's because so much focus and attention are routinely given to patients and *their* need for care—that far less energy gets devoted to the very people being asked to do the healing and nurturing?

Suffice it to say that because no one can sustainably give what they themselves don't have, healthcare professionals and organizations today must take steps to correct this. They must make it their intention to care about every single person who contributes to the success of their medical practice—large or small.

Josh Hartzell is a medical doctor himself. He has not only diagnosed the profound need for caring-inspired leadership in healthcare but has also identified the treatments, regimens, and remedies for the major ailments endemic to the industry: employee burnout, high turnover, and low engagement.

It's both ironic and important that some of the most compelling reasons why caring-inspired leadership affects people so deeply— and motivates them to put their hearts into their work—comes directly from medical science.

Please read on to learn how you can become an even more effective leader, one who leads with both your heart and your mind in greater balance. The rewards for mastering this work will be inestimable.

Mark C. Crowley, author of *Lead From The Heart: Transformational Leadership For The 21st Century*

The HealthCARE Leadership Pledge

Take care of your people and they
will take care of the mission.

*A*S A CARING-INSPIRED LEADER, *I deeply care about the people I lead and will do everything I can to support them. By caring for them, they will flourish, and they will ensure the success of our organization.*

As a caring-inspired leader, I deeply care about the purpose of our organization and its success. Our organization will positively impact the lives of those we serve through our actions.

I care as a leader and pledge to:

Take care of myself, personally and professionally.

Take care of my people and support them personally and professionally.

Be guided in leadership by my values.

Be present.

Be humble.

Listen.

Set high standards to help others achieve greatness.

Hold people accountable and give feedback to help them grow and improve.

Delegate effectively and for growth.

Invest in those I lead through mentoring, coaching, and sponsoring.

Lead for diversity, equity, and inclusion.

Advocate for those I lead.

Be a positive force of energy at work.

Recognize and thank those I lead.

As a caring-inspired leader, my legacy is composed of the people and lives I have impacted as a leader.

Introduction

*"No one cares how much you know until they
know how much you care."*
—*Theodore Roosevelt*

A S PHYSICIANS AND HEALTHCARE providers, we are called to a profession of caring for others. As leaders, we need to use that same desire to care for those we lead. Connecting to our roots as healers and caring for others is the key to effectively leading in this space. Caring-inspired leadership, the term for this approach to leadership used throughout the book, provides a way to ensure our patients get the care they need. It supports the well-being of those providing the care and training of the next generation. Being leaders inspired by caring is about creating cultures of compassion and excellence. This type of leadership is needed now! If you are reading this book, then I know you want to be that type of leader. The future is ours to shape with a new approach to leadership in healthcare—caring-inspired leadership.

Think about the best leader you have worked with. What do you remember most about them? My guess is that you remember how they cared about you. They cared just as much about you as a person as they did about your work. You worked hard and did not want to let them down because of how much they cared. Leadership is no longer about being the biggest or strongest or even the smartest. It is about getting the people who follow you to maximize their potential for their own growth and for the success of our teams, organizations, communities, and families. Just as you were inspired and motivated by leaders who cared, we need caring leaders to help us meet the challenges of today. The idea of caring as a leader may not be what you first envision, but as you read this book, you will see that when caring is placed at the center of what we do as leaders, it 100 percent makes sense. If we care as leaders, it should inspire and drive all the other actions we take.

We need effective leadership now more than ever. We are faced with numerous challenges at every level of medicine, from the patient's bedside to the C-suite. While this book is written for leaders in healthcare, the principles and ideas are applicable in any arena. The places we work need effective leaders to help our organizations thrive, whether that refers to providing patient care, providing electricity, providing services to others, etc. Our communities need leaders of integrity committed to helping them best serve those we live around and with. Our states and national governments need leaders who care less about being reelected and more about taking actions that best serve and care for their constituents. Our families need effective leadership so we can help our sons and daughters have the exceptional and meaningful lives that every parent wants for their children. This book provides a prescription to challenge us to be more effective leaders knowing that all of us impact others daily through our actions. If you are impacting or influencing someone else in your life, then you are a leader. This book is for you.

What gives me any credibility to write a book about leadership? I am fortunate to have been a student of leadership for over thirty years. I served twenty-five years in the United States Army and in military medicine. During that time, I learned from both amazing and not-so-amazing leaders, shaping and sharpening my approach to leadership. Many of these powerful lessons are shared in this book. I am convinced they can help you lead more effectively.

Let me share with you part of my leadership journey in more detail.

I have spent most of my life thinking about and studying leadership, specifically leading in military medicine. I didn't realize until recently that studying leadership was a hobby of mine. Over time, I have turned that into part of what I do professionally, but looking back, I appreciate that I have always been fascinated by and trying to learn more about leadership. This book will capture many of these stories.

As a kid, I was drawn to history. That may be an understatement...I *loved* history. When I was less than twelve, I remember lying in bed reading books about Abraham Lincoln, Daniel Boone, George Washington, Anne Frank, and other historic figures. I was attracted to their stories and how they led. I loved how Lincoln was able to overcome multiple failures to not only become president but also lead the country during one of the most important times in our history. I was inspired by the fact that someone who came from a rural area with a poor background could ascend to become president. It was motivating for a kid in Northwest Pennsylvania to think this was possible. Daniel Boone was a rugged outdoorsman and, much to the liking of my parents, it made me want to spend time outside, playing in the woods. George Washington, of course, was our first president and led the U.S. to victory in the Revolutionary War. He taught me about humility and being resilient when faced with adversity. Anne Frank taught me courage and optimism. These stories of leadership were compelling and sparked my interest to read more. Much to the chagrin of my two kids (currently ages 14 and 12), I try to get them to read about leadership and history as well.

Given my love of history and the military, I decided to pursue the Army as a career. In complete disclosure, my family was not exactly wealthy, so a secondary bonus was that the Reserve Officer Training Corps provided a path to a free education. That said, it wasn't exactly free, as I was obligated to serve four years of active-duty service once I graduated medical school. Once in ROTC, I was immersed in leadership. We had classes specifically devoted to leadership development, and we were always being evaluated and given feedback on our leadership.

Following college, I was fortunate enough to be accepted to the Uniformed Services University Medical School, which is the military's medical school. It was my first choice for medical school because I had decided that I wanted to make the Army my career. After graduating, I completed my medical training in Internal Medicine and Infectious Diseases. I was interested in both because they gave me the ability to take care of some of the sickest patients in the hospital. I also enjoyed learning about tropical infections and diseases related to travel. Understanding, treating, and ideally preventing infections are critically important in the military, as we have service members deployed across the globe.

I spent twenty-five years on active duty in the military, serving in a variety of roles before retiring in August 2023. This included multiple roles in medical education, including being a program director for the internal medicine residency at Walter Reed National Military Medical Center. I spent six months deployed to Afghanistan between 2009 and 2010 as a battalion surgeon with the 82nd Airborne Division. These experiences contributed to my leadership development and thinking about how to develop others as leaders.

For the past seven years, I have been developing a leadership curriculum for junior military officers. I have also been fortunate enough to teach about leadership at medical meetings nationally and internationally and to serve as an adjunct faculty member at the Massachusetts General Hospital Institute of Health Professions, teaching leadership to students from across the globe.

I by no means consider myself an expert on leadership development. In fact, one of my favorite quotes by retired Army colonel and former Vice President of Population Health at the University of Maryland, Dr. Chuck Callahan, is "Leadership experts aren't. If someone says that they're an expert, they may be selling something!" A friend, mentor, and two-time medical school dean who teaches leadership, Dr. Wiley Souba, says, "We never become leaders; we are always becoming leaders."

My hope is that you will let me be part of your leadership journey so we can explore why caring should be a foundational value that guides your leadership together. Leaders who care are more effective and create the environment to support those they lead so they can accomplish the mission. Ultimately, leadership driven from a place of caring is what is needed to best lead at this time in history, but I will let you decide that on your own, after reading the book.

The idea for this book took off after I was invited to be on the Leading the Rounds podcast to talk about leadership development in medicine.[1] I was asked what I had learned from medicine and how that shaped my leadership. After reflecting on nearly twenty years of being a military officer and a physician, my answer was that the key to leading is taking care of those you lead. If you care for those you lead, then they will accomplish the mission.

Too often, people talk about how they care about those they lead, but their actions fall short. This book takes the idea of caring as a leader and makes it real. It provides tangible steps to allow leaders to truly take care of their people, supporting them so they can flourish. In doing so, team and organizational performances improve.

From early in our careers as Army officers, we were taught about the importance of taking care of those we lead. Many may assume that leading in the military is about authority and giving orders that Soldiers, Sailors, Airmen, or Marines simply follow. This could not be further from the truth. During Army ROTC, instructors would routinely emphasize the importance of taking care of the men and women being led. How are their feet after a long road march? Do they have blisters? Did everyone have enough food? As officers, you only eat after those you lead have eaten. If your followers are sleeping in the field and getting wet, you should be sleeping in the field next to them. The importance of being present as a leader and experiencing what those you led were experiencing was paramount. If you want those you lead to follow you, you have to show them that you care about them. If you do, then they will do everything in their power to accomplish the mission.

"Mission First, People Always" Versus "People First, Winning Matters"

For a long time, the mantra in the Army was "Mission First, People Always." You cannot accomplish the mission without taking care of those you lead. You might be able to in the short term, but long-term organizational success is dependent on taking care of those you lead. This slogan, however, clearly put the mission before the people.

When I interviewed retired Major General Jeff Clark for this book, he explained that when he was the 82nd Airborne Division Surgeon, the division commander, Major General (MG) Mike Steele (who retired as a Lieutenant General), would repeatedly say, "When accomplishing our mission and taking care of our people and their families conflict, good leaders find ways to do both." Clark added, "If you're mediocre, you can probably do one or the other, [but] he expected us to be good leaders."

Personally, having worked with MG Clark, I know that this was more than just words. It was clear that he made both a priority. Generals Clark and Steele were clearly on to something—good leaders do both: accomplish the mission *and* take care of their people.

When General James McConville was Chief of Staff of the Army (top Army Officer), he, along with Secretary of the Army Ryan McCarthy, updated the slogan.[2] They summarized their leadership philosophy as "People First, Winning Matters." General McConville said, "We win through our people. People want to be on winning teams. People want to have a purpose in their life. That's why people must be a priority."[3]

This is a subtle but important distinction. The primary emphasis was on the people and not the mission. The directive was clear. Take care of our people and we will win. The number one priority was our people. Your number one priority should be taking care of your people in whatever arena you are leading. When you take care of your people, they complete the mission.

Anyone can issue orders, but that does not make you a leader. You are a leader when others follow simply because of who you are. Think of people you respect the most as a leader. If they asked you to do something, would you do it? My internal medicine residency program director, Dr. Greg Argyros, was beloved by us as residents. He pushed us hard and had extremely high expectations—it was clear he expected us to excel at medicine. There was also the expectation that we would work hard, and he did not feel sorry for us. My intern year in medicine was prior to the eighty-hour work rule, so we worked more than eighty hours routinely. If we made mistakes, we were held accountable. We knew how much he cared about our professional development and our families. He advocated to hospital leadership, without fear of backlash against him, to make sure we had what we needed to be successful. He listened to our ideas and empowered us. Changes were made to rotations and curricula based on our feedback. He created opportunities for us to shine through research, presentations, hospital committees, and ensuring we were prepared for life after residency. Every single act came from a place of caring. We knew he cared, and we would do anything for him. He was the model of a caring leader and still is, as you will see through his interview comments throughout this book.

Over the course of my career, I've seen many examples of caring leaders who have inspired and taught me how to effectively lead and run teams and organizations. These stories will be shared throughout the book to emphasize the lessons taught. It's never been the person who's the loudest, yelled the most, or made you do things. In fact, those are leaders who get tuned out after a while. It's the leader who is investing in you to develop your career and support your family who you want to work the hardest for. The purpose of this book is to help readers think about how placing caring at the center of everything we do as leaders allows us to be more effective.

Dr. Amy Oxentenko, who was interviewed for this book, talked about how we can implement intentional efforts of practicing caring as a leader to becoming caring leaders:

I have always cared deeply about the people I'm leading. It comes naturally. I suspect many caring leaders don't even have to think about this, as it may be a strength that allowed them to rise to the position they are in and is innately wired. They just do it. There are others who are looking to develop this skill set, recognizing it as a growth opportunity. Those individuals probably need to put some thoughtfulness into how to operationalize a plan so that it can be practiced with some regularity. At some point, you would hope it then becomes more natural so someone does not have to be internally reminded to find ways to be caring. It just becomes the thing to do. I'm certain it's teachable in that regard, and just something to think about and plan a little bit more methodically, at least to begin with, before it becomes second nature.

Leadership is like a muscle—the more you use it and practice, the stronger and more flexible you become. The purpose of this book is to help people develop the skills needed to be intentional about being caring as a leader. Each chapter ends with a Prescription for Caring in Leadership. The prescriptions include multiple tangible steps called "Caring Acts of Leadership" that you as a leader can implement. Each step is based on experience, advice from other leaders, and evidence about leadership. I have curated resources for each topic, drawing from leadership authors and teachers for those who want to take a deeper dive. Following the prescriptions for leadership in this book will make you a better leader and person, will improve your teams and organization, and will create followers who will be inspired to follow you.

As you read this introduction, I hope you are excited to change your life as a leader and the lives of those you lead. I am fired up to see how you will implement these ideas personally, for your organizations, and for your family and community.

Let's get started!

Biographies of Interviewees

I AM DEEPLY GRATEFUL TO the leaders who agreed to be interviewed for this book. Conducting these interviews was like getting a PhD in leadership education. They are tremendous examples of leaders who care deeply about those they lead. I wanted to introduce them to you at the beginning of the book so you had a sense of who they are upfront. Throughout the remainder of the book, I do not always give or highlight their position.

The titles and degrees people have and how we refer to them is important. This book is written for all leaders in healthcare, which is why I tried to capture voices of physicians of different specialties, allied health professionals, nurses, and other leaders within and outside of healthcare. When reading the book, if someone is a DO or MD, they will be referred to as "Dr." Those who hold a PhD or doctoral degrees in other professions will have their degrees listed after their name. The reason for using this approach is that I wanted to help readers recognize which lens someone was speaking from. Each caring leader is introduced with their brief bio below. Their lessons are woven throughout the book.

Greg Argyros, MD, MACP, FCCP
Retired Colonel, U.S. Army

Dr. Argyros is the president of MedStar Washington Hospital Center and the senior vice president for MedStar Health. Prior to this role, he served as senior vice president, Medical Affairs, and chief medical officer for MedStar Washington Hospital Center, providing overall clinical leadership and oversight, including quality of care, medical education, and research.

Prior to his arrival at MedStar Health in 2012, Dr. Argyros spent twenty-five years in the Medical Corps of the U.S. Army, most recently serving as chief of medicine at Walter Reed Army Medical Center and director of education, training, and research for the Joint Task Force National Capital Region Medical. In these roles, he was responsible for ensuring the successful merger of Walter Reed and the National Naval Medical Center.

Dr. Argyros graduated from the U.S. Military Academy at West Point and received his medical degree from the University of Pittsburgh. He completed his internal medicine residency at Walter Reed and was elected to Alpha Omega Alpha Honor Medical Society. He completed a fellowship in Pulmonary and Critical Care Medicine at Walter Reed. Board-certified in internal and pulmonary medicine, Dr. Argyros is a fellow of the American College of Chest Physicians. In 2012, he was named a Master of the American College of Physicians (ACP), an honor presented to physicians who demonstrate eminence in practice, leadership, or medical research.

Laurie K. Baedke, MHA, FACHE, FACMPE

Laurie K. Baedke is a faculty member, the director of Healthcare Leadership Programs, and the assistant dean of Physician Leadership Education at Creighton University. Ms. Baedke is a well-regarded speaker at international healthcare and continuing medical education conferences. She is also the host of a weekly leadership podcast, *The Growth Edge.* She holds a master's degree in healthcare administration and is a board-certified fellow of both the American College of Healthcare Executives and the American College of Medical Practice Executives. She has written two editions of a book, *The Emerging Healthcare Leader: A Field Guide.* In 2017, Ms. Baedke contributed a chapter titled "The Clinician Entrepreneur" to a book published by Oxford Press titled *The Handbook of Private Practice.* Her most recent book, *Mentor, Coach, Lead to Peak Professional Performance*, was released in February 2023.

Caroline A. Blackie, MS, OD, PhD

Dr. Blackie is the head of medical and scientific operations at Johnson and Johnson Vision. She leads a global team of talented leaders and innovators who help bring to life sight-enhancing and -transforming technologies. She is an internationally recognized speaker and subject matter expert in ocular surface disease and is widely published in the peer-reviewed literature. Her career as a clinician, scientist, and corporate leader spans diverse geopolitical, economic, and cultural environments (three countries, two continents) and has afforded her a broad spectrum of leadership opportunities. Her experience has taught her that whether she is serving in a mentor-mentee relationship or on a global team in a highly matrixed corporate context, sustainable success is achieved through daily commitment to creating and nurturing a conscious and caring culture. This is executed by diligently prioritizing people, then purpose, and then performance, in that order—not the reverse.

Charles Callahan, DO
Retired Colonel, U.S. Army

Dr. Chuck Callahan is a retired Army physician-executive who has served in a range of leadership positions over thirty-five years. He began as a pediatrician, then moved on to pediatric pulmonologist and pediatric intensive care physician. In the last decade of his military career, he served as the chief medical officer, chief operating officer, and chief executive officer of military facilities and health systems in the Washington, D.C., area. His global health experience includes the care of patients with Ebola in Sierra Leone. He is the author of more than 100 abstracts, articles, books, and book chapters and has been awarded more than two million dollars in research grants in asthma, telemedicine, and population health. From 2015 to 2024, he served as the vice president of Population Health at the University of Maryland Medical Center in Baltimore, supporting the medical center's efforts to improve the health and well-being of the people of West Baltimore. During that same period, he also provided city and state public health leadership during the COVID-19 pandemic. He and his wife of forty-three years live in West Baltimore, where he continues to practice pediatric pulmonology and to work supporting the community, endeavoring to live out a simple credo: love God, follow Jesus, care for others, and do good work well.

Jeffrey B. Clark, MD, MPH, MSS, FAAFP
Retired Major General, U.S. Army

Dr. Jeff Clark is a family physician with extensive executive-level leadership experience. He believes in building and serving with diverse, cohesive, highly productive teams by ensuring common understanding and collaborative, value-based decision-making. During his thirty-five years of military service, he assumed increasing responsibility in healthcare leadership and management by serving as CEO at the clinic, hospital, academic medical center, and regional levels, as well as COO and CMO at the enterprise level. Following retirement from the military, he served as a primary and community care officer for Medicaid, State of New Mexico. He currently serves as a Defense Health Agency senior leader mentor, the medical director for Semper Fi & America's Fund, and a chair of the board for *WarDocs: The Military Medicine Podcast.*

Angela Costa, RN, BSN, MPM
Chief Nurse Executive, Allegheny
Health Network (AHN)

As the Chief Nurse Executive (CNE) for AHN, Angela Costa serves as the voice of the organization's 6,000 nurses. Ms. Costa has led the implementation of best practices in nursing that has made AHN a preferred destination for nursing professionals. She works closely with the chief nursing officers at each of AHN's affiliated hospitals to innovate and improve the quality of nursing practice across the organization, as well as provide exceptional care to patients and their families.

Ms. Costa has helped implement and expand several nursing workforce programs meant to recruit and retain nurses and create new roles and schedules that meet nurses' personal and professional expectations. Throughout her career with AHN, Ms. Costa has served in roles of increasing responsibility, including most recently as the chief nursing officer of AHN West Penn Hospital, the vice president of clinical nursing operations, and the CNO/COO of Canonsburg Hospital. Ms. Costa's areas of clinical expertise include trauma, critical care, and neurology/stroke. She received her Bachelor of Science in Nursing degree from Duquesne University, and she later received a Master of Public Policy and Management degree from Carnegie Mellon University.

At West Penn, Ms. Costa also led the nursing team's successful journey to become Southwest Pennsylvania's only four-time Magnet-recognized facility—the industry's gold standard for nursing quality. Ms. Costa was also part of a select group of healthcare professionals invited to the White House to meet with President Barack Obama regarding patient care and access.

She serves on the Allegheny Credit Union board and is a member of the Hospital and Health System Association of Pennsylvania's Nurse Ambassador Advocacy Initiative. Ms. Costa also is active in the American Organization for Nursing Leadership (AONL) and Partner for Work, and she is a member of Palladium's board of directors.

Suzanna Fitzpatrick, DNP, ACNP-BC, FNP-BC, FAANP

Suzanna Fitzpatrick, DNP, ACNP-BC, FNP-BC, FAANP is a nurse practitioner at the University of Maryland Medical Center in Baltimore, Maryland, where she has worked since 2008. She is a clinical program manager with expertise in surgical patients, transplants, oncology, and emergency medicine. She began her healthcare journey as a paramedic, which she has continued doing as a volunteer for the past twenty years. Her educational background includes a BS from the University of Maryland, Baltimore County (2004) in Emergency Health Services; a BSN from Villa Julie College (2008); a Master's in Nursing in Acute Care (2010); a Post-Master's certificate from George Washington University in Family Practice (2013); and a Doctorate in Nursing Practice (2020) from the University of Maryland, Baltimore. Her doctoral work focused on teamwork and collaboration with emergency nurses. She was inducted as a Fellow of the American Association of Nurse Practitioners in 2023.

She has a passion for mentoring novice nurse practitioners in their transition into practice and in their professional development. She has written articles on teamwork, nursing leaderships, and transition shock for novice practitioners. She is a coauthor of *Innovative Leadership For Health Care,* a workbook that provides healthcare workers with frameworks and tools based on the most current research in leadership, psychology, neuroscience, and physiology to help them update or innovate how they lead and build the practices necessary to continue to update their leadership skills. In addition, she is an adjunct professor, teaching doctoral nursing students.

She is a co-founder of the Healthcare Leadership Community of the International Leadership Association, and she serves on several editorial boards, including the board of directors for the Society of Vascular Nursing.

Chelsea C. Hayes, SPHR

Chelsea C. Hayes, SPHR is a global corporate trainer and executive coach. Her Los Angeles–based firm, The Coaching Factory, specializes in interactive experiences in management, leadership, and inclusion. Her clients include powerhouse brands like PepsiCo, General Mills, Morgan Stanley, Eli Lilly, NBC, GE, Genentech, and Kendo by LVMH. She travels the world, listening to how people feel at work and then guiding them toward greater harmony.

Mark Hertling, DBA
Retired Lieutenant General, U.S. Army

Retired Lieutenant General Mark Hertling served for thirty-eight years in the U.S. Army as a tanker and cavalryman, serving at every level from tank platoon leader on the East-West German border to Commander of the U.S. Army, Europe, and the 7th Army. Mark served a total of thirty-eight months in combat—as a major in a cavalry squadron during Desert Storm, as an Assistant Division Commander in the 1st Armored Division in Baghdad in 2003 to 2004, and as the Commander of the 1st Armored Division and Multinational Task Force Iron in Northern Iraq in 2007 to 2008 during the surge. His other commands include the Army's Initial Military Training Command (Basic Training), the Army's National Training Center in California, the Joint Multinational Training Center in Europe, an Armored Brigade Combat Team focused on reinforcing the Korean Peninsula, and the Army's first Stryker Brigade. Hertling was also the Joint Staff War Planner (J7) during 9/11 and after.

After retiring from the Army, Mark became a senior vice president for a major healthcare organization in Orlando from 2013 to 2018. He was appointed to the President's Council on Fitness, Sports, and Nutrition by President Obama in 2014, and in 2021, he was appointed by President Biden to be a commissioner of the American Battle Monuments Commission, where he now serves as chairman. Mark was an adjunct scholar at West Point's Modern War Institute, and he now serves as a professor of Practice of Strategic Leadership at the Crummer School of Business at Rollins College. He is an executive member of the Dean's Alliance at Indiana University's School of Public Health. Since 2013, Hertling has served as a military and national security analyst for CNN/ CNN International.

A graduate of the U.S. Military Academy at West Point, he holds a master's degree from Indiana University and a doctorate degree from the Crummer School of Business at Rollins College. Mark is married to his best friend, Sue. They have two sons and five grandsons.

Jeff Hutchinson, MD
Retired Colonel, U.S. Army

Jeff Hutchinson, MD served twenty-five years as an Army Physician before retiring and moving to Austin. He has a BS in Chemistry from West Point and a Medical Degree from the University of California in San Francisco. His combat, clinical, and academic leadership experience provides expertise in strategic planning, communication, and education—including as a current advisor for the National Academy of Medicine Culture of Health Program. As an adolescent medicine specialist currently working at People's Community Clinic, a Federally Qualified Health Center, he cares for children and young adults ages ten to twenty-five. His mission is to help mission-driven individuals and organizations who want to have a positive impact on the arc of the moral universe leading to justice. He is a leadership and organizational consultant providing services across the country as an expert in diversity, equity, and inclusion. You can learn more about Dr. Hutchinson and his work at **www.wadealliance.com.** He believes everyone should strive to be both a lifetime learner and exerciser.

W. Brad Johnson, PhD

W. Brad Johnson, PhD is a professor of psychology in the Department of Leadership, Ethics, and Law at the United States Naval Academy. He is a faculty associate in the Graduate School of Education at Johns Hopkins University. A clinical psychologist, Dr. Johnson is a mentoring expert specializing in developing gender-inclusive mentoring cultures for organizations around the globe. Dr. Johnson is the author of numerous publications—including fourteen books—in the areas of mentoring, professional ethics, and gender inclusion. Recent books include *Good Guys: How Men Can Become Better Allies for Women in the Workplace, Athena Rising: How and Why Men Should Mentor Women* (both with David Smith), and *The Elements of Mentoring, 3rd Ed.* (with Charles Ridley).

Darilyn V. Moyer,
MD, MACP, FRCP, FIDSA, FAMWA, FEFIM
Executive Vice President and Chief Executive
Officer of the American College of Physicians

Darilyn V. Moyer, MD, MACP, FRCP, FIDSA, FAMWA, FEFIM is the Executive Vice President and Chief Executive Officer of the American College of Physicians (ACP). Board-certified in internal medicine and infectious diseases, Dr. Moyer was elected into

Mastership (MACP) in ACP in 2022, which recognizes outstanding and extraordinary career accomplishments. She is a Founding Board Member of the Gender Equity in Medicine and Science (GEMS) Alliance, former president of the Council of Medical Subspecialty Societies, and former member of the board of directors and immediate past chair of the board of directors for the Primary Care Collaborative. Dr. Moyer is a member of Women of Impact and is the 2020 Recipient of the American Medical Women's Association Elizabeth Blackwell Award, as well as the recipient of the 2020 Lewis Katz School of Medicine at Temple University Alumni Achievement Award.

Prior to becoming ACP's EVP and CEO, Dr. Moyer was a professor of medicine, executive vice chair for Education in the Department of Medicine, internal medicine residency program director, and assistant dean for graduate medical education at Lewis Katz School of Medicine at Temple University.

Alexander S. Niven, MD, FACP, FCCP
Retired Colonel, U.S. Army

Dr. Alexander S. Niven is a consultant in the Division of Pulmonary and Critical Care at Mayo Clinic and a professor of medicine in the Mayo Clinic College of Medicine and Science. He is the director of the Academy for Educational Excellence and serves as the education chair for both the Division and the Critical Care Independent Multispecialty Practice. Dr. Niven is the co-director of the Checklist for Early Recognition and Treatment of Acute Illness and Injury (CERTAIN), a global checklist-based program that improves processes of care and patient outcomes in the critically ill. He is also the medical co-director of the Mayo Clinic Pulmonary Function Laboratory in Rochester, MN.

Dr. Niven is a retired Army colonel and adjunct professor at the Uniformed Services University of the Health Sciences. During his twenty-one years of active-duty service, he held a variety of leadership roles, including medical director for the intensive care unit and respiratory therapy services, program director for an internal medicine residency, and designated institutional official and chief of education and research at the Army medical center level.

Amy S. Oxentenko, MD, FACP, FACG, AGAF

Dr. Amy Oxentenko is a professor of medicine and currently serves as the vice dean of Mayo Clinic Practice. She completed her IM Residency, Chief Residency, and GI Fellowship at Mayo Clinic Rochester, being a recipient of the IM Residency's Outstanding Achievement Award, GI Division's Bargen Award, and Institutional Mayo Brothers' Distinguished Fellowship Award. After joining the faculty at Mayo Clinic in Rochester, she served as program director of Mayo's GI Fellowship and Advanced GI Fellowship Programs, later transitioning to the role of IM Residency Program Director and serving as associate chair for education for GI and for the Department of IM. She then transitioned to chair of medicine at Mayo Clinic in Arizona in 2020. In the fall of 2022, she transitioned from her role as chair of medicine in Arizona to serve as vice dean of Mayo Clinic Practice across all practice sites.

She is a former chair of the American College of Gastroenterology's Women in GI and Finance Committees, she chaired the ACG Educator Task Force, and she has served on numerous ACG committees. She has co-created and co-chaired the ACG Train-the-Trainer USA Program and served as vice chair for the World GI Organization Train-the-Trainer Program. Dr. Oxentenko has served as a senior associate editor for *The American Journal of Gastroenterology*. She has been a member of the ACG Board of Trustees since 2017 and is now a member of the ACG Executive Team, serving as president-elect, with ACG presidency planned in October of 2024. She also serves as vice chair of the ACGME Internal Medicine Review Committee.

She has been the recipient of the Mayo's Department of IM Distinguished Contributions to Medical Education Award, Mayo Clinic School of GME Program Director of the Year Award, Minnesota's ACP Laureate Award, and Mayo Clinic Distinguished Educator Award. She was named the 2020 Woman Disruptor of the Year by Healio GI and has been named as one of the "Top 100 Alumni" by her undergraduate alma mater.

David Smith, PhD

David Smith, PhD is coauthor of the book *Good Guys: How Men Can Be Better Allies for Women in the Workplace* and *Athena Rising: How and Why Men Should Mentor Women*. He is an associate professor at the Johns Hopkins Carey Business School. A former Navy pilot, Dr. Smith led diverse organizations of women and men, culminating in command of a squadron in combat, and flew more than 3,000 hours over thirty years, including combat missions in Iraq and Afghanistan. As a sociologist, he focuses his research in gender, work, and family issues, including allyship, inclusive mentorship, gender bias in performance evaluations, and dual-career families. He is the coauthor of numerous journal articles and book chapters that focus on gender and the workplace.

Anne Thompson, PT, EdD

Dr. Anne Thompson is a physical therapist and educator. She has held leadership roles in clinical teams, healthcare, and academic administration. She has impacted patients and learners in her forty-five years through roles including interim vice president of academic affairs; interim dean, College of Health Professions; and chair of the Department of Rehabilitation Sciences at Armstrong State University. She has been a clinician and administrator in multiple healthcare organizations. She currently teaches in the leadership track of the PhD in Health Professions Education Program at Massachusetts General Hospital Institute of Health Professions.

Amy Vertrees, MD

Amy Vertrees, MD is a board-certified general surgeon, Army veteran, certified coach, author, and founder of the BOSS Business of Surgery Series. She served seventeen years in the Army, reaching the rank of lieutenant colonel and deploying three times to Afghanistan and Iraq as a general surgeon. After leaving the military, she was an employed surgeon who then created Columbia Surgical Partners, a private practice general surgery group. She discovered there were lessons that she was never taught in residency that were necessary for a successful surgical career. She created the BOSS Business of Surgery Series to fill in that gap and has used everything that she has learned to become a successful private practice general surgeon. The BOSS series includes a highly rated podcast, group coaching, 1:1 coaching, and the book *Become the BOSS MD: Success Beyond Residency*. You can learn more about her and her work at her website: www. bosssurgery.com.

Caring in Leadership and Why It Matters

CHAPTER 1

The Link Between Caring and Leadership

"I think that caring and leadership are synonyms. I never met a leader that I admired that wasn't also caring."
—Chelsea C. Hayes, SPHR

CARING-INSPIRED LEADERSHIP IS WHEN every action leaders take is done with the act of "care" in mind. Leaders care enough to take care of themselves, take care of the well-being of those they lead, be there, listen, set high standards, give feedback, and receive feedback. They care enough to invest in those they lead with mentoring, coaching, and sponsorship, and they care enough to be grateful. These actions become easier and more impactful when taken with the idea of caring for the individual as the driving force. Caring leaders prioritize people.

Being an effective, caring leader starts with taking care of ourselves and then caring about the people we work with and for. Leaders work for those they lead along with their own leader. They answer to and care about and support their boss, but in the truest sense, they should prioritize that they work for those they lead. This is an important distinction because it means that as a leader, your ultimate success comes from the success of those you lead, not always from making your boss happy.

Caring-inspired leaders care deeply about the mission of their organization. In medicine, this mission is ultimately about patient care. This includes the care of the patient's family members, as well as research, advocacy, and education of students, residents, and faculty. Too often, leaders think mission and people conflict, but in reality, they are intricately interwoven. Caring about your people and the mission should guide decisions and lead to success.

Dr. Jeff Hutchinson captured this during his interview:

> So what does caring really mean? We want to give it the altruistic term, like you said in the beginning—as doctors, we care about people, but care has to do with where your focus is. What are you concerned about? What do you care about? Do you care about your profit? Do you care about your people? Do you care about the customer? Care is not specific enough to say, "*That* is what makes a good leader," because all leaders care about something, but I think you need to hone it down to say, "do you care about the people in your organization as much as you care about the mission?"

I would add that if you *really* care about your mission, you also need to care about your people, because they are the ones who will accomplish the mission.

Dr. Amy Vertrees talked about how being caring as a leader is determined by where we spend our time and what we prioritize, and how that can be powerful:

> So what does caring mean? That I've assessed the situation. I've set my role in it, and I've deemed this is something that is

worthy of my attention. I have a desired outcome. When I care about something, I'm deciding this is a priority. I'm going to spend my time and my effort, my most limited resource... because if something means something to me, it's tapping into the purpose of why I'm doing this. I don't feel like I have to do something. I don't feel like I'm forced to do something. I feel like it's an active choice, and I'm bringing my whole self along. I'm doing it from alignment and interest and the idea of how I want to show up as a person. That's what leads to me being caring, and that is a powerful place to be.

What do we spend most of our time on? The things we care about.

As leaders, the more we understand our people, the more we can influence them and lead them effectively. This means prioritizing our people and spending time really getting to know them. This leads to our ability to align their goals and interests to those of the organization. It allows them to show up fully at work and be motivated to accomplish our important missions.

Retired Lieutenant General (LTG) Mark Hertling has led thousands of men and women in combat and emphasized caring as a cornerstone of leadership:

> It influences all the elements of leadership attributes, competencies, influence, methods, context. I don't talk a lot about that in my book, but I teach it a lot in every one of those areas. The requirement between "leader" and "led" is trust, and if you break down, trust. The only way that you can really generate trust from a leader to followers is if the followers feel they are cared for...If you look at all the influence methods everywhere, from directive to participative leadership influence methods—all of them have a different element of caring inside of it, or caring for the subordinates.

LTG Hertling emphasized the importance of trust in leadership. Think about who you trust in your life at work and at home. That trust is built around knowing they care about you. They consistently act in ways that demonstrate they care for you, and it builds trust. LTG Hertling emphasized how caring is a catalyst for developing trusting relationships:

> ...from the beginning of your career—whether it be military or medicine—to the time when you're a four-star general or the CEO of a hospital or the president of a medical system... In each one of those contexts, there are different ways that you care for the individuals you serve. You know that caring is reflective of trust and trust is the bedrock of leadership.

Caring is not only the catalyst for trust; it is the spark that can ignite every aspect of your leadership.

The Evolution of Caring Impacting Leadership

The idea of caring in medicine is present throughout history. Medicine is founded on the idea of caring for others. Hippocrates emphasized this, saying, "Cure sometimes, treat often, comfort always,"[1] and of course, he is the author of the Hippocratic Oath that many medical students still recite. Plato stated, "Caring about the happiness of others, we find our own."[2]

While these ideals are taught to medical students and other health professionals, they are often only talked about in relation to patient care. It's important to remember they are just as important when leading. Should we not comfort others as leaders? Should leaders not want their followers to be happy? Should we not teach future leaders?

The first emphasis on caring in leadership comes from the work of Robert Greenleaf, who coined the term "servant leadership" in his book *Servant Leadership: A Journey Into The Nature of Legitimate Power and Greatness* (1977).[3] He wrote that leaders need to serve those they work for. You flip the organizational chart upside down, and leaders are responsible for serving those they lead. He only wrote about the concept of caring on four pages,[4] but it was clear caring was central to his view of serving others. Early in the book, he states, "This is my thesis: caring for persons, the more able and the less able serving each other, is the rock upon which a good society is built."[5] Later, he talks about the importance of leaders caring and points out, "Most trustees I know just don't care enough. If trustees really cared, ideas and people would blossom all over the place."[6]

Leaders were responsible for serving those who worked for them to accomplish the mission. He argued institutions also had an obligation to serve those for whom their mission was intended. This is just as important today, as hospitals, private practices, and clinics all have a responsibility to serve and care for their patients.

So how is servant leadership different from leadership with caring as the foundation? A friend and colleague who is now a practicing cardiologist in Washington state, Dr. Lauren Weber (prior Navy Commander and proven military leader—check her out on the *Leading the Rounds* podcast[7] to learn more about the concept of followership and how it applies to leadership), provided some useful insights about the difference between caring and servant leadership.

She said, "Servant leaders care deeply but function to shelter their people. It can lead to poor delegation, an overburdened leader, and burnout."[8] She added, "Servant leadership should die a fiery death, in my opinion—we lost some of brightest stars to burnout because of its unrealistic expectations."[9] She contrasted that with caring-inspired leadership: "Caring as the inspiration for leadership is about fostering growth and balance. Much like a parent, you provide guardrails, feedback, opportunities for success and failure. But your commitment to the person never wavers—your greatest achievement is that they outgrew you."[10]

Servant leadership, while similar to caring-inspired leadership, is different (as we will discuss throughout this book). Servant leadership is generally defined as an approach in which leaders serve those they lead. Caring-inspired leadership, a more recent approach to leadership, is about taking care of the people you lead as the central part of your leadership. Caring-inspired leadership has a broader application to what we do as leaders when compared to servant leadership. Maybe it is a nuanced point, but when we care about those we lead, the chapter topics in this book become more important. For example, it makes being present, setting high standards, giving feedback, and recognizing people for their amazing work even more important, because not doing those things would demonstrate you don't care. Once you really care about someone or the mission, you feel more obligated to act.

James Kouzes and Barry Posner wrote one of the most influential leadership books of all time, *The Leadership Challenge: How to Make Extraordinary Things Happen in Organizations*, which is now in its 6th edition.[11] In their book, they talk about the five practices of leadership: model the way, inspire a shared vision, challenge the process, enable others to act, and encourage the heart.

The last practice was revolutionary in leadership development circles. They emphasized the importance of expecting the best from those you lead, recognizing followers, and taking a personal interest in those you lead.[12] The authors mentioned that when giving a workshop early on, they were even asked to not use the word "heart."[13] This speaks to how the idea of caring—and, more so, love—are not considered effective ways of leading by some. Kouzes and Posner doubled down and wrote the book *Encouraging the Heart: A Leader's Guide to Rewarding and Recognizing Others*.[14]

The book elaborated on the data supporting encouraging the heart and emphasized that the "best leaders care."[15] The book provides "seven essentials of encouraging" the heart.[16] It is packed with specific ways leaders can encourage the heart and practice caring as leaders. It is another book that needs to be on the bookshelves of all caring leaders.

Mark Crowley: Lead from the Heart

The book *Lead From The Heart: Transformational Leadership for the 21st Century* by Mark Crowley may be one of the most important books ever written on leadership.[17] If you are a healthcare leader, when you are finished reading this book, make it a point to read *Lead From The Heart*. We will talk about this later, but make this a book you give to others as well. It is a seminal work on the link between caring and leadership that blends data, stories, and ultimately advice on how to lead from the heart and care for those whom you lead. Crowley has become an influential voice in leadership with a podcast as well called *Lead From The Heart*. We need more people to listen and adopt these ideas.

In his book, Crowley talks about his evolution as a leader and how he came to the conclusion that leading from the heart was the most effective way to lead. He emphatically states, "It's simply irrefutable that leadership is failing specifically because it lacks heart[18]...What I've learned and concluded is that we need a new model of leadership for a new age—a paradigm that acknowledges the humanity, the hearts—in people."[19]

Heather Younger: The Art of Caring Leadership®

Heather Younger is the author of *The Art of Caring Leadership®: How Leading with Heart Uplifts Teams and Organizations* and a strong proponent of caring leadership®.[20] Shocking, since it is in the title of her book and she has trademarked the phrase! She defines caring leadership® as "taking daily actions in ways that show concern and kindness to those we lead" and wrote, "The more that leaders care for those they lead, the more those who follow them will feel that care and go over and above, out of loyalty and deep gratitude, for the benefit of that leader, that team, and the organization. This is as compelling a reason as I can think to pursue the art of caring leadership®."[21]

She provides multiple ideas about how to do this, as each chapter concludes with "The Art of Caring Leadership® in Practice," with actions people can implement to be more intentional about caring leadership®.[22]

How to Become a Caring-Inspired Leader

The books above describe the evolution of caring related to leadership in literature. For me, I first learned about the importance of caring as a leader from my parents. Many of the people interviewed for this book who are examples of caring leaders also talked about learning from their parents or other important leaders in their lives.

Chelsea Hayes said,

> I realized that caring leadership 100 percent starts at home.
> I have two parents who are both very affectionate with me.
> Very. They told me every day, "I'm proud of you." I saw them
> caring for each other. I saw them caring for me. I saw them
> caring for my siblings at any cost, and so it has to come from
> somewhere. It does not just appear. When I find leaders I
> really look up to, I start talking to them about their stories,
> and I hear similar stories—that they got this infusion of caring
> somewhere in their early life, and then it has continued to
> bloom beautifully. That's why people are drawn to them...
> Even if it didn't come from a parent or caregiver, maybe when
> the person is twenty, they get their first boss, and they're like,
> "Whoa, this person cares about me..." So that's why humans
> are so important to each other, because it still has to come
> from somewhere...The "caring seed" has to be planted. Each
> of us potentially has the opportunity to be the first caring
> leader that someone has...Not potentially, we *do*, every single
> day when we go to work, when we open our eyes, when we go
> to a coffee shop or pick up our kids...every single day, we have
> that opportunity.

Amazing that we all have the opportunity to positively impact
someone's career and life in that way, every day. The whole
purpose of this book is to inspire people to have this impact and
provide intentional steps on how to be a caring leader.

My mom worked at Walmart, and there were numerous examples
of how she and her coworkers took care of each other. Watching
them demonstrated to me the importance of taking care of those
you worked with when something bad happened. If someone
was sick or a family member died, people circled around them,
providing meals to their families. They would provide resources
and they would be there for support. It was clear they cared
about each other. My mom often talked about personal issues

other employees were going through and how she or others were supporting them. This left a clear impression on me about the importance of taking care of those you work with. When my mom died of breast cancer, the number of people who came to her funeral was astounding. Almost everyone had an example of something she had done for them, how she had supported them, or simply how her positive attitude was inspiring.

She was a caring leader as a parent as well. Let's take a sojourn here to tell a story about my mom, because it may give you some insight into why caring for others is so important to me. When my mom was diagnosed with recurrent metastatic breast cancer, I was in medical school. One of her coworkers (Pat Owen—now "Grandma Pat" to my kids) ended up helping to take care of her at the end of her life. They were amazing friends, and it was an exceptional example of caring. Her friend was right there alongside the hospice nurses until the end. I am forever grateful to Pat and the love and care she showed and continues to demonstrate to my family and everyone she interacts with.

My mom was amazing. Despite significant deficits from brain metastasis, she was always all about serving others. My birthday occurred just a few days before she died. She had an eye patch because the brain metastasis had impacted her vision, and she had difficulty using her hands. That did not stop her from making me one last set of chocolate chip cookies. Actually, it was a chocolate chip cookie *birthday cake.* This act of love has been a constant reminder to me of what it means to care for others.

Which people in your life cared for you like this? Imagine how it would impact our lives if we all cared for each other in this way. Every lesson we talk about within this book relating to caring as a leader applies not just at work but at home as well. My hope is that this book will improve your family, relationships, and communities.

What Caring Acts of Leadership have inspired you in your life? How would your leadership be different if you used that kind of care as part of your leadership?

Caring-Inspired Leadership in Medicine

The idea that caring as a leader should be the model for leading in medicine is a relatively new one. While I don't think anyone in medicine would argue over whether leaders should care, it is not the first thing most of us think about when leading. There are many leaders in medicine who do not have roles in direct patient care; these leaders may not have the same perspective as those caring for patients. Moreover, the idea of being a caring-inspired leader and making caring the basis of our leadership has rarely been described. Hopefully, after reading this book, being a leader driven by caring will become the approach that all leaders in medicine follow.

Professor Michael West from The King's Fund, a charitable organization to improve healthcare in England, wrote a book called *Compassionate Leadership: Sustaining Wisdom, Humanity and Presence in Health and Social Care*.[23] He wrote, "The purpose of compassionate leadership in health and social care is to help create the conditions where all those in our communities are supported to live the best and most fulfilling lives they can."[24] According to West, "When leaders demonstrate compassion, they provide support in a way that is consistent with the core value orientation of those they lead."[25]

Put another way, when healthcare providers lead from a place of caring, we are being true to ourselves.

Dr. Tait Shanafelt is the Chief Wellness Officer at Stanford and a thought leader on well-being and leadership in medicine. You will see many of his articles and research highlighted throughout this book. He wrote a paper in the journal *Academic Medicine* in 2021 titled "Wellness-Centered Leadership: Equipping Health Care Leaders to Cultivate Physician Well-Being and Professional Fulfillment."[26]

It is open access and a must-read. Shanafelt and his colleagues review the last seventy years of approaches to leadership, then offer Wellness-Centered Leadership as a new model.

Wellness-Centered Leadership consists of three elements: "care about people always, cultivate individual and team relationships, and inspire change."[27] They break the model into the required mindset, behaviors, and outcomes. The model provides valuable insights into caring as a leader. It importantly provides over forty recommendations of actions (behaviors) that leaders can implement to being intentionally "Wellness-Centered Leaders."[28] These are actions that you could print out and look at daily—if not weekly—to see how you can lead more intentionally. The article has case studies as examples to emphasize points. One quote worth sharing highlights the importance of caring as a leader:

> *"Caring about people always is the only reliable foundation on which to build relational leadership skills that inspire individual and team performance."* [29]

West and Shanafelt have moved the conversation forward in terms of caring as a leader in medicine. This book will build upon their ideas but is based on a slightly different perspective—the perspective that everything we do as a leader should come from a place of caring. If we care, then there are certain things we must do as leaders. After twenty-five years in the Army and using field manuals for many things, I thought this book should be like an Army field manual. Therefore, it provides tactical steps called "Caring Acts of Leadership" for you on how to be a caring leader and improve the lives of those you lead, your patients, your trainees, and you.

Caring: The Bottom Line

The idea of caring-inspired leadership sounds great, but does it really work? As a physician, I have always been told to practice evidence-based medicine. In other words, what is the evidence behind the decisions we make? While there is an art to medicine, data and research drive much of what we do. At the same time, there is a push toward cost-conscious care. We want to provide the most effective care while doing it in the most economical way. So, why am I telling you all this? Because using a caring approach to leadership is evidence-based, and most of the leadership strategies we discuss in this book are incredibly cost-friendly approaches to leadership. You don't need to buy employees coffee machines and foosball tables for the office; rather, you need to create an environment where they feel like they are cared for and have purpose and meaning in their work. (Of course, good coffee is always a plus!)

There are two great quotes I use when creating the case for a particular argument. They are provided here together because they share the same message in slightly different ways. The synergy between them creates a clear method for how to argue for change. Throughout this book, I will build the case for caring in leadership based on this approach.

The first quote is from Dr. Don Wilson, dean emeritus of the University of Maryland School of Medicine. He said, "Facts tell and stories sell." The second quote is from a friend of mine and former Army psychiatrist, Dr. Patcho Santiago. He said, when trying to get a decision made in your favor, "Don't bring feelings to a math fight."

In order to convince someone to do something as a leader, you often need to use a combination of data and stories. Data will provide the numerical support and often the business case for a particular proposal, while stories go straight to the heart. Emotions are a powerful influence in decisions, and sometimes— depending on the situation—the cost, even if more expensive, is offset by doing the right thing. Throughout this book, I will use a mix of data and stories to support the argument that leadership coming from a place of caring is the most effective approach to leading teams and organizations.

Prescription for Caring in Leadership

1. Reflect on and write out your story of caring-inspired leadership. Think of someone like a parent, teacher, coach, family friend, or someone else who cared for you in your life. How did that make you feel? Make a list of actions they demonstrated to make you feel that way.

2. Think of a time when a leader cared for you. How did it make you feel? What specific actions did they take to make you feel important and valued?

3. Talk to your team about the concepts of caring-inspired leadership. Have them answer the two questions above and then discuss as a group the behaviors that are identified.

4. Read Mark Crowley's *Lead From The Heart*[30], Heather Younger's *The Art of Caring Leadership*[31], Kouzes and Posner's *Encouraging the Heart*[32], and/or Michael West's *Compassionate Leadership.*[33]

5. Read Dr. Tait Shanafelt's article on Wellness-Centered Leadership, available via open access at https://pmc.ncbi.nlm.nih.gov/articles/PMC8078125/.[34]

CHAPTER 2

Dismantling the Myth of Caring Being Soft

"One of the criticisms I've faced over the years is that I'm not aggressive enough or assertive enough, or maybe somehow, because I'm empathetic, it means I'm weak. I totally rebel against that. I refuse to believe that you cannot be both compassionate and strong."[1]
—Jacinda Ardern (Former Prime Minister of New Zealand)

ONE OF THE FIRST things people will say when we start talking about the importance of caring as leaders is that you can't be "soft" on people or they will take advantage of it. When people hear the word "caring," some will think about being "soft" as a leader. They equate the word or idea of caring with being overly nice to people and not having the fortitude to make hard decisions. They claim we avoid the difficult parts of leadership because we care too much about the people we lead. This is not true. Being a caring leader means that we must embrace some of the more challenging aspects of leadership even more so, *because* we care. Dr. Amy Vertrees—surgeon, author of *Become the Boss MD*,[2] podcaster, and coach—emphasized in our interview that "leaders have to be able to do difficult things, and to be able to do difficult things, you have to tap into the immense strength of caring. "

Let's debunk the myth that caring as a leader is being soft. Think about a teacher, coach, or leader you had growing up. Many of you can probably identify one who had extremely high standards and continually pushed you to improve and excel. They did not mince words. Were they hard on you? Did they give you a good swift kick in the butt? Probably at times, if you needed it—but in the end, you knew they had your best interest at heart. This is a model for caring as a leader.

> *Dr. Amy Vertrees—surgeon, author of Become the Boss MD,[2] podcaster, and coach—emphasized in our interview that "leaders have to be able to do difficult things, and to be able to do difficult things, you have to tap into the immense strength of caring."*

Caring as a leader is not always going to look the same. Chelsea Hayes pointed this out, saying, "I think that people associate caring with some soft and fluffy thing, and that is incorrect. The way that I show care to you in a professional setting may be different than the way I show care to my sister, and both are important. There are many ways to care, and some are gentle and others are not as gentle. One act of caring has the ability to change our lives forever."

Michael West, in his book *Compassionate Leadership*, wrote, "Compassionate leadership may be mistaken for a soft and ineffective approach to leading in health and social care, but more courage is required to lead compassionately than to lead using command and control."[3]

Caring often means making difficult decisions that, in the moment, may potentially anger those you are leading. This means holding people accountable for high standards, giving difficult feedback, having challenging conversations, and even at times firing someone. It means challenging the status quo and, as Michael West and Suzie Bailey wrote about in a blog post titled "Five Myths of Compassionate Leadership," not taking the easy way out.[4] The motive and manner in which these tasks are done is what makes them Caring Acts of Leadership. One does not have to be a jerk when going about these tasks. If we really care about our people, our organizations, and our missions, then we have to do all of these things in a caring way. I would not call any of these leadership actions "soft."

> "*Compassionate leadership may be mistaken for a soft and ineffective approach to leading in health and social care, but more courage is required to lead compassionately than to lead using command and control.*"
>
> —**Michael A. West**
> *Compassionate Leadership: Sustaining Wisdom, Humanity and Presence in Health and Social Care*

Dr. Amy Vertrees captured this way better than I could when she said, "I think you are trying to challenge the perspective that caring-inspired leadership is fuzzy and soft. It's actually monumental strength." There is a reason why she wrote a book! She added, "Caring seems to be almost, at its surface, weak—like I'm at the mercy of somebody else. I think it's the exact opposite. I think caring is centered around us. Boosting ourselves up, our power of individuality and our power of choice. Allowing us to be the best version of ourselves."

Building relationships, having high standards, holding people accountable, giving tough feedback, and working creatively to create the best work environment are hard work—much harder than forcing people to do things. Leading by coercion, force, or threats is the easy way out.

Angela Costa, RN, BSN, MPM emphasized the importance of caring and being approachable:

> Caring is kindness. It's not softness. If I have to tell someone directly what I need to do or what they need to do, I can do that. The thing is that if you're mean, people won't approach you, and you won't know what's going on. It's a softness in my eyes that makes me more receptive and approachable to people. If I'm approachable, then I can help you. If you're not approachable, you won't find out what people need or what's happening in your unit. Your people just won't tell you.

In summary, if you are a jerk as a leader, you will miss important things because people will not be comfortable coming to you. People will not bring you their innovative ideas. People may simply leave to find another job.

> *"I think you are trying to challenge the perspective that caring-inspired leadership is fuzzy and soft. It's actually monumental strength."*
>
> —Dr. Amy Vertrees, Author of Become the Boss MD

Being a caring leader is more challenging than leading from a place of not caring. It is easy to not do the things above if you don't care about the people you lead. Retired Colonel Chuck Callahan, who has commanded military hospitals and now leads in civilian medicine, put it this way:

Caring-inspired leadership is the model of leadership needed most of the time.

> As a leader, I rarely had to be a "hard ass." The vast majority of the time as a leader is not about being hard; rather, it's a matter of creating resonance and not dissonance. Let's face it: creating resonance is not an easy task. Bringing different people together in healthcare to meet the mission is hard work.

The data on demonstrating caring as a leader would support these leaders' sentiments as well. Throughout this book, we are going to give examples and data pertaining to how caring as a leader impacts specific outcomes. What we will see, time and again, is that being a caring leader and supporting those you lead improves outcomes in healthcare and in business. Michael West, after reviewing the data in writing his book on compassionate leadership, wrote, "Research on climate and culture in health and social care internationally suggests that leadership cultures of command and control are less effective than more engaging and compassionate leadership styles and implies that compassionate and collective leadership approaches are likely to be the most effective."[5]

Laurie Baedke emphasized, "There is an abundance of research that confirms time and again that behavioral competencies outperform technical competencies in leadership performance. They're not easy to master. They're exponentially harder. But they matter, perhaps exponentially more."

Dr. Ruth Gotian, Chief Learning Officer at Weill Cornell Medicine and author of the book *The Success Factor: Developing the Mindset and Skillset for Peak Business Performance*,[6] calls these skills "power skills" rather than "soft skills."[7] Dr. Gotian and Sarah

Groover, a PhD candidate at Oklahoma State University Center for Health Sciences, wrote a piece called "Five Power Skills for Becoming a Team Leader" for *Nature*.[8] The five skills are teamwork, communication, commitment and reliability, adaptability, and open-mindedness and empathy. They write, "Identifying and developing 'power skills'—the crucial abilities that enable a manager to connect with people, communicate effectively, adapt to the unexpected, and be open-minded—can help you succeed in a supervisory role."[9]

They also talk about how talent alone will not help you be successful as a leader, "Being talented in your field is important, but your impact can be much greater if you know how to lead and motivate the next generation."[10]

To lead and motivate is going to require you to understand how to use the skills mentioned above and throughout this book. It's time that we all start using the terminology of power skills, given their importance. It's time we start developing our power skills. This book is a great place to start.

I served twenty-five years in the Army and spent an additional four years in the Reserve Officer Training Corps while in college. While serving in the military, I learned that leaders need to take care of their people. I talked about this in the introduction but will expand a little more here to emphasize the point that caring as a leader is not soft.

The military is considered to have some of the best and "toughest" leaders. As I have observed and learned from while studying these leaders over time, it has become crystal clear that the most effective leaders are the ones who care the most about their people and the mission at hand. While we can always force someone to do something, it does not work in the long run. As retired Colonel Dr. Greg Argyros, currently the president of MedStar Washington Hospital Center, said, "I can use a sledgehammer once." Paraphrasing, he goes on to say, "That might be needed if there is a burning platform, but ultimately, people will only follow you if they know you, trust you, and feel like they are part of the solution."

Dr. Argyros says a preferred way of motivating people is having them "feel like they are part of the solution and not just being talked to. That has helped me umpteen times in the ten years I've been in leadership positions."

Navy SEAL and author Jocko Willink is a scary guy. He's muscular, has a shaved head, and speaks *very* confidently. He talks about CrossFit and jiu-jitsu and served in some of the most challenging combat during the Battle of Ramadi in Iraq in 2006.[11] At first glance, based on his profession and interests, you might not think that he would be a loud proponent of caring as a leader. However, he constantly talks and writes about leaders needing to take care of those they lead.[12] I am 100 percent certain no one would call Jocko Willink soft. Many of the best leaders I have worked with in military medicine recognize the need to take care of those you lead.

A great example of the importance of caring as a leader is in his book *Leadership Strategy and Tactics*.[13] He has a chapter titled "Taking Care of Your People with Discipline."[14] He says, "Discipline is the best way to take care of your people."[15] He goes on to say, when discussing the idea of caring as a leader, that "...some leaders get very confused about what that means. They think 'taking care of your people' means making sure they are comfortable and happy, coddling them, giving them as much time off as possible, and not pushing them hard."[16] In Jocko's particular example, this is what it means to be ready for combat—and as he states, "If you really care about your people, you want them to go home to their families."[17]

Caring for our people in medicine means creating better lives for those we lead and our patients. We owe this type of leadership to both.

Retired Lieutenant General (LTG) Mark Hertling, the author of *Growing Physician Leaders: Empowering Doctors to Improve Healthcare*,[18] talks about caring for those you lead in his book. Describing effective leaders, he says, "He or she will successfully care for his or her soldiers."[19] During the interview for this book, LTG Hertling said,

> The first thing that comes to mind is almost a fuzzy approach of taking care of their needs and making sure that they get the right acknowledgment. All of that's true, but what I've learned in my career is caring goes a lot deeper than that. It sometimes requires the giving of tough love, the holding people to standards, the technique of letting them know that you are developing them as individuals. I do a drill in my physician leader classes and most times in any leadership seminar I give. I ask people to close their eyes and think of the person who they consider lit their fire or was the best leader they ever saw. I give them two minutes and tell them to open their eyes. It's an interesting drill, because people immediately think of someone, whether it's father, mother, and uncle, teacher, coach, colleague, someone who made a difference. When you start drilling down and asking the seven layers of questions about those individuals, you will find in most cases it's because those individuals cared in very unique ways. They were willing to give them critiques. They were willing to hold them to a tough standard. Whether it was a teacher who demanded more of them than any other teacher that they ever had, or a drill sergeant...it's not just the person that tells you what you want to hear or makes you feel comfortable. Sometimes, the most caring individuals are the ones who make you feel the most uncomfortable.

If the military and elite operational forces such as the Navy SEALs place a premium on caring as leaders, we should learn from their example. Dr. Amy Oxentenko provided a helpful way to think about this:

> We all know there are some skills that may be viewed as the soft skills, such as empathy, caring, and nurturing associated with leadership. And then there are the hard or firm skills, so to speak, which include financial acumen, innovation, and strategic or critical thinking. Those may work in a different part of your brain, but I don't think the two types of skills are mutually exclusive. I think a leader who is only approaching their role through finances, strategy, and innovation at the expense of everything else may be challenged in unique ways. They may have really great ideas—big, bold ideas—but if they're missing some of those soft elements, are they going to have people willing to follow?

Are you starting to see the pattern in caring as a leader? Rather than being soft, it is confronting the most challenging aspects of leading. I know you went into healthcare to take care of people. We are responsible for taking care of patients and their families—but we need to think more broadly about caring. We are also responsible for leading within our healthcare systems and schools and for educating the next generation of physicians, nurses, pharmacists, and other allied health professionals.

Since we care about our people and the mission, we need to be more intentional about being caring leaders. It should give us a revived sense of purpose and motivation to take care of each other so that we can take care of our missions in healthcare. Caring leaders in healthcare will generate followers ready to create the healthcare and education environments we desperately desire. We can do this together if we accept the challenge.

Prescription for Caring in Leadership

1. Reflect on leaders you have had in your life and career and think about how they challenged you and invested in you. Did they care about you? Did you see them as soft? What specific things did they do that you could do?

2. Think about some of the most challenging things that we do in leadership, such as setting high standards, holding people accountable for behavior and performance, giving feedback, and dealing with conflict. Are these easy? Hard? Anything "soft" about doing any of these?

3. Read Michael A. West's book *Compassionate Leadership: Sustaining Wisdom, Humanity and Presence in Health And Social Care*[20] or his blog post "The Five Myths of Compassionate Leadership."[21]

4. Discuss with your team the idea of caring-inspired leadership and if they think it means being soft.

5. How does being a caring leader impact your having high standards, giving challenging feedback, giving credit to others, and advocating to your boss for the people you lead?

CHAPTER 3

The Business Case for Caring as a Leader

"Caring is a strategic leadership competency that delivers real ROI."[1]
—Laurie Baedke

L EADERS OFTEN TALK ABOUT how their people are the most valuable resource in their organizations, yet many organizations and leaders fail to care for their people. They don't treat them as people, but rather as numbers or replaceable widgets. We focus on metrics like access to care, real value units (RVUs), and patient satisfaction. Maybe if we focused more on the people delivering the care, the metrics would take care of themselves? The data and many of our lived experiences would support this claim.

Anne Thompson, PT, EdD illustrated the idea of being a widget and that our work is not valued:

> I had an interesting discussion with a physician just a couple of weeks ago. He said, "I get the very definite impression that I'm replaceable, and I pointed out to the administrator that I was the last physician hired in the last six years. So obviously, I'm not that replaceable. They're not flocking to your door." I

think they don't feel cared for. They don't feel valued. They're not being rewarded for sticking with them. [Working through COVID-19 was] probably the most horrendous thing any of us have ever seen short of a war, and it comes back to caring as leaders. We're taking our eye off the ball and we're not taking care of our people. I fear it will only get worse because I have not yet seen the signs of increased care and support. If you feel valued, you're going to stick with it, but I think we've missed that. I'm not sure that we've been recovering in the ways that we need to. And you're right, it's not as simple as "Here's a T-shirt and an ice cream sundae." I think that that grew old pretty fast—but it doesn't have to be monetary. It could be done in so many ways. Care about them. They're not just a widget. [Don't make it so employees] get the sense of "I'm replaceable."

How many of you feel like your leaders see you as a widget? I know I have felt this way at times over my career. As a leader, have you ever treated your people that way–intentionally or unintentionally? How do we fix this? How would you show up at work, or how would those you lead show up at work if you felt valued and not just like you could easily be replaced?

The solution is to be a caring leader, according to Anne. "There are two things that you want in your leader. You want them to care about you. You want them to care about the mission. You want them to care about the people that you're serving, and you want them to be honest. Are you with me? I'll stick with that person through thick and thin."

Being a caring leader, in many ways, is as simple as letting the people you lead know you care about them and the mission. You are not just in it for yourself. You want them to do well. You want them to be well while the organization is succeeding. All too often, we are part of organizations where people are made to feel like they don't matter. This is not good for the people and ultimately not good for the organization.

Dr. Amy Oxentenko also brought up the idea of treating people like widgets:

> We're in healthcare. Whether you're a program director, a department chair, a dean, or a CEO, you're asking people to do tough things. You're asking them to work hard, in higher-level leadership, you're asking them to be accountable for patient targets and then financial metrics and all these sorts of things. You're asking them to do tough things. I think you get better buy-in, if that comes with caring as a part of that. It's not just all about the metrics, the numbers, the outcomes, but about how you make people feel. What are the concerns they have? How can you support them? There's going to be people willing to do the hard work if they know you're there to support them and you care about them, rather than just viewing them as a widget in a complex machine.

Amen! If we want people to do hard things, they need to feel valued. They need to feel cared for.

There is a growing recognition that our past ways of leading were not effective and we need to approach leadership with our workers in mind. The business world is acknowledging this, with many prominent leaders coming forth and talking about the importance of care and love as being two of the most important aspects of leading. The bottom line is that caring as a leader works.

Maybe you are still skeptical. Can caring as a leader really drive up profit and results? I saw a social media post by author and speaker Jon Gordon about the importance of Return on Investment in People versus Return on Investment generally. He stated in his newsletter, "As someone who has worked with the best companies and cultures on the planet, it's clear they all invest in their people and know it's their number one priority. After all, it's not the numbers and goals that drive the people, but rather the people who drive the numbers and achieve the goals."[2]

Let's look at some of the data and a few examples.

Heather Younger, the author of *The Art of Caring Leadership: How Leading with Heart Uplifts Teams and Organizations,* dedicated a chapter to "The ROI of Caring Leadership®."[3] She gives multiple examples from people she has worked with and interviewed on the impact of caring leadership®. She quotes the CEO of Service Express, who said, "...focusing on the people will deliver you not only the numbers you're looking for, but they'll beat them."[4] She attributed leading from a place of caring resulting in an increase in revenue from $3 million to $130 million.[5] That's an impressive return on investing in your people.

Heather ends the chapter talking about her interview with Garry Ridge, a legend in the business world for the way he runs the company WD-40.[6] If you have not heard him speak, you need to listen to him on a podcast.[7] Under his leadership, they have evolved from a $300 million dollar company to a $2.4 billion dollar one.[8] WD-40 has a global engagement score of 93 percent for employees, and "99 percent of tribe members [employees] say they love to tell people they work at our company."[9]

Do 90-plus percent of the people you work with feel that way about your organization? What would that level of engagement mean for patient care and provider and trainee well-being? What are the leadership actions that would create this sense of belonging and job satisfaction? The entire purpose of this book is to create caring leaders so these conditions can occur more often.

In the book *Lead From The Heart: Transformational Leadership for the 21st Century,* Mark Crowley provides a compelling argument for caring as leaders.[10] His book is a tour de force of data and stories about how caring for those we lead benefits employees and the financial bottom line. One thing that sticks out is his meeting and conclusions with the leaders at the nonprofit business think tank The Conference Board. He met with John Gibbons, one of their researchers and a former business leader. He pointed out that "Engagement, as we know, is a force that drives human performance."[11] What is the most important leadership skill driving engagement? Gibbons says the research examines "361 total leadership skills and behaviors that will be demanded of managers for the foreseeable future," and "ranking at the top— number one—is *having a caring nature.*"[12]

Are the people you lead fully engaged at work? If you want more engagement, be a caring leader. Take actions that will support them personally and professionally. Your investment by caring for them will have a positive impact on their lives and your organization's performance.

One last point from the business world: What is the number one driver of organizational success? According to Gallup, the people who do the work. Engaged employees. In the book *Culture Shock: An unstoppable force is changing how we work and live. Gallup's solution to the biggest leadership issue of our time,* the authors Jim Clifton and Jim Harter write, "Our employees and front-line managers control customer outcomes and daily cash flow more than any other single lever we can pull."[13] They report only about 30 percent of U.S. employees are fully engaged and that 70 percent of variance of engagement is related to the manager.[15] In other words, leadership drives employee engagement and results. In healthcare, frontline workers are even more important. It's not just about RVUs and access to care but patients' lives, trainees' lives, and the lives of everyone delivering the healthcare. If we want to have better outcomes in healthcare, we need to lead more effectively and improve how we care for those delivering the care and training.

These are just a few of many examples on how caring impacting leadership is making its way into the business world—not just making its way, but changing the approach of leaders with the growing recognition that companies that take care of their people are more successful.

Full stop! If business leaders are seeing the importance of caring in leadership, isn't this something healthcare leaders should be doing? We should be embarrassed that business leaders have figured out that caring as leaders is the optimal approach to leadership. Caring is our business in healthcare, yet we have often neglected to care for ourselves and each other. Each of us has the opportunity to infuse caring into our leadership in healthcare and change lives in a positive way through our leadership.

Caring-Inspired Leadership in Medicine

Leadership coming from a place of caring in medicine not only makes sense but is a model we should be comfortable with and thrive in. That does not mean it will be easy, as the principles and lessons in this book are far from easy. They are, however, rooted in caring. Medicine is not easy, leadership is not easy, life is not easy. We need caring leaders to improve medicine and to build better families and communities. As Mark Crowley writes in *Lead From The Heart*, "We have an unprecedented opportunity to reinvent how we will lead and manage people in our workplaces and to embrace the premise that when human beings are thriving, organizations naturally will as well."[16]

There is growing evidence that being a caring leader results in both better patient and financial outcomes. The patient outcomes will be weaved in throughout this book as we talk about the importance of leadership on burnout and how being a caring leader fosters worker engagement. This drives positive outcomes for patients, providers, and the business of healthcare.

Caring-inspired leadership is a winning model for all stakeholders in healthcare!

Professor Michael West from The King's Fund, a charitable organization to improve healthcare in England, provides evidence for what he calls "compassionate leadership" in his book *Compassionate Leadership: Sustaining Wisdom, Humanity and Presence in Health and Social Care.*[17] He has a chapter, "Compassion in health and social care: the evidence," in which he provides evidence for compassionate leadership resulting in better patient outcomes, patient experience, and decreased worker burnout.[18] He concludes the chapter stating, "Whatever our level of seniority in the organization, our compassionate leadership is key, therefore, to creating the conditions for compassionate care in service of our communities."[19]

Case Study of a Caring Leader

One of the best examples of a caring leader is retired Colonel Dr. Greg Argyros, who is currently the president of MedStar Washington Hospital Center (WHC) in Washington, D.C. Dr. Argyros oversees the largest hospital in Washington, D.C. He leads from a place of caring. Describing the importance of being a caring leader, he said,

"It is critical." Dr. Argyros outlined many things, including being present, getting to know your people, empowering the people you lead, listening, advocating for those you lead, investing in those you lead, recognizing people for jobs well done, and emphasizing your values. We will hear some of the stories of how Dr. Argyros operationalizes caring as a leader in this book. As he points out and models as a leader, "It's never about you."

Our job as leaders is to support the people we lead so they and our organizations can flourish.

Does caring-inspired leadership work? WHC has received many recognitions over the years, including A grades in "Social Responsibility, Health Equity, Value of Care, and Patient Outcomes" and being named the most socially and racially responsible hospital in Washington, D.C., from the Lown Institute in 2023.[20] They were recognized by NRC Health as one of the top 100 hospitals nationally for customer loyalty.[21] They are widely recognized as leaders in clinical care in multiple areas and are the number two–ranked hospital in the Washington, D.C., metropolitan area.[22]

Dr. Argyros attributes the success to their culture of taking care of their people. He states there are five strategic pillars at Washington Hospital Center: be the best place to work, offer the highest quality and safety for patient care, offer the best patient experience, be a market leader, and foster financial strength. What I love is how they go about accomplishing these. It starts with taking care of the people who do the work. Dr. Argyros points this out, stating, "If you do one, two, and three right, then you don't have to talk about four and five. They just take care of themselves."

Washington Hospital Center's success is pretty convincing evidence of the power of leadership based on caring. We need more healthcare organizations to focus on their people more than they focus on financial metrics. We have been putting our effort into the wrong things. If we build and support our teams, they will win!

Caring and Innovation

Innovation and quality improvement are essential for medicine. We are not going to solve the problems facing medicine unless we have the courage to try bold ideas. New innovations on how to deliver healthcare will be essential as we move forward, given the growing number of challenges that exist. These new models of care delivery as well as innovations in patient care itself enable us to provide more effective and efficient care. These innovations are fostered by leaders who care.

Michael West, in a paper titled "Caring to change: how compassionate leadership can stimulate innovation in health care" and his book *Compassionate Leadership: Sustaining Wisdom, Humanity and Presence in Health and Social Care*, outlines how compassionate leaders foster innovation.[23,24] He states, "Compassionate leadership creates the necessary conditions for innovation among individuals, in teams, in the process of inter-teamworking, at the level of organizational functioning as a whole, and in cross-boundary or systems working."[25]

The paper describes four elements (see table) to compassionate leadership: inspiring vision and strategy, positive inclusion and participation, enthusiastic team and cross-boundary working, and support and autonomy.[26] Leaders who care and follow intentional steps such as these can create the conditions for amazing innovation and progress in medicine.

Compassionate Leadership: Four Key Elements needed for Innovation[27]			
Inspiring Vision and Strategy	**Positive Inclusion and Participation**	**Enthusiastic Team and Cross-Boundary Working**	**Support and Autonomy**
Unwavering focus on high-quality continually improving compassionate care Inspiring and meaningful vision Shared understanding Clear, aligned, manageable challenges and tasks Alignment between workload and resources	Ensuring all voices are heard Creating psychological safety and encouraging teams to be compassionate to one another Valuing diversity including patient groups, positive attitude to differences Fair resolution of conflict	Working compassionately with other teams (inter-team compassion) Being supportive and collaborative Having a 'How can we help?' attitude	Creation of a positive climate- high levels of engagement, positivity and creativity Freedom to be autonomous, but with support Treating staff with compassion

Adapted from and reproduced with permission from the Kings Fund, Original source: West M, Eckert R, Collins B, Chowla R (2017). *Caring to change: how compassionate leadership can stimulate innovation in health care*. London: The King's Fund. Available at: www.kingsfund.org.uk/publications/caring-change (accessed on 28 August 2023).

Dr. Caroline Blackie brings these ideas to life with her leadership at Johnson and Johnson:

> In my work, innovation is critical for our business…Caring-inspired leadership creates a culture where people know they will be heard, that they have value, and that spreadsheets and milestones are not mission statements. Caring-inspired leadership feeds the innovation engine because it makes people feel courageous and inspired. They get big-time brave when they feel cared for…there is no one genius in the room. There is a team that needs to be able to see themselves as critical individuals and that they need each other to create something meaningful together. This can be sustainably achieved through caring-inspired leadership. People do beautiful things when you care for them. They get real, they get honest, and they get outrageously creative!

I think we all agree we want those we work with to be outrageously creative. We want to work in places where we are listened to and empowered to create meaningful change. How much better might our teams and organizations be with outrageous creativity? Are you willing to embrace caring as a leader to build this culture?

Costs of Not Caring

Toxic work environments are created by leaders who are *only* concerned about themselves and profit or success; it's the opposite of a caring culture. This is often at the expense of workers, who are treated poorly. There is often a lack of communication, dishonesty, unfair expectations, and a failure to reward or recognize people. I don't want to focus on this for too long, but it is important to point out that toxic work environments—or those that are otherwise not led in caring ways—lead to bad outcomes. You might be able to force people to do something in the short term, but leading by compliance will never beat leading by influence and getting commitment in the long term. When we don't have fully engaged healthcare workers, we are missing out on the care they provide and the solutions they bring to the table. Optimizing the work environment benefits workers and, ultimately, patients and trainees.

Dr. Caroline Blackie illustrates the risks of not caring:

> There's a saying that I learned years ago. It says, "What drives businesses is people. What drives people is how they feel at work." I never forgot that...Leaders who prioritize performance metrics over people cause harm to people in and outside of the workplace. Harm, even subtle harm, to individuals within an organization harms the organization itself. I think it is important to note that the "performance-over-people" leader resides in every one of us. I recognize her most in myself when I am under duress. It is natural to lead this way because performance metrics are where we focus our attention for delivering on our business goals. The leader who is driven solely by performance metrics and who sees only one path to get there—typically theirs—ends up either actively or passively disregarding how their people feel. They are deluded into thinking that a strong leader is one who can force people to "just get it done!" These leaders leave ash in their wake that can take months and sometimes years to address. I call them "learning angels." The emotional chaos they leave behind is a powerful teacher for precisely how not to lead.

Dr. Blackie raises a really important point. At times, we all feel the pressure to produce at work and to put the mission or work goals above our people. We have to resist those urges and recognize how our leadership impacts those we lead, their families, and our organizations. If people drive performance and organizational success, then we need to keep our eye on the ball and take care of our people. A failure to do so has led us to a crisis in medicine.

We are facing unprecedented rates of burnout, depression, substance abuse (composed mainly of alcohol), and suicide within medicine for physicians and nurses.[28-31] Burnout manifests as mental exhaustion, depersonalization, and a decreased sense of personal accomplishment.[32] Many people working in healthcare are tired of working in environments that don't support them, and they are leaving—or, worse, too many of them are taking their lives.[33]

Medscape reported in 2023 that 53 percent of physicians are burned out and 23 percent are depressed.[34] These are both increased from five years earlier, when the rates were 42 percent and 15 percent, respectively.[35] This is a crisis in healthcare, but not a surprising one, given the impact of COVID-19. Emergency physicians topped the list at 65 percent reporting burnout.[36] The best (if one can call it that) rate of burnout was among preventive medicine at 37 percent.[37] The Medscape survey of nurses reported that 52 percent of nurses had decreased job satisfaction following the COVID-19 pandemic.[38] Another study of 18,719 physicians by Jennifer Ligibel and colleagues published in *JAMA Network Open* in 2023 reported 37.8 percent met criteria for burnout and 32.6 percent reported an intention to leave their institution.[39] Sadly, 39 percent had a lack of professional fulfillment.[40]

These rates are staggering, but what may be more significant is the impact burnout has on healthcare. Burnout is directly linked to worse patient outcomes.[41-44] There is ample evidence that burnout among physicians and nurses leads directly and indirectly to worse outcomes in patient care. This includes decreased quality of care, medical errors, decreased patient satisfaction, decreased professional effort, and increased physician turnover. Each of these leads to incredible financial and personal costs to the organization, as well as consequences to patients.

The data is clear. We have a problem.

Burnout is culminating in physicians, nurses, and others leaving the field of medicine. We are already facing physician and nursing shortages, but these shortages are increasing at somewhat staggering rates. Moreover, as Dr. Tait Shanafelt and Clair Kuriakose reported in the *New England Journal of Medicine Catalyst Innovations in Care Delivery,* another 31 percent of healthcare professionals may be leaving in the next two years.[45] *Yikes!*

A cross-section multicenter survey study in JAMA Health Forum of 15,738 physicians and 5,312 physicians was published by Linda Aiken, PhD and her team in July 2023.[46] The study provides evidence of the problem and insights into what is needed to improve the situation. The conclusion stated, "…hospitals characterized as having too few nurses and unfavorable work environments had higher rates of clinician burnout, turnover, and unfavorable patient safety ratings. Clinicians wanted action by management to address insufficient nurse staffing, insufficient clinician control over workload, and poor work environments; they were less interested in wellness programs and resilience training."[47]

Shanafelt and Kuriakose highlighted the issue and impact. They said, "Rampant staff shortages, unrelenting burnout, and unsustainable workloads have led to a vicious cycle with no end in sight. Health care delivery organizations everywhere are facing one of the biggest challenges in a generation."[48] The problem, as they point out, is that without enough physicians and nurses, the work shifts to those who are left—which only further increases burnout and decreases job satisfaction. The authors end by quoting a clinical leader who said, "Clinicians do not want to be told what they need to do, rather administration needs to listen to what they need and actually DO SOMETHING about it."[49]

Burnout and depression are at similarly high rates in resident physicians in training.[50] The residents, who typically work the longest hours of anyone in a hospital, are paid embarrassingly low wages. A full discussion of the issues related to graduate medical education work expectations and payment of residents is beyond the scope of this book, but suffice it to say we are reaching a tipping point. Residents are starting to unionize and hold strikes to demand better wages and working conditions.[51] It says a lot when we have physicians (and, as we'll see below, nurses) going on strike. These professionals who always put patients first are at a breaking point. If we don't more effectively take care of them, we may be left without enough nurses and physicians to take care of our patients.

The financial burden of replacing or hiring a new physician is significant. Shanafelt and colleagues, in an article titled "The Business Case for Investing in Physician Well-Being" published in *JAMA Internal Medicine*, highlighted the issue, stating, "The business case to address physician burnout is multifaceted and includes costs associated with turnover and lost revenue associated with decreased productivity, as well as financial risk and threats to the organization's long-term viability due to the relationship between burnout and lower quality of care, decreased patient satisfaction, and problems with patient safety."[52]

The authors broke down the cost of replacing a physician given the factors involved and the lost revenue from time not working. They estimated the costs to be between $500,000 and $1 million dollars.[53] The article is sobering and should make senior healthcare leaders think about how physician retention is a financial driver.

Put simply, if we do a better job of taking care of our physicians, it will lead to better patient outcomes and improved finances for our organizations.

The situation is similar when we look at the nursing profession.

In 2023, over 7,000 nurses at two hospitals in New York went on strike for three days, demanding better working conditions and salaries. A nurse, Ashleigh Woodside, was quoted as saying, "We love our job. We want to take care of our patients. But we just want to do it safely and in a humane way, where we feel appreciated."[54]

Keep this thought about feeling appreciated in mind as we talk about the power gratitude later in the book. According to a report from Relias, the turnover rate for nurses in 2022 was 22 percent, and it takes about three months to fill a position.[55] Nationally, there have been nursing shortages resulting in organizations needing to pay staggering wages to traveling nurses. The nurses who are left are overworked and feel devalued. Consequently, some nurses have gone on strike, demanding better pay and working conditions. Rather than repeating this cycle, we need to develop ways to care for our nurses and create environments where they feel valued and are compensated fairly.

A research report from McKinsey & Company showed the number one reason why people left their jobs was uncaring leaders.[56] The next most common reasons were unsustainable work expectations, lack of career development opportunities, lack of meaningful work, and lack of support for employee well-being. Each of these top five reasons for leaving are addressed in specific chapters in this book. It is fair to argue that if people are ultimately leaving, they must not be as engaged as they could be leading up to that decision—and since engagement drives profits and (for healthcare) better patient outcomes, addressing these areas is critical.

Dr. Amy Oxentenko argues that caring has to be part of the solution to the workforce shortages, and I would add it would be part of the solution when addressing burnout as well. "I think it's going to get tougher in health care before it gets easier in terms of the workforce shortages, so that caring piece will go a long way toward the kind of loyalty that would be great to maintain with the workforce that has a lot of options."

> "I think it's going to get tougher in health care before it gets easier in terms of the workforce shortages, so that caring piece will go a long way toward the kind of loyalty that would be great to maintain with the workforce that has a lot of options."
>
> —Dr. Amy Oxentenko

While the data is convincing, let's end with a story. Behind every statistic for burnout and suicide, there is a human being, a colleague of ours who came into medicine to help others. This colleague could be you or me. It could be your child, parent, spouse, partner, or best friend. Unfortunately, most of us have had colleagues who have suffered from burnout or died from suicide. We have experienced the pain that comes from these stories.

Dr. Richard Boulay wrote a perspective piece for the *New England Journal of Medicine* called "Looking After Our Own" about his daughter's suicide attempt.[57] The system had failed her. When she felt like she had no way out, she attempted suicide. After her suicide attempt, her dad told a story of how her program abandoned her. They were more concerned about schedules and the program than her well-being. It is a somber read. Dr. Boulay concluded with this statement:

> Practitioners in other fields pride themselves on protecting one another. Firefighters race into burning buildings to rescue trapped comrades. Soldiers brave enemy fire to retrieve the wounded from the battlefield. Yet we purported healers tolerate stacks of body bags filled with our dead colleagues, after people like me have failed to understand the depth of their suffering.[58]

How long will we let this go on without stepping up to advocate for, fight for, protect, and care for our own?

As you read the rest of this book, remember that the central idea is that being a caring-inspired leader will improve the lives of those we lead in healthcare. If we improve the lives of those who care for patients, it will lead to better patient care. This book provides practical suggestions in every chapter about how, through caring, you can lead more effectively—because we must do better. We have the ability to change the narrative and create better inspiring stories in the future. We must do so as soon as possible.

Prescription for Caring in Leadership

1. Discuss with your direct reports whether they feel cared for at work and whether leadership makes them feel like a priority. If so, why? If not, what would change that?

2. Make a list of leadership actions that make you feel cared for at work. Ask yourself if you are doing these actions for those whom you lead.

3. Seek feedback from your team about whether or not they are engaged at work and if they feel supported. Ask them

for specifics about what you could do more of as a leader to support them.

4. Read *Lead From The Heart*[59] by Mark Crowley, or commit to listening to one of his podcasts each week or month.

5. Read *The Art of Caring Leadership: How Leading with Heart Uplifts Teams and Organizations*[60] by Heather Younger, or commit to listening to one of her podcasts each week or month.

6. Give copies of this book to your team and read it as a group.

Being a Caring-Inspired Leader Starts with You

CHAPTER 4

Care Enough to Take Care of Yourself

"In no relationship is the physician more often derelict than in his [her] duty to himself [herself]."
—Dr. Johnston, As a Physician.
Washington Med Ann 1902; 1:158-61.[1]

YOU CAN'T LEAD OTHERS effectively if you are not well yourself. We have to recognize that "self-care is not selfish."[2] We tell patients it is important for them to take care of themselves. If they don't take care of themselves, how can they take care of their kids? How can they take care of their parents? How can they be the best versions of themselves where they work? We need to listen to our own advice!

I purposely put this chapter early in the book because the idea of taking care of ourselves as leaders is often an afterthought—but we need to prioritize our own well-being to keep us in the fight and to model self-care to those whom we lead.

Laurie Baedke, author, podcast host, and Director of Healthcare Leadership Programs at Creighton University, captured the importance of taking care of ourselves as leaders. She said we must "lead ourselves first, and this includes self-care." Here is her sage advice:

> Especially for high-achieving professionals and for leaders, that practice of self-compassion is vital. Give yourself a little bit of grace and be vulnerable to own your shortcomings. Frame these moments as turbulent, but not terminal. When we suffer a gaffe or make a mistake or miss a deadline, how do we process that moment? Perfectionistic tendencies and our ego can cause us to perseverate or flagellate. People-pleasing and shame can cause us to deflect or avoid. A care for self and a curiosity to learn from each moment in life can productively apply the assessment of mistakes and successes alike for future positive performance. I think it's an important part of the care equation to really think about. If we're going to care for others as a leader, we really have to care about ourselves and invest time in loving ourselves and appreciating what is good about us, and owning what's not.

I'm fond of saying, "Own your awesome, and acknowledge your awful." This is a call to action to claim your strengths and share them liberally, but also to understand where you can get in your own way or the way of others, and work to grow or improve or collaborate more strategically with others in a way that models humility, accountability, and self-love or self-care. Leaders, your actions and behaviors and beliefs are setting the example for others

> *"If we're going to care for others as a leader, we really have to care about ourselves and invest time in loving ourselves and appreciating what is good about us, and owning what's not."*
>
> —Laurie Baedke

who follow you at work, at home, and in your community. Are you modeling a realistic and authentic and kind view of yourself that you'd want your amazing junior colleague or impressionable child to adopt for themselves?

What are *you* modeling? We need to look at it through this lens. It is definitely about our own health, but it is also about what we are saying to those we lead. If we neglect our health or families, others may see that as necessary to be successful. We can break this cycle in medicine, but it is going to require many of us to approach our health and work differently.

The problem is almost everyone in healthcare puts the needs of others above their own. The system around us is collapsing, but because of how much we care about our patients, we figure out ways to make it work. We develop multiple workarounds to solve problems because we don't want to let our patients, their families, or our trainees down. This altruistic attitude and increasing amount of work expected of everyone coupled with systems issues has resulted in staggering rates of burnout, depression, and suicide. A clinician in a nonprofit clinic in the United States quoted in the 2023 *New England Journal of Medicine Catalyst* survey by Shanafelt and Kuriakose highlights this sentiment:

We cannot continue to rely on the altruism of health care workers to make up for the lack of staff, support, and resources. We cannot continue to bully primary care and other cognitive specialties that provide high-value care but at a lower rate of compensation and reimbursement than procedural specialties. If our current health care workforce is not engaged and enthusiastic, our ability to attract new students into health care fields will wane.[3]

There are many other papers and resources that document the rates of burnout, depression, and suicide within medicine. This is a huge problem, and if you're not aware of it, then please go look at more data. We cannot afford to have physicians, nurses, and other healthcare providers leaving the field of medicine. This is creating a crisis in medicine that will impact patients as well as all the people providing the care who remain to do the work.

We need to care for ourselves and our colleagues in the same way we care for our patients. If we don't, then healthcare will struggle to recruit people to the field, and many more will leave. The business world is talking about thirty-two-hour work weeks, and we still think eighty hours is reasonable for resident physicians taking part in their training following medical school. Some argue it's not *enough* for trainees. Many staff physicians and nurses are working more hours than their nonmedical friends who have less school debt and less education and are making more money. The practice of medicine has reached a tipping point, and it is not sustainable.

How do we care for ourselves and each other? We can't solve well-being with events or training, but rather by making it a way of life. We need to use a well-being lens as a filter for every decision we make for ourselves and for our organizations. "How does this decision impact the well-being of me and my team?" Ask that question with every decision you are making.

Does leadership matter? What role do leaders play in the well-being of those within the workforce? If you are not familiar with the work of Dr. Tait Shanafelt, the Chief Wellness Officer at Stanford, then you need to read up on his work. He has done some groundbreaking research looking at the impact of leaders on burnout and job satisfaction.[4] Leadership directly correlates with the satisfaction and well-being of those we lead.[5] A paper by Jennifer Ligibel, MD and colleagues also demonstrated that supportive leadership behaviors, alignment in personal and organizational values, and perceived gratitude were inversely related to intention to leave.[6] Effective and supportive (caring) leadership matters.

You can also ask yourself these questions and use your personal leadership story to provide evidence for the power of effective leadership.

How motivated did you feel and how satisfied were you when you had a boss (leader) who was not effective? A boss who did not support you? A boss who did not recognize your work? How did you feel when you had a boss who did support you? We thrive at work and home when we have bosses who support us personally and professionally.

Leaders should think about these five areas of well-being (as identified by Gallup)[7] for themselves and those they lead:

1. Career
2. Physical: good health and energy
3. Community: where you live
4. Social: relationships
5. Financial[8]

This list identifies areas where we can be more intentional and strategic about well-being. All too often, we think we will take care of ourselves later, only to wait until it is too late. We make mistakes because we are fatigued or burned out. We ruin a relationship with a spouse or partner. We fail to form bonds and miss out on events with our kids and friends. We simply miss out on life.

Unfortunately, I, like many of my colleagues, treated being tired and busy as badges of honor. I was lucky, as this never really led to significant burnout, but it does for many. We need to prioritize *our* health, and, as leaders, we need to prioritize the health of those we lead. We should celebrate those who prioritize their health and well-being rather than question their dedication, which happens at times. Earlier in my career, I would become upset with colleagues who would leave work early to do personal things or not work as hard as I thought they should have. I was wrong. *They* were the ones who had it figured out.

Prioritizing our own wellness will look different for each of us, but we should consider the areas mentioned in the Gallup poll.[9] I will not spend a lot of time on each area, but I do want to mention a few ideas, as well as one critical point. **We model wellness for those we lead.**

Prioritize Health

What does health look like for you? It has taken me over twenty years to answer this question, but here are some of my personal priorities for health:

- I prioritize exercise. It's good for me, but more importantly, it's medicine for my soul. I feel less anxious and stressed when I exercise.

- I make sure I get seven to eight hours of sleep a night. Earlier in my career, I was only consistently getting five to six hours, which was a mistake. I realize now how much sharper and less moody I am when rested.

- I love to eat, so having good meals is important.

- I prioritize time with my family and especially my kids.

- I take time to read and learn what I am interested in.

Do I always stay on track? No, but I am also better now at recognizing when I am off track and self-correcting. I am better at giving myself permission to make myself and my family a priority.

Make sure you are getting your routine health maintenance. Just like cars, if we don't get our oil changed, tires rotated, and brakes and pads changed, then things will go wrong. Don't wait until something breaks to work on it. Make this a priority for those you lead as well. I embarrassingly had no primary care appointments during my twenty-year Army career. Fortunately, I was relatively healthy, but this is certainly not what we recommend to our patients, so why would we allow it for ourselves?

I mentioned fitness is important to me, and you should make fitness your friend. Over time, I have realized that if I don't exercise, it leads to me having a shorter temper, not thinking as clearly, and, quite honestly, just overall not feeling well. We are all busy, so you may need to get creative with this. I have a colleague who has started to hold meetings while walking outside. These extra steps and fresh air make a difference. I have been known to do push-ups in my office. It not only keeps me awake but allows me to sneak in a workout. Consider having your team do a workout together. Put exercise on your schedule. Remember, you are role modeling this for others.

Make Sleep a Priority

Sleep is a personal issue for me—hopefully, my story will make you think more about your sleep, in addition to the data above. It took over ten years to find out I had sleep apnea. My colleagues made fun of me for falling asleep almost every day at our noon lecture. This would be part of our end-of-year skit, when the residents in our medicine training program made fun of faculty. I finally got a sleep study after a colleague mentioned how it had changed their life. I still remember my former medical school classmate and sleep physician texting me and saying, "Dude, I feel bad for you. Your sleep is terrible."

I didn't realize the impact sleep was having on my performance and family. Sure, I got a lot done, but I now wonder how much better I could have been if I had been well-rested. Knowing how I feel today in terms of energy and being awake—I really wish I could have that time back. I also became much less moody at night with my kids. I wish one of my residents or colleagues would have simply asked me if I was okay and if I had thought about seeing someone because I always looked so tired.

Sleep Is Not for the Weak

There has long been the idea that there are somehow superhuman leaders who don't need to sleep. General Stanley McChrystal famously talked about only needing a few hours of sleep each night.[10] Dr. Anthony Fauci talked about surviving the early days of COVID-19 with little sleep until his wife called him out on it and helped him realize he needed more sleep.[11] In his book *Essentialism: The Disciplined Pursuit of Less*, author Greg McKeown talks about "Protecting the Asset" (we are the asset to making the world better), stating, "One of the most common ways people—especially ambitious, successful people—damage this asset is through a lack of sleep."[12]

He has an entire chapter in his book devoted to the importance of sleep (Chapter 8) that is worth reading.[13] Most of us in medicine have gone without sleep and even bragged about it at times. We need to look at sleep as a foundational element of well-being as leaders in healthcare.

A study by Captain Lyddia Petrofsky and her team published in the journal *Military Medicine* in 2023 looked at sleep among military leaders.[14] The study reported that while lack of sleep decreased performance, it was often not prioritized. One participant stated, "We're always saying as leaders, you know, sleep, nutrition, this and that. And then we're some of the worst offenders."[15]

This is an important point. We need to be role models about sleep. This is good for our own health and clinical and leadership performance. Maybe even more importantly, it sets the standards and expectations related to sleep for those we lead.

Petrofsky and her colleagues give examples of how leaders need to "set the example for change" and "share personal sleep values."[16] One leader interviewed for the paper stated, "We're just talking about it right now. But we're not walking what we are talking. So, until we change that culture and how we do things, it really doesn't mean much." Another leader commented, "I openly communicate the priority that I put on my sleep. I encourage those in my direct sphere to also prioritize it."[17]

Data shows when leaders prioritize sleep, it helps those they lead improve their sleep. An article by military sleep experts stated, "Leaders that incorporate sleep and fatigue management into the planning and execution phases of operations will help facilitate mission priorities and prove a force multiplier."[18] A randomized controlled trial of training in sleep leadership among thirty-nine Army platoons demonstrated that training leaders on sleep has the potential to improve the sleep habits of their entire unit's sleep.[19]

Each of you will need to decide how to approach sleep personally and for those you lead. Don't neglect it because the data is clear: sleep is a worthwhile investment. Try to get at least seven or eight hours each night. Be as creative as possible to help those who you lead to get sleep too. Can you adjust schedules? There will be times when we have to go without sleep, but we need to recognize that consistently not sleeping is not good for us or for those we lead.

Bottom line: Prioritize your sleep as a leader and make sleep a priority for those you lead.

What's Your Strategic Plan for Life?[20]

Let's shift gears and talk about well-being related to our careers. Our careers overlap with our well-being in every other area of our life. That should be a prime reason why we need to think about how we approach our careers and the impact it has on other areas of our life. Too often, we just let life happen to us rather than taking control and being proactive about how we manage our life and career.

There are innumerable books written about time management. I was introduced to a life-changing idea by author and Navy SEAL Jocko Willink on his podcast, aptly called *The Jocko Podcast*.[21] The idea is that you should have a strategic plan for your life. Once you have a strategic plan, you should make tactical decisions every day to support that strategic plan. We tend to spend a lot of time focused on the daily tasks without thinking about how they support our long-term plan. The same is true for organizations. Being busy should not be our goal, nor a badge of honor. Being effective and having an impact is what we should shoot for. Eliminate as much as possible among the tactical things you do on a daily basis that do not support your strategic plan. This same approach should be used for your organization, where you prioritize what is important and try to eliminate other things.

I have paired this with ideas from James Clear's book *Atomic Habits*.[22] Why did I pair them? When thinking about our careers, we need to start with the big picture and be strategic. Then we need to figure out what habits and daily activities best support us reaching our larger vision for life. Rather than just meandering through our days, we must make conscious decisions and take intentional actions to reach our goals.

The biggest takeaway I had from *Atomic Habits* is how small acts over time build up.[23] The idea that if we get 1 percent better every day, over the course of a year, we are exponentially better.[24] Over the course of several years, we become astronomically better. The small, incremental steps we take every day may not be noticeable on their own, but if we are strategic and disciplined enough to do the small, tactical steps, they will add up over time. If we are not strategic about what we do, it often results in us being incredibly busy without necessarily being productive. We are missing opportunities to lay down the building blocks of future success.

What does this look like in real life? What do you want to accomplish and be known for? It is critical to try to answer this one question. If you know what you want, you will waste less time on what you see others doing and what others want you to do. I have come to this realization over time. Let me use myself as an example. I have realized that my real purpose is to develop others as leaders. While I still love taking care of my patients, my primary goal is to create leaders in healthcare who will transform the way we provide care, educate trainees, and take care of each other. This means that I have stopped doing almost any research related to infectious diseases. I pass on opportunities, committees, or other work that are interesting but not aligned with my primary goal. I give up some really cool stuff at times, but I get to focus strategically on the one big thing that means the most—like finishing this book! I hope you will agree it was worth it.

Prioritize and Make Saying No a Habit

Prioritization is key to effective time management and reaching strategic goals in life. Most of us were never trained on how to be strategic or to maximize our time. Rather, we learned it by trial and error. For me, that was lots of errors. I would recommend you read the book *Essentialism* by Greg McKeown.[25] It is a relatively short read (saving you time already) and will give you multiple strategies to be more effective with your prioritization and time management. He will also help you answer the question from the prior paragraphs about what is most important. Essentialism is "... about learning how to do less but better so you can achieve the highest possible return on every precious moment of your life."[26] Is that not an appealing thought?

McKeown has an entire chapter on saying no. He writes, "The right 'no' spoken at the right time can change the course of history."[27] If we are going to be strategic about our daily tasks, then we have to become experts at saying no. We have to have the ability to respond when presented with opportunities.

The hard part is knowing how you discern when to say no and how to avoid saying yes and regretting it. Many people are worried about the fear of missing out (FOMO). A piece of advice: *let go of FOMO*!

McKeown gives this advice: "If it isn't a clear yes, then it is a clear no."[28]

Generally speaking, it is a good habit to hit the pause button when asked to do something. Don't give an answer or respond to that email request immediately. Here are a few phrases I have found helpful, adapted from an article by Dr. Sarina Schrager and Dr. Elizabeth Sadowski (see their table below):[29]

> "Wow, I am honored you would think of me. Let me think about it to make sure I can give you my full effort."

> "Thanks, this sounds like a great opportunity, but I would like to review it with my boss (mentor)."

> "This is definitely something I am interested in. I just need to look at my ongoing commitments before I can give you an answer."

> "This is terrific and I would love to help. Is there something I am currently doing that we could move off my plate to allow me to dedicate the necessary time to this?"

Now you have time to think before committing. Use your strategic life lens to see if it supports your long-term goal. If it does not, then decline the request. Not only does this prevent you from doing work that may not align best with your long-term goals, but it potentially keeps space open for an even better opportunity. A friend and Chair of Family Medicine at the Uniformed Services University, Colonel Dana Nguyen, has been part of a group of women who meet once a month for their "Committee of No." The women meet to discuss different opportunities and whether they would make sense for the individual. They collectively provide each other advice. Most of us would probably benefit if we had a Committee of No in our lives!

Dr. Sarina Schrager and Dr. Elizabeth Sadowski wrote a great article, "Getting More Done: Strategies to Increase Scholarly Productivity," that has many useful prioritization tips and a table meant to help you decide whether you should say yes or no.[30] The table is included here to provide you with a useful checklist or approach to making your decisions. As a leader, you can use this table and provide the article when mentoring others.

How to Decide Whether to Say "Yes" or "No"

Does this request fit with your career goals?

Would the work use your skills?

What is the long-term benefit of this work? Could it lead to other work that is more closely related to your goals?

What is the timing of this work? Does it need to be done within a week, a month, or can it be done more long term when you may have more time

Can you be involved in part of the work but not all?

Are you able to give up another responsibility in order to take on the new request?

Is the requestor someone who is your supervisor or who can influence your career?

Would saying "no" jeopardize other parts of your job or career goals?

Adapted from and used with permission from authors and publisher. Reference: Schrager S, Sadowski E. Getting More Done: Strategies to Increase Scholarly Productivity. J Grad Med Educ. 2016 Feb;8(1):10-3. doi: 10.4300/JGME-D-15-00165.1. PMID: 26913095; PMCID: PMC4763375.

Be Present at Home

What is your strategic plan outside of work? How does that help you prioritize your decisions? Part of well-being is our relationships with our family and who we are in our communities. We need to be present for our family and friends. Some of us are guilty of prioritizing work and careers over our families. I am guilty of this too! My biggest regrets in life are not being present for my family. I missed my college roommate's wedding because I was studying for exams in medical school. I went to a meeting to present a talk instead of going to my wife's promotion to captain in the Public Health Service. I feel tremendous guilt for putting my own selfish needs above those of others or thinking something else was more important. You are either there or you aren't. You only get one chance to be present. There are no replays or do-overs.

If you are like me and missed important stuff, don't beat yourself up anymore. Give yourself grace and forgiveness. Move forward with intentionality to prioritize family and friends. In an ideal world, we would be at everything for friends and family. The idea of being home every night for dinner and never missing a kid's event is, for many of us, not reality. Rather than throw our hands in the air and say, "Oh well," we should do our very best to be there as much as possible. We need to set boundaries with work and have certain non-negotiables. For me, that has been blocking my schedule to help coach my kids' sports teams. We have been able to spend many hours together because of this. Note: Coaching your kids in sports may not be the best idea, especially as they get older, but that is a discussion for a separate time.

One of the best articles I ever read on this was titled "Important vs. Urgent" by Colonel Mark Blum, who was the commander of the 212th Field Artillery Brigade at the time.[31] I first saw this article when I was a young Army officer, as it was sent around many circles in the military and has since been shared more widely. He was reflecting on the end of his career and wished he had spent more time with his family. The lessons he shared were helpful. He said he would have spent more time at home when his kids were little, went on more vacations, skipped work social engagements to be with family, and help more with his kids' schoolwork.[32] He would be "more absorbed in their problems." There is always more work to be done, but where should you be? He gave three rules to help determine if you should be somewhere:

1. It is important to someone who's important to you;

2. Your personal presence makes a difference; and

3. The opportunity is not going to come around again.[33]

These are effective rules to help you prioritize. One last quote from Colonel Blum to reflect on and motivate you: "The object for all of us is to make sure we run out of career before we run out of family." [34]

As a leader, it is important for your own well-being to be at these events. Put these events on your calendar and then don't give them up for anything else. Schedule around them. They should mean a lot to you, as they definitely mean a lot to your friends and

> *"The object for all of us is to make sure we run out of career before we run out of family."*
> — Colonel Blum

family. If you prioritize these things as a leader, those you lead see this and feel less pressure to avoid prioritizing them in their own lives. If you are at work super late or early, it can send the message that you expect that of others. Be explicit about what you expect. Set the expectation with your team that they will be present at major life events—and for that matter, as many important events as possible. Kick people out of the office. It is generally easier the higher we get in the leadership food chain to have flexibility in our schedule. We need to create flexibility for those we lead. We need to help them prioritize their lives outside of work. If they are not taking care of their family lives and themselves, it will ultimately hurt their performance and our organizations. Not to mention it is simply the right thing to do as the leader.

Let's end this chapter with some advice from Suzanna Fitzpatrick, DNP, CRNP. She talks about the importance of putting yourself on the to-do list: "Put yourself on your own to-do list. You might not always get there, but put it on there every day. I'm focusing on myself. You know I have a to-do list every single day. It's just for my running, lifting, reading, and piano lessons."

*You decide what, but start putting something for yourself not just **on** the to-do list but at the **top** of the list.*

Prescription for Caring in Leadership

1. Spend some time reflecting on what healthy (mentally, physically, spiritually) looks like to you.

2. Commit today to actions that will keep you healthy so you can take care of those you lead.

3. Make sleep a priority.

4. Mentally, what do you need to do to get better? What should you be reading? What could you be practicing? Do you have a coach?

5. Block time on your calendar for exercising, reading, time with friends and family, and vacations. Stick to that just as much as you stick to work items.

6. Put yourself on your to-do list each day.

7. Consider reading *Essentialism* by Greg McKeown.[35]

CHAPTER 5

Care Enough to Prepare

*"The best preparation for tomorrow is
to do today's work superbly well."*
—Dr. William Osler[1]

H OW MANY OF YOU think leadership is critically important? How many of you spend a significant amount of time thinking about, studying, and working on your leadership skills? Why do we spend so much time focused on clinical malpractice and not leadership malpractice? So much of what we do in medicine requires effective leadership. We deliver team-based care that requires leadership skills. We implement quality improvement and patient safety initiatives that require leadership skills. We are part of systems that are responsible for educating health professionals, which require leadership skills. If you are reading this book, then you are spending time developing your leadership skills. Kudos to you, and thank you for that investment—but generally speaking, most of us who work

> *Why do we spend so much time focused on clinical malpractice and not leadership malpractice?*

within the field of medicine have not spent a lot of time developing our leadership skills. Most systems we work in don't invest in leadership development. This needs to change at all levels for us to be more effective.

Caring as a Leader Starts with Preparing

If we care as leaders, parents, spouses, partners, and teammates, then we have to take the time to prepare. We have to put in the work. The long hours. The time studying, the sweat on the court, the field, the track, and the weight room. We have to care enough to take care of ourselves, as already mentioned. This means we prepare for everything we do. You can't prepare for a crisis once the crisis has arrived. Will you be ready for your life-defining leadership moment when it arrives?

This really hit home for me when I listened to the *WarDocs* podcast with my friend and medical school classmate, retired Colonel Dr. Ramey Wilson.[2] He spent the majority of his military medicine career supporting our troops across the globe. He had a decorated military career in operational medicine, deploying multiple times. The Army Chapter of the American College of Physicians named the operational medicine ward after him in recognition of this expertise in Operational Medicine. Each year, we give the Colonel Ramey Wilson Award for Operational Excellence to an exemplary Army internal medicine physician.

Dr. Wilson is a warrior. Take the time to listen to his podcast and learn more about his experiences and lessons of leading. The lesson that stood out to me the most was "Be prepared."[3] This really hit home because he made the point that as Military Medical Corps officers, our job was to be prepared to care for the sons and daughters who volunteer to go downrange and serve in austere and often dangerous environments. As Military Medical Corps officers, to paraphrase Dr. Wilson, we are responsible for the well-being of these individuals. We want to be able to look a mom or dad in the eye and say we did absolutely everything we could to keep their child alive.

Preparation may not always be about life or death, but preparation *is* always about someone's life! You never know how your preparation for leadership is going to influence and change the arc of someone's career or life. Are you taking that responsibility seriously? Can you look them in the eye and tell them you were fully prepared to teach them, coach them, care for them, and lead them?

To be completely clear, in the practice of medicine, our preparation does impact someone's life. We have to be sure we are prepared clinically. I don't want to lose sight of the fact that providing direct patient care is our top priority and we have to be prepared to provide the care patients need. That is our promise to them. That said, given the impact leadership skills have on all that we do, we need to be more prepared as leaders. That should be our promise to those we lead. Preparing to lead could be as simple as making it a habit to listen to a leadership podcast once a week on the way to and from work. It could be reading a book related to a leadership challenge you're facing at work, such as how to have a difficult conversation. It could be talking to a mentor or a coach. To prepare means making an intentional effort to improve our leadership.

Dr. Jeff Hutchinson during our interview emphasized this point about developing ourselves as leaders and developing those who will be taking our places:

> I think the best leaders care about building other leaders and about being replaced. The military taught me that. We could disappear at any moment, and if you were hoarding all the

information, hoarding all the power, then the organization is going to have a very difficult time recovering. It will, but it does so much better if you've built up people to say, "If I go down, someone else is going to pick up the ball and keep going."

Current State of Leader Development in Medicine

The bottom line is that leadership development is not a priority in medicine, but it needs to be prioritized just like developing clinical skills. While there are examples of organizations that do this well, these are outliers. I have spent a lot of time talking to friends and colleagues within and outside the United States, and there is a gap in leadership development. Currently, the Association of American Medical Colleges and the Accreditation Council for Graduate Medical Education do not have a specific requirement for teaching leadership during medical school or residency training.[4,5] Sure, there are items that fall under what could be considered leadership, but there is not a specific requirement. The CanMEDS Framework—which is the standard set by the Royal College of Physicians in Canada—has identified "Leader" as a specific role for trainees.[6] If leadership is critical to positive outcomes in medicine, why is there not more of a focus on preparing trainees for leadership? Every physician needs to be trained on how to be an effective leader.

What about other healthcare professionals? While a full review is outside the scope of this book, it is clear that most healthcare professionals recognize the importance of leadership development for their professions. Nursing schools have a requirement for leadership development. The accrediting body asks that "The curriculum provides experiential learning that enhances student ability to demonstrate leadership" and that leadership development is integrated throughout the curriculum.[8]

An Institute of Medicine report, "The Future of Nursing: Leading Change, Advancing Health," was reviewed by Barbara Brunt and Bette Bogdan in their paper "Nursing Professional Development Leadership," published in StatPearls in 2023.[9] They highlighted the recommendation, supporting "education programs for leadership development to prepare nurse leaders at all levels with the leadership acumen to transform the healthcare system."[10] The important point to note is "at all levels."[11]

Leadership needs to start at the bottom and work its way up. Our healthcare systems become more effective when we have effective leadership at all levels.

Allied health schools have similar recommendations recognizing the importance of leadership among all healthcare professionals. Pharmacy schools are required to ensure "development of professional self-awareness, capabilities, responsibilities, and leadership."[12]

Physical therapy schools are required to train learners in leadership development: "Describe where and how the physical therapist professional curriculum includes content and learning experiences in ethics, values, responsibilities, service, and leadership in the ever-changing health care environment."[13]

Most leadership preparation and development falls to health systems or individuals. Unfortunately, most health systems do not have the resources to adequately address this issue. There are some exemplars, but this still leaves the majority needing ways to improve their leadership. For better or worse (maybe even richer or poorer), there are an unlimited number of ways to improve your leadership skills (e.g., courses, degrees, books, podcasts, mentoring and coaching). It only starts when we recognize the importance of preparing for our roles as leaders.

Preparation as a healthcare leader has three parts. It requires you to prepare for your clinical role, prepare yourself as a leader, and then prepare and develop the next generation of clinicians and leaders. Each of these requires specific attention to detail and discipline to ensure we are prepared for the required roles and responsibilities. Just like the practice of clinical medicine, there are no shortcuts to leadership development. We have to make this part of who we are and give it the time and effort it demands.

> *There are no shortcuts to leadership development. We have to make this part of who we are and give it the time and effort it demands.*

The easiest way to learn about leadership is by taking advantage of the leadership moments we are part of everyday. We can look at everything we do through a leadership lens and determine what lessons we can learn from it.

During her interview for the book, Chelsea Hayes said, "Every single day of my life. I learned from everyone, everywhere. My niece is three, and she teaches me so much about leadership and what kind of woman I want to be and hope to be. So yeah, I'm always looking for teachers."

I love this example because it illustrates that we can learn from people in restaurants, coaches, teachers, and the people we work with and for. If someone drops a tray in a restaurant, how does the team respond? How do they pick each other up? How do they communicate? The same lessons apply in healthcare. Observe each situation and ask yourself, "Do I want to add that behavior to my leadership tool belt or avoid it?"

If you do this, you become more equipped to lead.

If you care about preparing for leadership, make it a priority. We prioritize what we think is important, and how we spend our time is the real test of what is important. Make leadership development a habit for you and for those you lead. I am a huge fan of James Clear's book *Atomic Habits*.[14] Small and frequent input leads to huge effects over time. If you invest thirty minutes a week learning how to become a more effective leader, that is over 1,500 minutes per year. Make it an expectation of those you lead that they are intentionally spending time developing the leadership skills of those they lead. We should be asking those we lead during annual reviews how they are developing themselves and their teams. Talk about leadership development with those you lead and make it part of your culture.

Developing leadership development programs—or, at a minimum, setting time aside to teach and talk about leadership—needs to become the standard in healthcare organizations. While the desire to pursue leadership development is an individual decision, organizations should make it easier for those who want to become more effective. We have already seen that there is a return on investment for more effective leadership. Everyone has different resources, but look at how your organization can make intentional efforts to better prepare leaders.

We are all going to move on at some point, so what are you doing to systematically develop your bench and succession plan? These initiatives could be big or small. They could be as simple as inviting speakers on leadership every month. They could be courses offered a few times a year, or they could be year-long leadership development programs. You can also start small and grow your leadership development platform as you go. The important part is that if we care about our patients and each other, we have to care about leadership development.

One of the most effective ways you can prepare as a leader is to read. General James Mattis famously said, "If you haven't read hundreds of books, you are functionally illiterate, and you will be incompetent, because your personal experiences alone aren't broad enough to sustain you."[15]

There are many great books that can provide advice on almost any topic on leadership. The number of leadership books that exist is overwhelming, so in Appendix A, I provide a Prescription for Caring in Healthcare Leadership Reading List to help guide you with books I think will be meaningful. The recommendations coincide with the chapters in this book. Also, part of the reason I wrote my book was to condense a lot of what I think is important for healthcare leaders into one book. Consider this book your leadership starting line.

Here are a couple of tips to help make the most of your reading for leadership development:

- Make it a habit to take notes in the book.
- Mark pages with tabs or folded corners so you can go back to important points.
- Write notes to yourself in the back of the book, or even start using note cards to categorize different leadership topics so you can review them over time.

- Host leadership book clubs. Consider doing a book club outside of your organization, where you may feel more free to speak openly about struggles you are having at work.

For several years, our internal medicine residency at Walter Reed has done a leadership book club for the book *The Culture Code* by Daniel Coyle.[16] Each year, we give a copy to our Chief Residents who are new graduates and junior faculty who help lead the program for a year before moving on to other things. We spend time as a group reviewing the book and discussing how we can implement the ideas within our program. This helps us continually build our culture using the book as a guide. We generally meet for dinner and review the key concepts, so not only is it building leadership skills but fostering connections.

Daily Preparation

We have focused a lot on what I consider long-term preparation early in this chapter. I want to finish the chapter by talking about the daily acts of preparation that are important as a leader. Preparation is a sign of respect for the time of those we are leading. If you are a teacher, are you preparing for your students? Are you adequately preparing for meetings? In the military, we have a mantra that is instilled in us from early in training—*Proper Planning and Preparation Prevents Piss Poor Performance.*

We need to prepare for the task at hand to more effectively utilize our time and the time of those we are leading. Is the best version of yourself showing up each day? You might fool people some of the time, but ultimately, people know if you care enough to be prepared. Dr. Jeff Hutchinson talked about this in terms of meetings. One Caring Act of Leadership is to "make sure that

JOSHUA D. HARTZELL, MD

meetings are meaningful." This means preparing and ensuring that the meetings cover "what is important to the people" and "where to spend time." If we care about the people we lead, we need to prepare—whether it is for a meeting, a clinic, teaching, or something else.

I want to end the chapter with a couple of quotes. One is from retired Major General Patrick Donahue, who once said about leading in the Army, "We are leaders in the world's most intellectually demanding profession, where the cost of crappy preparation is the death of your people and the fate of your nation. Put the physical and intellectual energy in; we need you. Preparing for leadership is a lifelong endeavor."[17] The second is from Nancy Koehn in her book *Forged in Crisis*. In her book, she talks about five leaders who dealt with crises: Ernest Shackleton, Abraham Lincoln, Rachel Carson, Frederick Douglass, and Franklin Roosevelt.[18] She says leadership is not something that a few people are born with—rather, courageous leadership develops from within as leaders discover a purpose to motivate others.[19] She consistently talks about their self-development as leaders: "The harder they worked on themselves, the better they became as leaders."[20]

The same holds true for careers in medicine. Poor leadership leads to worse patient outcomes, less effective training, and burnout among providers. Burnout among providers impacts our relationships and families outside of work. We have a responsibility to prepare and lead effectively. Our hard work and preparation as leaders changes lives.

Prescription for Caring in Leadership

1. Set aside at least thirty minutes to one hour per week to study leadership. This could be reading a book, article, or blog, watching a video, or listening to a podcast.

2. Make a commitment to read a certain number of leadership books each year. Set the goal and hold yourself accountable, or find a friend to hold each other accountable. My challenge is for you to make it a goal to read at least two leadership books each year.

3. Create a leadership folder on your computer. Every time you find a good leadership resource, put it in there so you can go back to it when you need it and share it with others. You can use these resources to coach them and help them with their own leadership development. I have a Word document as well where I put links to particular articles that I like to give to people so that they're easy to find when they come up.

4. Commit to taking a course on leadership or attending leadership sessions at your professional meetings in the next year.

5. Find a coach to help build skills in an area where you need to improve as a leader.

6. Talk to your mentor about leadership and how to improve.

7. What does preparation look like for you in the role you are in or the role you are preparing for? What are you currently doing to prepare? What do you need to do to prepare?

8. Think about ways to develop the leaders that work with and for you. How are you preparing those below you to lead? Consider these items:

   a. Meet with them specifically to talk about leadership.
   b. Invite speakers on leadership development.

    c. Send out articles or podcasts about leadership.

    d. Do a leadership book club with your team.

    e. Host a dinner at your house to talk about leadership.

    f. Support them in attending a leadership development course.

CHAPTER 6

Care About Your Values
and Purpose

*"The values that matter to you most
are reflected in your behavior. How
you behave is how you lead."*
—Dr. Thomas Varghese Jr.

L EADERSHIP STARTS WITH YOU. This may sound cliché, but it's true. Sometimes we need to be reminded of the simple things—and just because something is simple does not mean it is easy. Leadership requires that you know who you are, what motivates you, and what shapes your actions. To be an effective leader, you have to spend time getting to know yourself and why you lead the way you do.

Almost every leadership book will have a section at the beginning on developing a better understanding of who you are as a leader and what your values are. A few of my favorites, which I pull examples from in this chapter, are *The Leadership Challenge* by James Kouzes and Barry Posner,[1] *True North, Emerging Leader Edition* by Bill George,[2] and *Dare to Lead* by Brené Brown.[3] I highly recommend reading them, as I have found that repetition in thinking and reflecting on this has helped me to solidify my own understanding of my values and their importance. While each is written with different voices and examples, they all point toward the importance of knowing who you are as a leader, knowing what drives you (purpose), and ultimately having your values guide your actions. We cannot cover all we need to in this chapter, so my hope is that you will be inspired to go read more about values and purpose and use some of the resources/references that are provided for a deeper dive.

Know Yourself

To be effective leaders, we have to know what drives us. We have to understand why we make the decisions we do and why we act the way we do. A friend, colleague, and former two-time medical school dean, Dr. Wiley "Chip" Souba, has written and spoken frequently about the inward journey of leadership. According to Dr. Souba, "Becoming a world-class leader involves much more than becoming a more proficient or a better strategic thinker. Most fundamentally, the process is about personal transformation. All great leaders are on a continuous inward journey to transform themselves and their organizations."[4]

The first step, according to Dr. Souba, is to "construct your life story."[5] What events in your life have shaped you to be the person you are? This is very similar to Bill George in *True North,* who titled Chapter 1 "Your Life Story."[6] He writes, "...they become great leaders, using their gifts to help others. This could only happen if they first understood themselves and their life stories."[7] Both Dr. Souba and Bill George talk about the importance of reflecting on your life experiences and spending time thinking about how they have shaped you as a person and as a leader.

Have you ever thought about why you act a certain way? Why do you lead the way you do? I have included a figure to help you think about all the different people and experiences that have helped shape who you are. Every one of these people and events has influenced who you are and, as a result, how you lead. Bill George and Warren Bennis have talked about how crucibles or great challenges that people face in their lives shape them.[8,9] Dr. Souba states, "Great leaders use difficult situations, trials, and tests in their life stories to extract meanings that shape their self-concept."[10]

Understanding these influences is an important part of being an effective leader. Spend some time and think about each of the items in the figure and how these have impacted you.

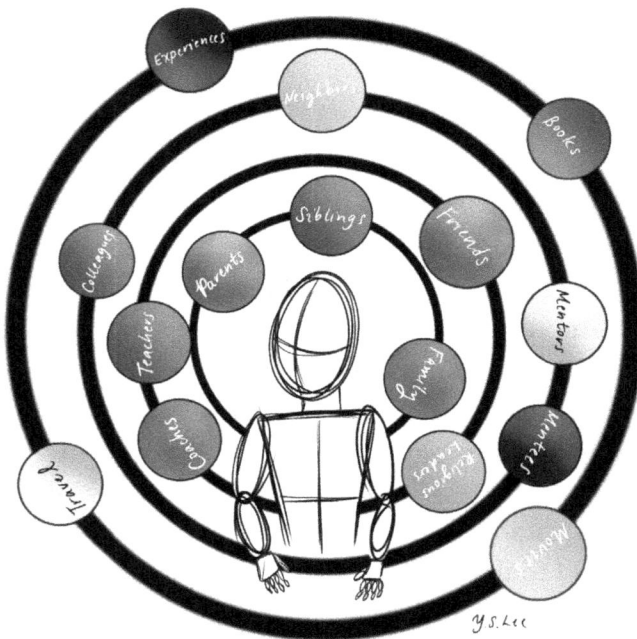

The ways we develop and lead as a result of our life experiences is not always positive. Souba points out that "the events and incidents that we select to construct our life stories can get in our way, hold us back, and hamper our growth and development."[11]

Bill George states, "By reflecting on their stories, leaders understand how important events and interactions with people have shaped their approach to the world. Discerning our stories and then reframing them as necessary enables us to recognize that we are not victims, but people shaped by experiences that provide the impetus for us to become leaders."[12]

As you continue to grow as a leader and as a person, it is important that you think about what is shaping your actions and how you may need to adjust to be more effective. If you want to achieve your purpose in life as a leader, you have to continue to grow and evolve.

Know Your Purpose

As a leader, what is your purpose in life? Bill George has famously, in leadership circles, coined this as a leader's North Star.[13] It is the reason you lead. To be an effective leader, it is important to understand what you want to achieve. I am not talking about how much money you will make, the number of papers you will publish, or the position you will rise to. I am talking about what drives you as a leader. What impact do you want to have, and what legacy do you want to leave?

Having a firm understanding of your purpose is important as a leader, as told to me by Dr. Jeff Hutchinson during his interview. He gives us an example of how purpose guides us as leaders:

> Why do you want to be a leader? If your why is because you think that's what you're supposed to do, you're not going to be as effective. If your why is because you care about the

organization, you're going to be more effective. If your why is because you see a greater good that you can do in this organization than you could do anyplace else, you may not get to where you want to be, but you're going to be a caring leader and have a fantastic impact.

Prasad Kaipa provides an excellent example in a 2012 *Harvard Business Review* blog post.[14] He highlighted the life and leadership of Dr. Govindappa Venkataswamy. He is an ophthalmologist who has brought free eye care to millions of people. If you have not read about him, you should, as he is an amazing example of a leader driven by caring. His North Star was to "eliminate needless blindness by providing appropriate, compassionate, high-quality eye care for all."[15] Using this as his vision, he was able to lead and create systems to provide affordable (free in most cases) eye care across the world. According to Kaipa, Dr. Venkataswamy has "trained 15 percent of ophthalmologists in India and thousands more from over 69 countries. The work from this one man is said to have touched 40 percent of eye care patients in the developing world to date."[16]

Wow! One man with one purpose has had an amazing impact driven by his North Star.

Dr. Jeff Hutchinson talked about his purpose in military medicine: "Knowing that when I cared about my group, I did great...The example for that is in the Army. When I think about trying to change some of the statistics, the racialized medicine in military medicine, it gave me an energy and a purpose and a goal unlike any of the other ones."

My North Star is to positively impact others' lives. This was shaped by my parents, who consistently demonstrated helping others growing up. My dad used to help take care of one neighbor's pigs while the farmer went on vacation. Caring for pigs, I assure you, is a smelly business and makes an imprint on you. My dad was also on call to help people if they had bats in their house. This freaks me out, now that I know more about rabies, but it was routine when I was growing up. He would volunteer with scouting events and help others he worked with if they needed something. He was always helping someone. I was also driven by a youth baseball coach, Daryl Jones. He was a former Major League Baseball player who had come back to our small town and dedicated his life to coaching. He was more than a coach, as he inspired each of us to be better people and have high aspirations for our lives.

When my mom was diagnosed with breast cancer, I saw firsthand how people can suffer with illness. I made it a point to ensure that whenever I could, I would help alleviate suffering in others. Every action I take is one I hope positively impacts others' lives. This could be through patient care, teaching and mentoring, or leading. It could be by leaving an absurdly high tip for a waiter at a restaurant. It could be by coaching a youth sports team. It could be by smiling at someone and saying hello while walking down the street or through the hospital. You never know when someone simply needs an act of kindness that positively impacts their life.

Ideally, your purpose will align with your place of work. If it doesn't, you may struggle, as we tend to be more motivated when we are working toward something that is important to us. If they don't align, you may need to consider whether you are in the right spot. Obviously, there are lots of other considerations—like financial stability for you and your family—but aligning your purpose with your organization's purpose can be a powerful combination.

What is your North Star, your guiding light on your leadership journey? Identifying this is an important part of understanding who you are as a leader and guiding your leadership. As Kaipa highlights, "North Stars align our energy, emotions, and actions in the service of our vision."[17]

Know Your Values

Once you know your purpose, you have to know what values will allow you to achieve it. Think of it this way: your purpose is your destination, and your values are the compass keeping you on the right path. They should be the lens (see image) through which you look at problems and that help you decide what action to take as a leader. Unfortunately, most of us don't spend a lot of time focused on our values.

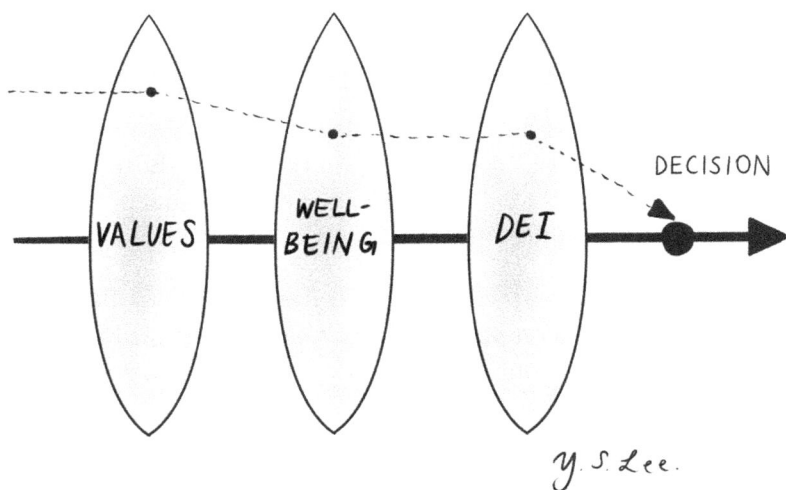

Image: Decision Making Lens. Consider your decisions by examining them through your values.

I have delivered numerous talks on leadership and generally speak on the importance of values. When I ask the audience how many of them know which values drive them or if they have thought about their values, rarely do I get more than a few hands. Most of us have never been asked, and many have never been a part of formal leadership development programs. Thinking about our values for many is often relegated to posters on the walls or internet banners. As learners are taught about values, however, they start to see the power of how they shape us as leaders and organizations. They allow us to be more intentional about the way we lead and show up for others.

Suzanna Fitzpatrick, DNP, CRNP talked about the importance of knowing your values and how they serve as a guide for her and her organization. As we will get into more below, she also points out that our values come alive through our actions:

> I try to be somebody that you know what my core value is at all times. It's every part of me. My core value is loyalty. There's no question. It's my friendships. It's my patients. It's my family. It's my way of teaching. All of that is me. You might not always like it, because I'm going to be loyal to those things, and you know the extra things, maybe not as much. I try to live by those things.

> When I ask people to do things here, because that's what they know. The mission of the organization is about community. I help the community by volunteering. I am a longtime volunteer. I am committed to investing in the development of novice healthcare providers and helping to make them feel like part of the organization. I try to speak the vision with my actions, and I encourage other people to do that too.

You can find lists of values in *The Leadership Challenge*,[18] as well as in Brené Brown's book *Dare to Lead*.[19]

My core values are caring, courage, and well-being. I cheat somewhat with "caring" because you can put "care about" in front of other values to emphasize them. Almost everything else we do as leaders involves caring: care about setting high expectations, care about giving feedback, care about recognizing others, etc. While caring is one value, it supports all the other things I find important about leadership. If you care, then it changes the way you approach other values and the behaviors they drive. As you can see, if you didn't figure it out from the title and what you have read so far, I think caring is important.

We also have to be courageous as leaders. This is not about physical courage in healthcare, but moral courage. We have to have the courage to speak truth to power, courage to be vulnerable, courage to be humble, and courage to have difficult conversations with those we lead.

Finally, well-being is critical to each of us—the well-being of an individual leader and also of those we lead. My promise to everyone I lead is that I care deeply about your personal and professional well-being. I intentionally put personal well-being first because if you are not doing well personally, it's hard to be well professionally.

Think about your own values and what resonates with you. Spend time identifying your values and let them guide you as a leader. This requires some deep work in reflection as you think about what is really important to you. In many ways, your leadership values will be your brand as a leader. How do you want to be identified as a leader? If you identify your values and then take action to demonstrate them, they become reality.

Values Guide Action—Developing Caring Acts of Leadership

Values are the guide for the decisions we make. Knowing our values should help us as we are confronted with numerous leadership challenges and decisions. We have to live out our values as leaders—otherwise, they don't mean anything. Brené Brown famously wrote in *Dare to Lead* that we need to take values from "BS to Behavior."[20] As you think about your values, start pairing them with concrete actions that bring them to life. What tangible steps can you do each day to bring your values to life? For the rest of the book, we are going to talk about Caring Acts of Leadership. These are actions that bring your caring as a leader to life.

Unfortunately, values often become nothing more than something on a poster in the hall or a banner on the internet, when they should be powerful guides for decisions and building your culture. Major General Clark provided an example of how values helped guide actions when he was the Director of Walter Reed National Military Medical Center:

> The centerpiece of our Walter Reed strategy was *an extraordinary experience for every patient, every time.* Right? We made that the centerpiece of our strategy icon. You may remember the icon with the Patient in the center, and Our People across the top, you know, so it was very easy. It kind of rolled off your tongue. Our patients are in the center. Our people are at the top...we tried to live that. I tried to role model that.
>
> I will never forget—at one of our morning staff meetings, we had a complex decision to make. Our leaders had different opinions on what we should do. We had discussed this challenge for several minutes when Captain [Navy] Phil Purdue, our chief of surgery, said, "We just have to keep our

patient in the center." And there was a moment of pause, and then it became obvious what we needed to do. All Phil did was remind us of what we said we were going to do, and when we didn't let other stuff get in the way, we quickly came to a decision that was in line with what we had already established as important.

Values and Action Define You as a Leader and Shape Culture

There is a direct connection between your values, your actions, and the culture of your organization. Our cultures are shaped by the actions or lack of action that is taken within our organizations. I have never been a huge fan of the inspirational posters that espouse different leadership characteristics—just think about the soaring eagle or penguins lined up following a lead penguin. (Don't ask how we ever got to penguins being a symbol of leadership! I couldn't tell you!) Action and behavior matter and form our work environment. Culture is what it *is* like to work somewhere, not what we want or think it *should be* like.

In the book *Management Lessons From Mayo Clinic: Inside One of the World's Most Admired Service Organizations,* former Mayo Clinic Chief Executive Officer Dr. Glenn Forbes stated, "If you've just communicated a value, but you haven't driven it into operations, into the policy, into the decision-making, into allocation of resources, and ultimately into the culture of the organization, then it's just words."[21]

Dr. Alex Niven, a current pulmonary critical care doctor at Mayo Clinic, talked to me about leaving the Army after over twenty years of service and going to Mayo Clinic. He was given a month to learn about the culture and system before starting patient care. This emphasized to him just how important their culture is as an organization. How many places have you worked that spent time focusing on teaching about and reinforcing cultural values?

To make values and actions become culture, you need to be intentional in your actions. Spend time talking to your teams about your values and their values. Talk about shared values within the organization and how these values guide daily decisions and actions. Recognize people for living out these values. Catch them doing great stuff and modeling the values you want, then point these out to others. The more time we spend on our values, the more we *have* the culture we want, as opposed to simply wishing we could create it. Building an effective culture is not magic but is the result of daily intentional effort to build the culture you want and need to thrive.

> *Building an effective culture is not magic but is the result of daily intentional effort to build the culture you want and need to thrive.*

Your Personal Leadership Philosophy

As we close this chapter, I want to challenge you to develop your own leadership philosophy, capturing the items we have discussed above. In their book *The Leadership Challenge*, Kouzes and Posner ask, "What is your leadership philosophy?"[22] A leadership philosophy is simply a written statement about who you are as a leader, your values, what you expect from your team, what will not be tolerated, and what your priorities are for the organization. The document serves as a "leadership compass" for you as a leader and for your followers.[23] Research by Kouzes and Posner has demonstrated that leaders who are clear about their leadership philosophy score 25 percent higher when rating their own leadership effectiveness.[23] Maybe even more importantly, leaders with a clear leadership philosophy versus those who are not clear were rated 40 percent higher in effectiveness.[24] Developing your own leadership philosophy of values and expectations is a valuable process as a leader.

In the military, with each new commander, we were often introduced to and given their leadership philosophy. This was a one-page summary of their expectations and what was important to them as a leader. It was an introduction to who they were (including their family and other things, such as hobbies), what they expected, and what was important to them. Developing a leadership philosophy is a great way to think about who you are as a leader and communicate that to your team. The philosophy can then guide your actions as a leader and the actions of your organization.

According to Tom Deierlein, a West Point graduate and decorated (Bronze Star and Purple Heart) Army ranger who has written about developing leadership philosophies, "When you write and follow your leader's compass, you will be a more effective leader and experience less stress. You will energize your people and set them free. Your people will admire you for being authentic. You will be on course for leadership success."[25]

Appendix B has a worksheet designed to help develop your own leadership philosophy. I would recommend you read the article by Tom Deierlein,[26] as it is one of the best resources I have seen. Once you have developed your philosophy, you should share it with those you lead. This can be done in person, via email, during group presentations, or even through a video message or podcast. Most leaders I have known send it out so that everyone can have a copy of it to refer back to.

Think about how caring as a leader will be part of your philosophy.

Caring-inspired leadership allows us to lead authentically in healthcare. We should embrace it and be ourselves as we work to reshape the way healthcare and medical education are delivered.

Prescription for Caring in Leadership

1. Identify three personal values and write them down. Post them so you can see them where you work. Reflect on them daily or at least weekly to determine if your actions are supporting who you want to be. What Caring Acts of Leadership do you need to do more of to bring your values to life?

3. Discuss your values with your team and have them identify how those values can become Caring Acts of Leadership. For example, if a team member identifies respect as a core value, then a Caring Act of Leadership could be that before a decision is made, everyone on the team gets to provide input. This demonstrates respect for the ideas and opinions of the team.

4. Develop your leadership philosophy. Share this with your direct reports and talk about why it is important. See the Leadership Philosophy Guide in Appendix B to help.

5. Read at least one of the books mentioned in this chapter and on the Prescription for Caring in Healthcare Leadership Reading List in Appendix A.

Caring Acts of Leadership

CHAPTER 7

Care Enough to Take Care of Those You Lead

"Shouting 'self-care' at people who actually need 'community care' is how we fail people."
—Nakita Valerio[1]

WELLNESS IS A LEADERSHIP issue. We need to stop blaming people for not being resilient enough and address the systemic drivers of burnout, low morale, depression, and suicide. While each of us has an individual responsibility for wellness, we need leaders at every level to institute creative change within the system to better support all of us. An example might be allowing telework for employees to eliminate their commute time and allow them to have flexibility with family and personal events, or ensuring everyone gets a break for a meal while they are on a scheduled shift in the hospital. We need tangible solutions and not more resiliency training for individuals.

Leadership consultant and coach Chelsea Hayes introduced me to the idea of "community care." The term, as defined by Heather Dockray, is "basically any care provided by a single individual to benefit other people in their life. This can take the form of protests, for which community care is best known, but also simple, interpersonal acts of compassion."[2] These could include simple acts like a "text when you just need someone to talk...someone grabbing groceries for you...somebody coming and doing your dishes and watching your kids while you are grieving."[3]

In her blog post, Dockray wrote, "Self-care alone can't solve systemic issues. For that, you need community care."[4]

To fix the pandemic of burnout in medicine, we need to better support each other within our community through Caring Acts of Leadership. We need a seismic shift from our leaders to fix our system.

This means we need to look at things like clinic work schedules, clinic and hospital processes, insurance reimbursement structures that are less time-consuming, sick leave and parental leave policies, and mental health support for healthcare providers. We need leaders who can innovate and develop system changes that will improve not only patient care but the lives of healthcare providers. It is our time to lead and develop a system that supports healthcare providers, rather than just expecting us to make it work.

Over time, I have observed different leaders and taken ideas from them to help support the well-being of those I lead. Some of these are simple, but they can be impactful. Major General Jeff Clark said we have a privilege to lead, and "You must care about them... and you have to demonstrate it; otherwise, people do not have the

> *It is our time to lead and develop a system that supports healthcare providers, rather than just expecting us to make it work.*

opportunity of knowing their leaders and organization care about them as individuals and fellow human beings."

In this chapter, we will talk about specific strategies that leaders can implement at any level to better support those they lead.

Some of my earliest leadership lessons were from Army Reserve Officer Training. I was taught the importance of taking care of my soldiers. "Leaders eat last" is a strategy that ensures everyone else has food. Another unwritten rule is to check the team's feet on a long road march. The bottom line was that you as the leader were responsible for their well-being. The mission could not be completed if your soldiers were not able to perform. Sound familiar? Our mission in healthcare cannot be completed if those we lead are not able to perform. It is not just that—our job as leaders is to set the conditions for those we lead to perform optimally at work *while* flourishing at home and in their communities.

> *Our job as leaders is to set the conditions for those we lead to perform optimally at work while flourishing at home and in their communities.*

Care for Your People, Whatever They Need

Taking care of your people requires knowing them and figuring out what they need to be successful. We are going to talk about some work-related items below, but before we dive into those, as leaders we need to recognize the need to care for the whole person at work. This means we need to identify what we can do to best support the lives of the people who work with and for us. We are not responsible for every aspect of the lives of those we lead, but we can play a role and often can be of immense support. If we support the lives of those we lead and care for them, they will want to be part of our organization and will want to work hard.

Angela Costa, RN, BSN, MPM provided two examples that frankly make me want to go work for her. This is the first:

> You must know your employees. One day, an employee came into my office when I worked on the North Side of Pittsburgh. The North Side is a diverse area, with households of all socioeconomic backgrounds. Many of our nurse aides came from different backgrounds, and they all had different struggles and different family situations. Single moms in particular have a hard time juggling schedules and come to work with so much on their mind. I remember the employee came into my office in tears, saying how the SWAT team was in the house next to hers and her son was home by himself. She was so worried about her son's safety, so I insisted on driving her home so she could be with her son. You really have to care about others that you work with. At that moment, we had to forget about work and care about the human being—my employee had to get home to her son.

The second story is about supporting her employees during the holidays:

> We've often helped our employees during the holidays. It's important to support your team year-round, of course, but it's especially important during the holidays. Everybody, every family, goes through rough patches, and when they do, it's important to come together as a team and support each other. Sometimes that means emotional support— picking up your teammate when they aren't feeling their best. Sometimes it means chipping in to help them buy their kids extra Christmas gifts. It's important to get to know your employees on a personal level so you can help them when

times get tough. When you care for your employees, they become better employees because they know it's all about caring. Everybody wants to know that someone cares about them.

Listening to the way she supports those she works with made me tear up a little. She goes from taking someone to a house with a potential SWAT team to playing Santa Claus. I suspect her employees would run through a wall for her, and it is no surprise that her caring as a leader has resulted in her being elevated to the senior ranks of nursing leadership. She made a phenomenal point about why taking care of your people is important:

> As leaders, we have to make sure that people feel supported in their lives away from work so that they can function better in the work environment. You're not going to get the best out of people if their mind is somewhere else. You're not going to get them to provide great care for patients if they are distracted. Employee wellness leads to better patient care; a better employee experience leads to a better patient experience.

If we care for our people, we get the best out of them. If we support their personal lives, they are able to show up fully at work. If they are not distracted at work, patient care is improved. Isn't the goal to deliver the best patient care? This starts with taking care of those delivering the care.

Reconnaissance and Action

How do we know what our people need? We need to make finding out a priority. This can be as simple as walking around and asking or as complex as holding town halls. There should be some continual effort to identify needs. Measuring well-being and being held accountable for it is a Caring Act of Leadership.

JOSHUA D. HARTZELL, MD

Once you identify needs, you must take action to fix things. As leaders, we need to put our resources into our people. Sometimes these are system fixes. Sometimes these are simpler things. The bottom line is making well-being a priority for those you lead.

Here is a great example of how Angela Costa, RN, BSN, MPM supports her team. They do an annual survey and make changes based on the feedback:

> The survey showed that our team members were feeling dehydrated and hungry because they didn't have a chance to drink and eat during their shift. Why would staff not get a meal break? It's an assignment every day on the assignment board. Staff members shouldn't be coming in to work and asking for the opportunity to eat. As it turns out, some people didn't want to take a lunch break because they were worried about who would take care of their patients. Nurses would rather deprive themselves than deprive their patients. So, we had to reinforce for them that taking a break to eat will allow nurses to take care of their patients better. We also installed new hydration stations and new snack machines, providing better and healthier meal-on-the-go options. I have made it my mission to make sure that everyone has a chance to eat. The message we are sending is "take a break." Eat, sit down for five minutes, decompress, and at least get away from all that stress that's hitting you in that nursing unit. We owe it to our nurses to make sure they can have their meal breaks.

She gave some sage advice about why this is important: "Happier employees make happier patients."

We are good at taking care of others, and not so good at taking care of ourselves. Leaders can play a vital role in helping those we lead prioritize their health. We need to leverage our caring nature and make it part of our leadership. We can support the well-being of those we lead by reminding them—or, even better, making it an *expectation* of them—to do the things they need to be healthy, mentally and physically. We need to model these behaviors!

The Road to Well-Being

The book *Drive* by Daniel Pink reshaped the way I approach wellness from a personal and organizational perspective.[5] This book changed my life. I would like to think it has changed the lives of many others as well. Since reading the book, I have taught these ideas to hundreds of physicians across the country, getting them to think about ways to bring these ideas to their organizations. Motivation is the opposite of burnout.

Pink's main idea is that employee motivation has evolved over time, going from Motivation 1.0, which was essentially basic human needs, to Motivation 2.0 (rewards and punishments), to Motivation 3.0, which is driven by intrinsic motivation.[6] The latter consists of autonomy, mastery (expertise), and purpose.[7] Over the course of my career and study of leadership, I have found implementation of Pink's ideas are a useful model to approaching well-being and improving morale and engagement at work. They provide a framework that gives us concrete ways to approach wellness. Rather than just talking about needing to improve well-being, there are tangible steps we can take, as I outline below.

By giving employees autonomy, they are more likely to feel motivated. Pink uses multiple companies as examples and demonstrates how these companies flourished by giving people who work for them more autonomy.[8] In healthcare, we struggle to create autonomy. We have shifts that need to be covered, procedures that need to be done, and classes that need to be taught. I will not argue any of these points—and yes, there are times when we all have to sacrifice some of our time for our patients, students, or organizations. The question we need to ask ourselves is, where are the spaces and time in which we could create flexibility? Could we alternate work schedules? Could we create schedules that give people protected time to work on projects?

When I was a rising junior faculty, a mentor used to say, "Associate Professors are made on nights and weekends." But if academic advancement is important, why should we not actually give people time to do the work, rather than make them use their own? The work they do could support advancements in medicine and teaching. Innovative ideas will support quality of patient care.

Maybe we are looking at this all wrong? With the brain power we have in medicine, if we gave people more time and space to think, we could solve more of the problems we have. And maybe we would have a less burned-out workforce—a workforce who is now leaving medicine.

As leaders, consider giving some amount of time to those you lead to work on their own stuff—or simply to take time off to recharge. While I was an internal medicine program director, we elected to give all of our trainees an extra half-day off a week every fifth week during their ambulatory clinic block. Could you give those you lead even a couple hours off, intermittently? Would you want to work for a leader or organization who did that for you? Giving people protected time to work or take care of themselves is a Caring Act of Leadership. This will pay dividends in the long run for well-being, work production, and retention.

If people feel like they are working to the top of their ability and improving their skills, they tend to be more motivated. Sound familiar? How many times in healthcare have we heard someone say that they feel like they are doing tasks someone else should do? How excited do people get when they have the opportunity to work on their professional development?

The idea of developing mastery to motivate followers just seems brilliant. Think about your best boss and favorite place you have worked. I suspect that it was a place or person who was investing in your professional and personal development. We appreciate and want to work harder for people who invest in us. For organizations and leaders, the more effective your people become, the more effective your organization becomes.

People will raise objections to this idea. They will say, "We don't have the money. We don't have the time. It is their responsibility, as physicians, nurses, and physical therapists, to have ongoing professional development." What is your role as their leader? What role does your organization have in terms of mastery for those who work within it? I have helped people give a business case analysis of how investing in those you lead makes financial success.

Let's take the example of going to the Stanford Clinical Teaching Program. The program teaches faculty how to deliver a local faculty development program on clinical teaching. It is a seventeen-hour course that, once you complete a month of training, you can deliver locally. I was sent to this course as a junior faculty, and it probably cost our institution around $20,000. That's some sticker shock! But since that course ten years ago, I have taught well over 150 faculty development workshops and served as an assistant dean for faculty development and as a program director.

I would credit the course with many of my skills. Serving in leadership positions alone would probably have been worth the investment, but what about the teaching from what I learned in the course? I have taught over eighty residents and faculty. It is hard to find a similar faculty development course, but if you had to pay someone to teach it or send people to the course, it would likely be around $1,000 per person. So, the investment in me returned well over $60,000 to our organization. Leaders need to think more strategically and creatively about how professional development has a return on investment.

There are so many ways leaders and organizations can invest in mastery. Every leader can and should be mentoring and coaching (we have a chapter on this later). Leaders directly enhance the careers of those they lead in terms of mastering skills through coaching and creating opportunities. Do you have a system in place for mentoring? Do you or could you have a coaching program for professional development?

What systems do you have in place for ongoing professional development? Look at these and see if they are on target. Do your invited speakers cover what your staff need? How much input do staff have into topics covered? Are you hitting topics they may not be getting in other places? For example, how much time is spent on leadership development? How often are you sending people to ongoing professional development courses? How often are you nominating people for specific career-enhancing opportunities? I have been fortunate to have taken multiple Harvard Macy courses because people invested in me. These were profoundly impactful for my professional development as an educator and leader.

This should be a metric every leader at every level has measured. What are you doing to develop the mastery of those you lead? Make this part of every performance review and highlight examples of excellence within your organization.

Power of Purpose

Pink's final component of intrinsic motivation is purpose.[9] The idea is that if people are doing work that matters, they will be motivated. He is not alone in this belief. At the 2022 BLUEPRINT Leadership Summit, Doug Conant (CEO of ConantLeadership) and Liz Wiseman (author of *Multiplier* and *Impact Players*—put these on your leadership reading list) made the statement, "People don't burn out because they're working too hard; they burn out because they're having too little impact."[10] Author Jon Gordon adds, "We don't get burned out because of what we do. We get burned out because we forget why we do it."[11]

Let's hear from some of the people interviewed for this book. Suzanna Fitzpatrick, DNP, CRNP emphasized the importance of remembering why we do what we do and how that motivates and inspires us:

> I don't know every nurse in the world, but every nurse I've ever spoken to will tell you that they come into healthcare because they want to help people, because they have a drive to help others, and that sort of comes with that caring lens of caring for others…I came to a hospital during COVID-19, and there was this high level of nursing burnout and retention… you miss many people. Miss them when they wake up in the morning and—what made you want to be here?

> What made them want to be a nurse? What made them want to be a leader in their organization? What made them want to be passionate about the mission and vision of their organization? And luckily enough, I have not lost that. I've never felt anything but gratitude and love for my profession.

Her example highlights how purpose fuels us at work. The ability to connect with a larger purpose in life gives us energy. Fostering this connection to our purpose is important for us and those we lead.

Dr. Jeff Hutchinson drove this point home when talking about how, as leaders, we need to have intrinsic motivation: "The more intrinsic the motivation, the more we're doing something because doing it is what gives us energy and strength, the longer it can be sustained. I think that can help with burnout because, as we help other people realize the intrinsic value of medicine, it reminds us of why we're doing what we're doing. It's a leadership necessity."

Everything we do in healthcare and teaching has purpose and meaning. That said, we often lose sight of this, and we rarely recognize people for the purpose in their work. We take for granted the amazing work that we do. I wrote about this in a blog post for KevinMD.com a few years ago.[12] Essentially, a resident had saved someone's life overnight, having successfully coded them several times. My response was...well, isn't that what we are supposed to do? My reaction was a real wake-up call to me that we need to do better at *thanking* those we work with, emphasizing the value and purpose of their work.

We need to help those we lead recognize the purpose they have in their work. We need to do a more effective job of recognizing those in healthcare for the life-changing work they do on a daily basis. We had a bolus of this during the COVID-19 pandemic, when healthcare workers were hailed as heroes, but that time has faded. We are back to the norm where, all too often, we don't give ourselves credit or recognize the meaning of work by others in healthcare. Make it a habit to talk about the value and purpose of the work people do. We will delve into this more later, in the chapter on gratitude.

Do not abuse purpose and meaning to get people to work more than they should. There is, unfortunately, data that some leaders will abuse employees who are generous. Stanley et al. published a paper, "The Dark Side of Generosity: Employees with a reputation for giving are selectively targeted for exploitation."[13] They state, "…we find consistent evidence that managers are inclined to take unfair advantage of employees with reputations for generosity, selectively targeting them for exploitation in ways that likely, and ironically, hamper long-term organization success."[14]

The lesson is that while it's beneficial in the short term, abusing your people ultimately is a failing strategy. Leaders have to ensure that while pursuing their own well-being and fostering the well-being of those they lead, they are not abusing the idea of purpose to get more out of people.

Tactical Steps for Well-Being

I am not a fan of doughnuts, and while I have started to do yoga—because, as I get older, I recognize the importance of flexibility—neither is something I want my organization to provide to support my wellness. What I want, and what almost everyone wants, is to not have our time wasted and for people to respect our time. I also want to be provided with the resources to be able to do my job, to have opportunities to grow and learn, and to be recognized when I do a good job.

If we care about people, we should care about the work they do and their time. We must be okay with them setting boundaries and working toward work-life integration. Some of us have not done this well in our careers and don't always respond well when others do. We look at them and think they are not making a full effort. We should be encouraging them and applauding them for achieving better balance or integration. This is going to be a huge mindset shift for many of us, but it is where we need to go.

We must give people permission to take time off, take time to go to medical appointments, and take time to exercise. Sometimes we need to force people to take time off. We need to model taking vacations and actually being on vacation. We need to arrive and leave work at reasonable hours. If you stay at work every day until 7 p.m., you may be giving the impression that this is what you expect of others. You can either leave early—which is probably good for you—or be explicit with those you lead that you don't expect them to be here. Yes, walk around the office and the clinic and tell people to go home. You may need to do this several times until people take you seriously. When people do these things well, we should applaud them and recognize them for it. Here are a few examples of what you could say:

"I am really glad you spent time with your family yesterday."

"It's great you got to the gym this morning. What are you working on?"

"How did your daughter do in her game last night? Did they win? How did she play?"

"How was your vacation? It must have been amazing to be in Pittsburgh for a week!"

Leaders should work to actively protect people's time. We can, in doing so, avoid last-minute emergency due-outs. One year, right before a long four-day weekend, we got a data call that was needed for the Tuesday that we returned. This would mean doing part of the work over the long holiday. Why? Was it urgent? No. Was someone going to die if it was not done by Tuesday? No. Was there any consideration by those asking for the data and the urgency of it on the impact on the lives of those being asked to collect the data? Well, I cannot answer that question directly, but my sense was no. The information could have been asked for earlier or asked for later the following week. These timelines that we end up imposing on others are a significant source of frustration and burnout. It takes control away from those who had planned their time effectively, since they *still* lose the ability to use their time the way they had planned.

Lieutenant General Milford Beagle, who, at the time of writing this book, was the Commanding General of United States Army Command and General Staff College, had a practice called "Lamps Out Time."[15,16] The memo set the expectation for everyone in the command that all work would be done by Friday at 1500 (3 p.m. for all you non-Army types.)[17] In the memo, he stated, "People are the Army's greatest strength and most asset. Therefore, taking care of people is one of our priorities. As part of that mission, we must do all we can to create a healthy work environment by helping our soldiers achieve better work-life balance...Lamps Out Time is one step in that direction. A small way to inject some balance into the lives of our workforce."[18]

The memo was created to allow soldiers more time with their families or to take care of personal issues. *Wow!* This is true leadership! What could something like this look like in your organization?

One important point Lieutenant General Beagle made when sending this memo: When taking care of our people, it does not always mean that we give people time off.[19] In fact, there will be times that we need their time. A few things to consider as a leader: "Am I using the time of my subordinates in the most effective and efficient way? Are there ways I can give time back to them for their own well-being?" If you have to call someone in for a shift or if you know you just made someone work on the weekend to complete a task, is there a way to compensate them for that time? "I know you had to work over the weekend to get that done. I want you to leave and take the rest of the day off today." We need to rethink the way we manage our people's time.

Try to avoid night and weekend emails. When we send messages at night or on the weekends as leaders, it often creates the sense that we want a reply. Even if we don't, most of the people who work for us feel pressured to respond—or they read the email and are distracted by the tasks they now know lie ahead. A few things can be helpful. First, if possible, just avoid sending emails at night or on the weekend. A trick I learned was to use the "delayed send" feature on email. I write the emails and schedule them to go out the following morning or Monday morning. This way, I do not put any pressure on those I am leading.

Be explicit about your expectations as a leader. Because I have two kids who have tons of activities, my schedule can be somewhat erratic. I try to be at all their events. This means leaving work early sometimes for a practice or game. This also means that I am writing emails early in the morning, late at night, or often on the weekends. If not using the delayed send feature, you can also tell your people, "I don't expect you to respond to emails on the weekend and nights. I will call or text if there is something urgent." Then, only call or text if something *is* really urgent!

All of my chief residents (first-line supervisors for internal medicine trainees) were incredibly hard workers. They always put in more hours than should be expected. They really cared about our residents and the mission, but this could come at a cost to them personally. As an internal medicine program director and their supervisor, I made it a point to say,

1. "You don't need to be here. You can work from home if you need to."

2. "I will never question where you are and what you are doing. I know you will work hard."

3. "I expect you to take time for your own work, fitness, and leisure/vacation."

Despite this guidance, there were times when I literally had to kick my chief residents out of the hospital. I told one chief I would fire her if she did not take the day off the next time her kids had a day off from school. She knew I would not fire her, but she did ultimately take some time off!

I know because I made these mistakes. I felt guilty about not being home, and I never wanted to create that environment for those I worked with. The goal is to create an environment where people feel safe and good about taking time for themselves and their families.

To close this chapter, I wanted to again highlight the work of Stanford Chief Wellness Officer, Dr. Tait Shanafelt. He published an incredibly impactful research study on the qualities of immediate supervisors that decrease burnout and improve job satisfaction.[20] This paper should be mandatory reading for healthcare leaders and used as a reference to support possible wellness initiatives. It includes this list of ten ways to support those you lead to improve their well-being and morale:

1. Holds career development conversations

2. Inspires me to do my best

3. Empowers me to do my job

4. Is interested in my opinion

5. Encourages employees to suggest ideas for improvement

6. Treats me with respect and dignity

7. Provides helpful feedback and coaching on my performance

8. Recognizes me for a job well done

9. Keeps me informed about changes taking place

10. Encourages me to develop my talents and skills[21]

Reference: Shanafelt TD et al. Impact of organizational leadership on physician burnout and satisfaction. Mayo Clin Proc. 2015 Apr; 90(4):432-40.

They found the composite leadership score based on the ten items above had a significant association with both burnout and satisfaction.[22] Several of these items increased satisfaction by more than 30 percent and decreased burnout by almost 20 percent.[23] For example, "Encourages me to develop my talents and skills" led to a 39 percent increase in job satisfaction. Being interested in someone's opinion decreased burnout by 16 percent and improved job satisfaction by 37 percent. "Empowers me to do my job" improved satisfaction by 40 percent! These strategies are all things that every leader can do.[24]

These should be posted on the desk of every leader. These are data-proven strategies that leaders can implement to improve job satisfaction and decrease burnout. These align well with the work of Pink, as each of these items falls under autonomy, mastery, and purpose.[25] If you want to support your people, improve morale, and decrease burnout, make these ten steps your starting point.

Prescription for Caring in Leadership

1. Perform an act of community care for someone. Send a text message of encouragement, make dinner for a friend, help someone with a task you know they need help with. Any act supporting someone you know is an act of community caring.

2. Identify specific strategies to promote autonomy, mastery, and purpose for those you lead. Talk to those you lead about ways to make these part of your investment in those you lead and your organization.

3. Commit to avoiding sending emails and text messages after hours and on weekends.

4. Applaud and recognize someone for taking time off. Point this out during meetings to emphasize to others how important it is.

5. Place Dr. Shanafelt's list of ten leadership qualities on your desk or a wall in your office, and make sure you are doing these things on a daily basis for those you lead.[26]

6. Give Dr. Shanafelt's list to those you supervise who lead others, and ask them to talk about how they are doing these things for those they lead. Make it an expectation that they are doing these things.[27]

7. Read Daniel Pink's book *Drive*.[28]

8. Read Shanafelt's article reference above.[29]

CHAPTER 8

Care Enough to Get to Know Your People

*"Finding out what caring means for each
individual on your team is essential. It's not
important. It's the oxygen of the team."*
—Dr. Caroline Blackie

SOLDIERS DON'T JUMP ON grenades for the Army—they jump on grenades for their buddies to the left and right of them. We must have this indoctrinated in us in the Army, because Dr. Jeff Hutchinson shared a similar idea. "We don't go to war because of the cause of freedom. We fight because of the person next to us, and that's what you have to do, for most people remind them of the person next to them that they're fighting for."

People we work with and for will go above and beyond because they care about their relationships with their leaders and coworkers. In healthcare, this means better patient care and better lives for those on the healthcare team. As leaders, we have to work to develop these relationships and help the people we work with feel that connection to each other.

There is no separation of work and family. What we do at work impacts how we feel and act at home, and what we do at home impacts how we feel and act at work. We don't have work lives and personal lives. We have lives. Dr. Caroline Blackie emphasized this point: "My words reflect my 'heart thoughts.' We can't separate the heart from the mind. Caring-inspired leadership demands bringing your whole self to the job. Choosing otherwise is choosing to do only a portion of the job."

Leadership is about relationships. These connections build a sense of team and influence. The more you know the people you lead, the more they will want to work hard for you. If, as a leader, you are strictly working via a transactional relationship with those you lead, then you are going to be missing things that could impact their performance and, consequently, the performance of your organization. We have to recognize people will show up to work based on how their life is going. You cannot separate the good and the bad. It would be naïve to think our personal lives don't impact our work performance. How, as leaders, do we best support and care for our people?

> *"Showing someone that you care about them as a person, and not for the work you can squeeze out of them, is key."*
>
> —Dr. Oxentenko

Dr. Amy Oxentenko captured this point much better than I did:

> I think that how you care for others as a leader says a lot about you. I deeply value the relationships of people I work with and the people I have led. It's not just those five minutes of check-in before the official meeting starts. It's taking the time and meeting a past mentee for a coffee, or making time when they reach out with a question or for advice. It comes down to not

only answering the question but keeping an open-door, open-email, open-phone-line sort of availability. Showing someone that you care about them as a person, and not for the work you can squeeze out of them, is key. We're all holistic people that have lives outside of our work, and those things influence how we show up and what we bring to work every day.

How many of you want to have Dr. Oxentenko as your boss, knowing she values relationships and will care about you as an individual?

Leaders who know and understand their people have more influence. We don't need to be friends with those we work with—it is *leader*ship, not *liker*ship. However, effective leaders understand who their people are and what makes them tick. We don't need to be therapists for coworkers and those we lead, but we need to make sure we are aware of challenges they may have in their lives that are impacting their performance. We may need to connect them to resources to help them be the best versions of themselves at work.

Personal connection and knowing your people allows you to lead them based on what you know about them—not just who they are as workers but who they are as people. The better we know our people, the better we can support them. Developing these relationships builds trust, and it makes everything else we do as leaders easier.

Mark Crowley, in his book *Lead From The Heart,* talked about the importance of personal relationships, saying, "When I made time to more personally know the people who worked for me, it had the effect of significantly elevating their achievement...If you want exceptional results from people who work for you, you need to make a personal connection with them."[1]

This means we need to think about how we intentionally build these relationships. Do we set aside time to meet and talk to people? Do we make sure we are walking around and seeing what is going on at work and in the lives of those we lead? This is time well spent.

Heather Younger, author of *The Art of Caring Leadership*®, wrote,

> Those we lead have a deep desire to feel safe and bring their full selves to work. When we accept them for what they bring to the table, including baggage that we carry; we empathize with them; and we pay close attention to the things that are important to them, they know it. They will grow from such relationships, model it to others, and be willing to do what it takes for the leader and team to be successful.[2]

What I love about Heather's example is that if we care for those we lead and foster these relationships, then that same approach ripples through our organization.[3] The leaders we lead will take the same approach with those they lead. Caring about the whole person then becomes part of your company culture. Imagine an organization where people feel valued and cared for. What would that do to patient care? What would it do for the lives of those delivering the care? You don't have to imagine this as a leader. You can make it happen.

Demonstrating Caring as a Leader by Getting to Know Your People

Let's spend some time on what it looks like to get to know people at work. The examples below illustrate some tactical ways as a caring leader to get to know your people. Think about how you can incorporate these into your organization so employees feel valued, cared for, and motivated to be there.

Be intentional about getting to know your people. Spend time to develop these relationships. This means devoting time as a leader to be with your people—not just in the clinic, or in the operating room, or in the office. We will develop relationships through our daily activities, but we need to set aside additional time to meet with folks.

Caring Through Meeting

One effective way to show you care is to spend time with them. Have meetings specifically to get to know them. Learn what drives them and how you can support them while working to accomplish the mission.

Dr. Blackie gives examples of using meetings to facilitate learning about people and connecting people at work. The first idea is about using prompts to foster connection:

Who is this person I am working with? What things do they like? How do they spend their down time? What are their hidden talents? To facilitate this learning, we use pictures and photographs assembled on a single slide and speak to the team about the visuals. I love baking, so my photographs almost always include at least one baking conquest. Others on my team like to paint, hike, travel, play music, etc. We repeat this process at various times throughout the year. The pictures and the words we use to describe them are a powerful portal into who we are and what we love, and it brings us to life. When we learn about each other, we can foster meaningful connections. I'll use myself as an example. Because of the joy that baking brings me, my team proactively shares their experience of baking with me. For example, I have received recipes and spontaneous photos from random events with beautiful cakes and pastries, I am asked questions about baking, I receive frequent encouragement about baking! And I love it. The team shares in this way across all members and all relevant topics. We talk about travel tips, concerts, favorite trees, parenting, cultural norms (we have an international team), etc., all of it.

> We also share about heartbreak and loss. This is the natural outcome of a safe and caring environment. The hard conversations, where people willingly share genuine and meaningful pain, is part of the process. Earlier in my career, this was more difficult for me to manage. A healthy and caring team culture creates and delivers a sacred space to bear witness to a team member's pain. This space can help immeasurably with the personal integration of life's challenges: death, funerals, grieving, betrayal, failure, etc. Witnessing hardship and sistering, when needed, is core to our humanity. "Sistering" is a woodworking term that is used to describe how a weakened or fragile floor joist can be strengthened by attaching a strong additional beam on either side. When we "sister" for each other, we are not trying to fix the person in distress; we are bolstering and protecting them. We'll pick up the work. We are fully here for them. Using a couple of personal examples, I told my team immediately when my father died unexpectedly in 2021, and I shared when my husband was going through chemoradiation earlier this year. My sharing gives others courage to share. This is life. All of the ups and downs are happening together, daily. Private pain creates disconnection; shared pain does the opposite.

> We also share recovery. Life moves forward and so do we, both as a team and as individuals. Timelines around recovery are highly individual. Some people need twenty-four hours. Some people need twenty-four days or twenty-four weeks or months. I have learned if I'm playing the long game—and I am—there is always a way to incorporate the whole person in a way that works for everyone. This is an example of caring as a leader.

Notice how Dr. Blackie goes from what interests people to pain they might be experiencing. The depth of connections at work will vary, but you cannot get to deep connections if you don't start with building basic connections. These connections take time and intentional effort to get to know those you lead, as well as for them to get to know each other. These connections create an environment where people can feel safe and supported at work.

Dr. Blackie gives another example using what she calls "skip meetings," demonstrating how to meet not just with her direct reports but everyone on her team. She described them as meeting:

> ...once a quarter or once a month, depending on what the opportunity is, directly in a one-to-one with every single member of my team so that they get comfortable sharing more of what they think and feel about their context at work. I don't ask them questions like "How are you getting along with your coworkers?" It's about creating an environment where we have open conversations that are low pressure and where we can talk about anything...Sometimes we're just talking about the weather and the sports...Other times they're talking about a crisis that they're going through. I can never predict what is going to come up. It is about being available for whatever needs to be said and heard.

How do we get people to the point where they are willing to share, whether it be in a group meeting or an individual meeting? Does everyone have to share? When and how do I share? These are questions that may come up when you are thinking about what these interactions might look like at work. Dr. Jeff Hutchinson provided some great advice:

> In clinic meetings, when I would run the Adolescent Department, we would go around and everyone talked about metrics and how many patients are seen. I would never talk about that. I would talk about what was challenging this

week. Sometimes, especially when my wife went through the cancer diagnosis…I would say I was very grateful for everyone for stepping up when obviously I wasn't as here at present as I could have been. I think that let the group know that it is human to have times when you are just not a hundred percent. It wasn't the same day, but it was later on, people would say, "I'm having a hard time in my family, and this is just not the best time for me."

Someone being comfortable enough to say that in a group like that really told me that I was making a difference and letting people know that not only I care, but everyone in the group had at least some level of compassion and caring.

Dr. Hutchinson went on to talk about how, as leaders, we can be vulnerable, but we have to understand the situation. We may show vulnerability and humility in different ways. Vulnerability creates the space for others to be vulnerable, but we have to consider the situation. We must accept that not everyone wants or needs to share and be vulnerable. Like most things in leadership, the situation should guide the action. Dr. Hutchinson's point is summarized here:

For some people, the connections they make at work are so important because that's where they spend most of their lives, so you want to give them the opportunity to make those connections. For other people, work is just a means to an end, and for whatever reason, they don't want to open up and share. So, caring can't be seen as just how vulnerable you are. It can be "I'm here on time. I volunteer for other stuff to do." There can be lots of other ways to show that you care. Everyone doesn't have to show they're caring the same way.

So, to finish—as a leader, if you're not comfortable sharing, it doesn't mean you need to become more emotional. The most effective leaders do have some vulnerability, so figure out what part you're willing to be vulnerable about. This could mean being vulnerable by saying, "I don't understand this part of my job," or "I know I can't be everywhere, and I can't watch everyone the way that I want to. I can't mentor everyone the way that I want to." There's something we all fall short in, and that can be the vulnerability that we share. Then, we have to accept the fact that not everyone can show vulnerability and still be considered a leader. So, you have to take everything in context. If on your first day, you're crying and saying, "You know this is me. This is the raw me," you may not have a team to follow you.

We need to form connections around what people want to share and not force things. Suzanna Fitzpatrick, DNP, CRNP shared a similar story, emphasizing the importance of connection and how it is different for everyone:

> I want you to show your best self. I want you to give yourself grace that every day, your best is not the same. I want you to give me grace for the same. I think you know that is a key part of caring, and I don't think everybody needs to share all of their things...We all have to have some self-preservation. I don't want to talk about Thanksgiving, when I cried because I miss my mom. But having moments where you can connect with people in their way, whatever that may be, [is important. It's okay if] you're an introvert, you don't like a lot of conversation at work, or you don't want to share because you're suffering a trauma. Figure out a way to connect with other people in the space that feels meaningful to you and meaningful to them.

The Power of the Check-In

Many of us like our space at work and do not want to be micromanaged. We also want to know that our boss cares about our work and values what we do and who we are. You can help create this sense of value and caring by checking in on your people. You can also use check-ins to make sure people are doing okay when something bad happens, if someone seems off, or to say "thank you" when someone is doing great work.

Laurie Baedke, director of Healthcare Leadership Programs and assistant dean of Physician Leadership Education at Creighton University, emphasized the importance of getting to know those you lead and how to use check-ins. When teaching her students, she makes it a point to get to know them, but also to make sure they understand the power of connection between leaders and followers:

> *Cura personalis* is a Latin phrase that translates to "care for the whole person." When I think about why caring matters in leadership, I think about this in the way that I show up as an academic and as a program director. In the Executive MBA program, I tell each of my students when they come in, they're adult learners, they're mid-career professionals, they're physicians and surgeons and clinical and non-clinician leaders. Our objective in onboarding and walking each student through their academic journey is to get them to that point where they, of course, grow in their knowledge and skill and attain competencies and achieve a graduate degree. That's their academic formation, but *cura personalis,* care for the whole person, means that I am equally invested in your personal formation, your leadership formation.
>
> For example, this might mean asking my student Josh, "Josh, are you okay today?" Josh has been a little bit radio silent on the discussion board these last couple of weeks. Is everything okay with Josh? Or, being the type of leader who, outside of an academic realm, sees one of your team members or colleagues, senses that something is off, and checks in on them, saying, "Are you batting a thousand today? Are you alright?" Because if we don't attend to all those other factors, we're missing the whole picture. Life happens, in myriad ways. If we've got a head cold to beat the band and we feel sick

as a dog, we can't operate at 100 percent. If we've got an aging parent or just had to make the hard decision to say goodbye to the longtime family pet—those are tough days, right?

I've had students who have gotten personal cancer diagnoses while they're in their EMBA journey. Their spouse has navigated a cancer treatment journey. They've buried parents. Those students are not 100 percent in those moments, and the empathic, caring leader responds accordingly. In my academic program and as a leader, *cura personalis,* care for the whole person, is an objective or approach to get you through this assignment, this course, this program, adapting to assess what matters most today. When [you] care as a leader, that gives you the grace and the space to stay whole in life, and I think that when we do that, it demonstrates compassion, it is kind, and it's the right thing to do.

Baedke hits a home run talking about slowing down to take the time to check in on the people you lead:

I think one of the most powerful things that we can do to demonstrate care for others is really just care...one of the best ways that we can show care is to slow down and check in on people, and then make time to receive their response. It lets people feel seen. It demonstrates that we value them. When we think about how much of any given leader's day is "just go, go, go, answer questions, respond to emails, put out fires," it's counterintuitive to slow down and reach out in those ways. But it's really vital that we do, because the power of demonstrating that care, even if it's the most miniscule moment, if it is sincere, it then translates into follower trust.

This is a great example of how we can often neglect to care for those we lead while focusing on getting the work done and not caring for the worker (or learner, in this case). Take the time to check in on your people. It will help them feel like you care, and you may learn things that allow you to better support them.

Dr. Oxentenko shared a story about working with a new intern on the GI service during July. Dr. Oxentenko explained that when she was a resident, she had a really rough experience, and it made her question whether she should pursue GI as a specialty or not. She did not want an intern to feel unsupported. During her time with the intern, they had some challenging patients and scenarios, and she was worried about how the rotation may have impacted her. They talked about it during their time together. Dr. Oxentenko circled back after the rotation to check in and met with the intern for coffee. She continues to meet with her and help her prepare for fellowship applications.

This is showing you care about those you lead: being there and investing in them. I have to assume having a very senior and established leader take the time to check in and meet makes the intern feel incredibly supported.

I know this feeling because I have experienced it. A few years ago, a chief resident in our program died unexpectedly. It was a very challenging time, personally and professionally. I was really struggling as a leader. Dr. Art Kellermann, the dean of the School of Medicine at the Uniformed Services at the time, reached out to me via email. I had previously worked for him as an assistant dean, but we had not spoken for quite some time. The title of the email was "You matter, I care."

He provided some comforting words of support and his personal contact info, making himself available to talk. He didn't know how much that encouragement and just knowing he cared was needed by me. I still have the email. I gained a lot of respect and admiration for him because of how much he cared. He was a busy dean, but he took the time to care for someone he knew and had led. Each of us has this opportunity to check in and support those we lead—or, for that matter, a colleague. It can have lifelong career and personal implications.

People will never forget how you support them through personal tragedies. As the residency program director, we had family members die, relationships end, pets die, and miscarriages, among other things. These are stressful life events, but these are happening to the people we work with all the time. How do you support your people through these times? My mom died of breast cancer during medical school, and what I remember is the leaders at the school supporting me. They were not concerned about the rotations and making sure I completed my assignments. They were concerned about *me*. That was over twenty years ago, and I still remember. Supporting people during these challenging times is the right thing to do, and it builds trust and relationships like few things can.

Connecting Through Meals

It is a military tradition that senior leaders invite the members of their teams to their houses intermittently to eat. Throughout the course of my career, I remember having dinners at many of our senior leaders' homes. As an ROTC cadet at Duquesne University, our battalion commander, Harry Griffith, invited us to his home to talk about our careers and life in the military. When I was an intern, the hospital commander had a barbeque for us at his house. One event that stands out most was during my intern year of medical training. I was working over the holidays, as was my future wife. My attending, Colonel Charles Oster, invited us both over to his house. We greatly appreciated this, as we were obviously not home for the holiday, but being there with his family made us feel at home. Despite being years later, I remember all of these dinners and appreciate how these senior leaders took the time to get to know me and care about me. They also created the space for me to better connect with colleagues—and, in one case, my future wife!

Dr. Alex Niven, a retired Army colonel who now works at Mayo Clinic, described one experience he had while in the Army, further illustrating the value of these meals and being intentional about getting to know those you lead. This story about a hospital commander captures many of the points here about getting to know those you lead and why it is important for the individual and their family:

> He had us over to his house several times and always made a point to start the conversation with something informal to break the ice before we got in the business of the day. He was very deliberate in terms of how he approached these issues. We had beers together, but it wasn't like friends...We had casual conversations, but those conversations were for a purpose: to clearly build a strong relationship and a sense of trust between each of us and him. For him to share a little bit about himself was very effective in terms of inspiring a common sense of purpose and mutual sense of—I'll use the term "admiration," because I think we all respected him and respected his leadership style. That translated into a greater level of engagement and us serving a more effective role. So certainly, you can order people around, and they will do the jobs that they're paid to do, but so many things that we ask people to do are above and beyond their job description...You know how great it is when you're in an environment where people actually know your name. Ask you about your kids. Find out how the job is going and when you're frustrated with something, help you with that, so you can do your job better and easier. So you can go back and spend more time with your family and kids. I think that's pretty awesome. When I think about the caring role the leader has, that's the first and most obvious example.

This story captures the impact of leaders who connect with their people. It fosters trust and motivates them.

The Work Family: Care about People and Their Families

One way to approach your work environment is to consider it part of your family. We spend as much time—or more—with the people we work with than we do our actual family. The more we care about and take care of each other, the more successful we will be as individuals and as an organization. As alluded to earlier in the book, this is not all sunshine and roses but means that we deeply care about the personal well-being and professional success of each person we work with.

The way people feel about work directly impacts the way they treat people outside of work. This means that as leaders, we impact not only those we lead but their families and communities. If someone leaves work and is dejected about their work environment, how do you think they will treat their spouse, partner, parents, kids, or neighbors? We need to think about leadership and the larger impact that it has on those we lead. We are all connected. We would be better off if we saw each other as being connected and treated each other in ways that build each other up.

What does it look like to care for people at work like they are family? Here are a couple of examples.

My wife recently told me a story in which her coworker's dad was in a cardiac ICU. Her coworker told her that she would still be able to make several meetings they had coming up in the next several days. My wife, of course—because she is an amazing caring leader—said, "We got you covered; don't worry about it." The question is, why do so many people feel so compelled to put work ahead of being with a sick parent in an ICU? What does it say about us as individuals and the cultures that we create at work where that is the expectation? We need to create work environments where family comes first, because we know that people can't focus on work if they are worried about a sick parent.

Author Brad Johnson, when talking about exemplars of leaders who care, described how one leader, Steve Trainor, took care of him during a time of need. Brad was going through some health issues, including chemotherapy for a cancer he was dealing with:

> Fifteen years ago, I had a major health issue. It was really unanticipated. Steve was just so kind, there at the right moment, and I think recognized a couple of things. Number one: I just needed somebody to sit with me at that moment. Think about it out loud. Express care. See how I was doing frequently. You know, another part of the care, and that was kind of circling the wagons at a time when maybe the stress of all of this was preventing me from making good decisions about how much I should take on or what I could continue doing. Especially as I was going through some treatment. It was Steve who could gently, in a very caring way, say, "Hey, let's get you to step back from that," or "That's just not genuinely, really, not that important right now. We can let that slide for a few semesters, that just doesn't matter right now." I think if he hadn't taken the initiative to say that, I'm not sure I would have been quite so good with boundaries and prioritizing self-care. Those two things about Steve's leadership personified the care issue.

Brad's boss helped him prioritize his health and set boundaries. Essentially, Brad's boss told him that he did not need to do certain things and that he should focus on his health. What I love about this story is that Brad did not have to ask for it. His boss made it an expectation that Brad would take care of his health. The lesson is that, as bosses, we should not wait for people to ask us for time off or less work. The fact is most people, especially in healthcare, will just not ask. Let's create cultures where we can support people and make this happen proactively.

To help create this family environment, you can focus on things that are important to the members of your organization. You can celebrate personal events. This helps the team get to know each other and builds bonds. This should be done with sensitivity as to what people want to share, but you could consider sharing if someone gets married or has a child, or if someone does something really exciting outside of work, like plays in an orchestra, leads a fundraiser for the community, or completes a marathon or other sporting event. You can decide what is important to your team and what you think would be valuable to share. When I was the internal medicine residency program director at Walter Reed National Military Medical Center, we started buying and giving onesies when babies were born. They had the logo and "Welcome to the Team." It was a simple gesture, but one that signified we cared about the employee and their family. The "Welcome to the Team" saying was also an intentional reminder that families are part of the team.

What innovative ways might you be able to incorporate care based on who your people are and what they appreciate? How can you create connection and demonstrate caring?

Can You Care Too Much?

If you care about the people you lead, then you have to care about what happens to them outside of work. Yet, can we care too much or get too close to them? You will hear people say that we need to keep a distance so we can still make the hard decisions. David Smith, PhD, when talking about the idea of having emotional distance from those we lead, said,

> That's very twentieth-century leadership. I think that was part of the model that maintained this gap between leaders and followers. It was expected and desired to maintain that gap, to not have connection. To not have attachment. I think in healthcare—certainly in other professions, like the military— you could see why people may have come up with that, because you're going to deal with challenging situations that can be very emotional. It can be hard on you as a leader, but that's why it's leadership. It is hard, and if you're doing it well, I think you have no choice but to feel some of it.

Retired Lieutenant General Mark Hertling illustrated this point:

> We have to get to know the people we lead to better understand them and to lead them, but at the same time, there is a separation. You know, you're not going to see a lawyer be overly familiar with their paralegals or their administrative staff. Anytime you have a professional relationship. When an individual is a professional, like a physician or a nurse or a soldier, they understand that there has to be an understanding of the individuals that they're working for, a true knowledge of what makes them tick. There also has to be—and this is a hard part to explain, and most people who aren't in professions [like this] don't get this—there has to be a separation between work and personal life, because the personal life can influence the work life in terms of professional decision-making, and that's when it becomes dangerous.

The last point about being dangerous is that if we get too close to those we lead, we may fail to make hard decisions that impact them. We are not going to be making decisions like LTG Hertling sending people into combat, but leaders are often faced with hard choices. This is something we need to be aware of. At the end of the day, sometimes we have to make these challenging decisions when we know it may impact someone we care about—yet, it is our responsibility to the patient, our system, our society.

Leadership is hard because we cannot fix everything and will not be able to help everyone. We will mess up and say the wrong things or offend people. For self-preservation, we have to understand that despite how much we may care and how much we might try to help people or fix the organization, it won't always work. Brad Johnson talked about this:

> I guess the question is, have I been somebody who showed up at that moment, done the triage, really been present? Done everything I can to sit with them and express care about them? Ultimately, things may not turn out well for them or their career...I think that's a challenge as a mentor. For example, I'm not taking my mentees home with me in a way that's disruptive.

We have to ask ourselves if we did our best and if we did give ourselves grace. We then fight the next battle for those we lead and our organizations, knowing we will win many more than we will lose.

Do Not Fake Caring

The whole point of this chapter is that we need to really care about the people we lead. We need to address an important point about caring at work and getting to know our people. You cannot fake caring about people, and if your motives for getting to know people are only to use that information to your benefit, that will quickly be identified by those you lead, and you will lose influence. People have a radar for insincerity. You might be able to fool people for a brief period, but they will figure you out before long. Your desire to develop and foster these relationships at work needs to come from a genuine desire to know and care for the people you lead.

Retired Major General Clark drove this point home during his interview:

> What I had to remind myself—and we had to remind each other—was, why do you take care of your people? And some people say, "Well, they work harder." Well, they may, but that's not why you take care of them. You take care of people, you create conditions for the folks in your organization and yourself to prosper, because it's the right thing to do, because that's what leaders do.

Strategies to Get to Know People and Connect People at Work

Let's end the chapter with some tangible ways you can connect with your people. We have talked about some of these above, and others are discussed elsewhere in the book for other reasons. Some of these will be specific to the individual. Some will be applicable to their families as well. This is a short list, so be creative and think outside the box about how else to create connections between you and those you lead, as well as between them.

1. Walk around leadership

We will talk about walking around in the next chapter on presence, but it is worth mentioning here too, as it has significant value in getting to know people. If you are a leader and people don't know what you look like, then you have a problem. When you are out walking around, it gives you a chance to learn about your organization, but also your people. Take this opportunity to try to learn a little bit about who they are as individuals. Depending on your role, you are not going to have a deep relationship with everyone, and the closer you work with someone, the deeper that relationship will be. That said, you can still get to know people at all levels. The more they see you, the more likely they are to share with you.

One strategy aside from work topics, as Dr. Pat Young said, is to talk about the Three F's: Family, Food, and Fun. You can always ask people about their family, what they like to eat, and what they like to do for fun.

2. Hold individual and group (team) meetings

Data from Gallup suggests that just one meaningful fifteen- to thirty-minute conversation with employees a week has a significant impact on worker engagement.[4] Make time to meet with those you lead. This is a chance to get to know them a little, as well as address work-related issues that we discuss later in the book, such as expectations, feedback, and thanking them for what they do.

Think about ways to budget time for meeting with the people you lead individually or as a larger group. Depending on your position, you may not be able to meet with everyone individually. That said, you can and should meet with as many people as possible individually, as that time allows you to learn and shows you care. If you cannot meet individually, then think about having group meetings. These can help you learn about the people you lead and can help them learn about each other.

For example, if you are the department chair, think about having a meeting with groups of residents. If you are a chief nursing officer, think about meeting with groups of charge nurses or meeting with all the new hires in the past three months.

3. Make check-ins a habit

Don't wait for people to come to you. Make it a habit to check in on people. This may or may not lead to a larger discussion, but it opens the door. Take the time to intentionally reach out to people you lead or mentor and see how they are doing. Check in on a colleague who has started a new position. You can do this if you know something happened to them, or you can also just do it randomly. "How are you? Anything you need to talk about? Anything I can help with?"

One thing I like to do is write myself reminders. If I know something has happened to an individual—a bad patient outcome, they were sick, or something happened to a family member—I will make a note on my calendar to follow up with them. Without the note, I would assuredly forget, so I put it on my schedule.

Checking in does not always have to be about negative things. Make yourself reminders to check in for other reasons as well. This might be to check in on a new employee. It might be to ask a colleague how they are doing with their newborn. It might be to check in on the progress someone is making on writing their book. These check-ins keep you connected and show you care.

Every time someone asked me about the progress of my book, it motivated me. I appreciated that they remembered I was working on it, and their check-in reminded me that it was important. Writing is hard work, and these energy boosts helped get me to the finish line.

Who do you need to check in on today? Make a list of three to five people each week you can contact.

4. Break bread together

Eating together can create bonds. Whether you have people over to your house, eat at a park, or go to a restaurant, it allows you to spend time together and get to know each other. There are many ways to do this. I have seen people do leadership breakfasts, where the leader of a team will just go eat in the cafeteria or a designated space and invite others to join him or her. The same can be done for lunch. You could set up coffee and a continental breakfast in a designated location, and the leader could be there to meet and greet and chat with people. If the coffee is good—and, for that matter, even if it is not—you will likely draw a crowd in the healthcare setting. You just need to create the space for connections.

You could have an ice cream social. If you want to go healthy, you could have a frozen yogurt option. Break out the ice cream and toppings and create the time at work for people to get together. Depending on where you work and the convenience, consider inviting families and kids to take part. Leaders can even take the role of serving the ice cream before socializing.

Allow people to bring part of who they are to work, and maybe even their own traditions and cultures. Have a chili cook-off. Host a lunch and make it an international day when people can bring in dishes that they like from their families or cultures. We hosted a few Spooky Bake-Offs at Halloween to bring people together and get to try fun Halloween-inspired desserts. Cater dinners at major holidays or have people bring in food.

5. Play sports together

Getting people to play sports together or go to a sporting event could be another option. There is something about sweating and suffering together that brings people together. You could pick almost any sport, depending on your team. Meet for Frisbee once a week. Play flag football. For small leadership teams, you could consider doing an event together, like a Ragnar Relay or Tough Mudder. Recognize that not everyone on your team may be able to participate or want to participate, so be sensitive to this and inclusive when planning.

6. Book clubs

Books offer a window to discussion. The books you pick could be work-related or simply fun books that might be a blast to read and talk about. I am part of a leadership book club, and we recently read a comedy. We did not talk about leadership for this month, but we had a ton of fun doing it. Pick something that people will want to read, either for fun or something that will spur meaningful discussion. The point for this book club is to get people together. If possible, and if funds are available, consider buying the book for those who want to participate. You could even choose *this* book to start your new book club!

These strategies are just a few ideas to get you started on better knowing those you lead and building relationships. Which ones, if any, you decide to use is up to you. Some may not make sense based on your team, and some you may not be comfortable with or able to do. It may not be practical to have people over to your house. You may not like sports. It's not important which strategies you use, but it is important that you make getting to know the people you lead a priority.

It is critical to point out that you should not expect people to do things after hours for work. Don't make it mandatory fun to come to a particular event if not during routine work hours. If you are scheduling events after hours, think about ways to give that time back to those you lead, if at all possible. We don't want to damage well-being in the process of trying to create connections at work.

Prescription for Caring in Leadership

1. Reflect on a leader who took an interest in your personal life. How did that make you feel? How did it impact your engagement and relationship with that leader? How could you emulate that leader to more effectively lead someone else?

2. Pick at least one of the six ways to get to know people listed above and implement that strategy with your team:
    a. Walk around leadership
    b. Hold individual and group (team) meetings
    c. Check in with people
    d. Break bread together
    e. Play or watch sports together
    f. Start a book club

3. Implement Dr. Blackie's example of having people give a picture during meetings, and spend a few minutes describing why it is important to them to get to know each other better.

4. Start a meeting by asking each person to talk about one thing they did outside of work in the past week.

5. When you meet with people, make it a point to ask them about their interests outside of work: "What is one of your favorite things to do besides work?"

CHAPTER 9

Care Enough to Be Present

"In every command tour I had, trooping the line—those daily walks around the building, the base, or the camp—always yielded great insights into how well the organization was doing and how well I was leading."
—Admiral William McRaven
The Wisdom of the Bullfrog: Leadership Made Simple (But Not Easy)[1]

WHEN WAS THE LAST time you physically walked through your department, clinic, or medical school? If you are a department chair, clinic chief, CEO, senior hospital executive, or dean or other educational leader, when was the last time you walked through your hospital? Would people recognize you if they saw you? Seriously, if you are a senior leader in your organization, would members of your organization recognize you if you were in the elevator together? It's hard to drive and instill values within an organization when people don't even know who you are as a leader. Even if they know who you are by name recognition, how do you build trust if they never see you or hear from you directly?

Presence is going to look different for every leader at different levels, and certainly the CEO of a hospital can't spend all day every day visiting people—but he or she *can* make a concerted effort to get out and be with the people working on the front lines. Someone who's a mid-level manager or a charge nurse might be able to spend much more time with his or her direct reports. The bottom line is, leaders need to be present. Brad Johnson noted, "Nothing expresses care quite as much as somebody who just makes the time. That communicates more than words." We vote with our time about what matters most to us. If those we lead are the most important thing to us and we care about them, then we need to spend time with them.

Full stop—this goes the same and more for your family.

Dr. Chuck Callahan talked about the importance of being present as a leader. He said, "You have to look people in the eyes so you can really see how they are doing. When you look often enough, you can sense quickly when something's not right with someone." To emphasize his point, he shared a story of when he was in a pediatrics morning report (academic conference for trainees) and noticed from across the room that one of the residents looked upset and was fighting back tears. He stepped out and paged her to another room, where she had the opportunity to compose herself and then rejoin the group. Neither mentioned the event, but she apparently knew what he had done. Years later, a colleague of that resident told Dr. Callahan how much that moment had meant to her. This is a prime example of how you miss the opportunity to care for those you lead if you are not present and how the demonstration of caring can have a significant impact even beyond the individual directly affected.

When I was asking my friend retired Colonel Ramey Wilson (from Chapter 5 on preparation) about the importance of presence, he said, "You don't know if you don't go."[2] Bill George in *True North, Emerging Leader Edition* similarly states, "As a leader, are you working side by side with your team members? Do you model appropriate behaviors and provide constructive feedback? Do you know enough about their world and context to make useful suggestions? This is sitting sidesaddle to learn, make suggestions, and encourage them rather than judging them from a distance."[3]

Retired Major General Jeff Clark shared the importance of walking around as a leader, which further illustrates the impact:

> One really needs to walk around. You really need to spend time out and about. For me, it was the most fun and rewarding part of leadership. It wasn't "I must go walk around." It was "When can I stop doing what I'm doing so I can go walk around?" My wife, Sue, and I would walk around on Sundays. We'd start at the top of the hospital, and we would hit every floor—every ward, starting with behavioral health, L&D, lab, pharmacy, X-ray, ED, etc. Walk all the way down...I was not there primarily to see patients...The purpose was to speak with the staff, to talk to individuals and just see how things are going...shake hands, ask what I can do, say "Thank you." There's no rocket science here. You learn a whole lot about your organization. You just listen and you think, "Jeez. Hmm! Let me file that away," because tomorrow morning, Monday morning, I can ask, "How can we do better in this area?" But it was mostly just to walk around and listen to folks. By listening to folks, you can learn things that create conditions to improve mission/people.

In the book *Encourage the Heart* by Kouzes and Posner, they call this Care By Walking Around (CBWA).[4] They learned the term from Tom Melohn, who was the president of North American Tool and Die.[5] I love the term—leaders at all levels should make CBWA a part of their Caring Acts of Leadership.

These stories emphasize the key elements of presence as a leader, which include the ability to learn from those doing the work, being present to offer help, the ability to give feedback, the ability to emphasize values and purpose, and the ability to demonstrate gratitude. Despite being in a more dispersed working world, leaders have to find ways to be present to effectively lead. Leaders need to model presence and make it an expectation of those they lead. This is how you can scale presence within an organization.

Be Present to Gain Respect and Credibility

There is a classic leadership mantra that leaders shouldn't expect others to do what they are not doing. While we all have our roles and responsibilities, it is important for us to still get dirty at times. If you are a healthcare provider and in a leadership position but are no longer providing care, you can start to lose credibility. I am not saying that you cannot lead effectively if you are not providing care, but I can tell you that when you are standing shoulder to shoulder with those you lead, it builds tremendous respect. You will much less likely get the comments, "He doesn't know what it's like anymore."

Dr. Amy Oxentenko captured this:

> You remove any perceived differential between you and the people that you're leading when you are willing to roll up your sleeves and do the hard things you are asking them to do. Those actions are very powerful. Let me give an example. When I was moving to Arizona, taking on the Department of Medicine chair role, we were in the first few months of the pandemic. Like others, we had huge inpatient coverage issues

and needed to pull our outpatient subspecialty staff into the hospital to help our hospitalist colleagues. I had never practiced inpatient medicine at the Mayo Clinic in Arizona before, since I was new to that campus, and I didn't know my way around the hospital at all. There were so many staff who felt anxious and apprehensive about volunteering to do this inpatient coverage, given their subspecialty expertise, years out from training, and largely outpatient practice. It was greater than twenty years removed from my time practicing general internal medicine in an inpatient setting, but when I sent out that memo and the signup list, I plugged my name in first on the list to show that I was willing to do it. Yes, I was just as apprehensive as everyone else for the same reasons. It comes down to others seeing you take those initiatives without you calling them out and highlighting them, because if you have to make a point to highlight it, then it becomes less authentic.

We have to remember that each of us has our job to do. While I appreciate a hospital director or CEO who still takes care of patients if they are a healthcare provider, I don't want them doing patient care all the time. I want them to effectively lead our hospital.

Be Present to Support

Bad things happen, in life and in medicine. From a work standpoint, there are bad patient outcomes whether we do everything correctly or not. There are times patients die unexpectedly. There are times when things don't go as planned with a procedure or a family interaction. Outside of work, people deal with the loss of loved ones or illness in their families. People will remember how you supported them during difficult times and defining moments. How are you showing up as a leader during these times to support the people you lead? How are you caring for them?

In healthcare, we need to support each other. Retired Lieutenant General Mark Hertling shared an emotional story with me about his time in combat and how his chief of staff at the time, Colonel Bryan Watson (ended career as Major General—two stars), exemplified being present to provide support. It illustrates how being present as a leader sometimes means supporting other leaders and not just followers. It also means being vulnerable as a leader and having empathy, because both build trust. As you will see in his story, these traits are not always easy for us as leaders and followers to show:

> That may get me a little emotional, but there was a day in January of 2008 when we were in Northern Iraq. I had just come back from a battlefield circulation to about ten different areas, because we were in the middle of a major operation, and every single one of our brigades was involved. On that particular day in January 2008, we had eight deaths in six different locations in a span of about five hours. As you know, this is nothing compared to what the Ukrainians are experiencing right now—but for a counterinsurgency fight, when you have eight battlefield deaths in one day, that's a pretty hefty toll. I came back to the headquarters knowing about seven. In fact, I was in one location where two of them had died because an improvised explosive device had collapsed a house and crushed a couple of soldiers. I was about 100 yards away when it happened.

> I landed in my helicopter back at the headquarters in Tikrit early in the evening, and Bryan Watson, the Chief of Staff of the Division, came out to meet me and he said, "Hey, sir, we had another death." I immediately thought he was talking about the last one I had heard about on the radio as I was flying back.

> I said, "Bryan, are you talking about the one in the 3rd Armored Cavalry Regiment? I already heard that report."

He said, "No, it was another one since the one in the 3rd Armored Cavalry Regiment."

I said, "When did that happen?"

He said, "About three minutes ago."

I went up to my office in the headquarters building and just slumped in my chair behind my desk. We had been in combat at that time for about three months. It had been a continuous lack of sleep and constant fighting. We were in a tough mission where it was a very dynamic and complex environment. Sitting in the chair, I put my head in my hands, and the emotions were overwhelming. I don't even think Bryan knew this, but I heard the door to my office open, then slowly start to close, and I looked up, and I saw Bryan going back out because he must have seen me getting emotional at my desk.

I'm thinking, "Okay, that was smart for him to do that, because I don't want the chief of staff of the division seeing the division commander sitting in his office crying about the death of his soldiers."

Well, about three minutes later, the division chaplain walks into my office, and I mean he just walks in, which is very much against Army protocol. He just came in and sat down. By that time, I had pulled myself together, but he could tell I was still emotional. The chaplain said, "So, boss, the Chief says that you might need me." I just looked at him, and smiled, and that terrific chaplain gave me some great chaplain advice. He said, "Hey, boss, I know you're the division commander, and I'm the division chaplain for all your soldiers...but I'm also your chaplain too." We talked for a while, and then he offered to pray with me for the soldiers we had lost that day.

After the chaplain left, I walked over to Bryan's office. His office was right across the hall from mine, and I just stuck my head in.

I said, "Hey, Chief, thanks for getting the chap for me. I needed it."

He didn't even look up. He said in his gruff voice, which all of us knew was a way he camouflaged his feelings, "Boss, I don't know what the hell you're talking about. I'm busy. Leave me alone."

How can you—you know, you as a leader—how can you put a price tag on that kind of caring and dynamics within an organization?

When bad things happen, it's vital you check in on your people. We have bad outcomes with patients, and we have bad times in our lives. We talked about this in an earlier chapter, but it needs to be emphasized again: all of us (even the three-star generals) need people to check in on us and support us. We need to be present to support those we care for and lead.

Be Present to Learn

A colleague and friend, Navy Captain Dr. Mike Kavanagh, said he learned from someone else to "deliver the mail." He would pick up the mail and deliver it to people he led, giving him a reason to go see how they were doing. The higher we move up in leadership positions, the harder it is for us to remain in touch and maybe to fully understand what is happening on the front lines. If we are not present, it becomes challenging for us to really know what is going on. We are relying on others to give us information, and that information is filtered. Unfortunately, leaders are sometimes told what people think they want to hear and not what they need to hear. We talk about this more during the feedback chapters, but it is a real risk to you as a leader. It is important for you to do your own reconnaissance.

Have you ever heard yourself saying, "My boss just doesn't get it. I would love for him or her to come work in the emergency room for a day. My boss has no idea what it is like to be on call overnight. My boss doesn't have to call insurance companies between appointments to get approvals for medications. My boss doesn't have to skip lunch because one of the other nurses called out sick today."

Get the point? There are many things that happen within healthcare that require specific expertise. It is impossible to think that leaders should know everything, but that does not mean they should never show up.

Dr. Chuck Callahan talked about his time when he was in senior-level hospital leadership. He kept a pair of scrubs in his office so he could quickly go to visit places in the hospital where senior leaders seldom show up, like the location responsible for the sterilization of surgical equipment, usually in the basement of most hospitals. People always appreciated the visit. If you want to improve as a leader, sometimes just showing up more and listening is a great first step. Dr. Callahan shared another lesson from retired Brigadier General Mark Thompson: "Be present and positive." Show up and bring positive energy and appreciation.

Be Present to Help

When you show up, listen, and learn, it will often provide the opportunity for you to help. Your reason for being present is to help your team be more successful. As you gain information, you may identify an issue that you were previously unaware of. You can provide resources or ideas of ways to solve problems. Sometimes this can mean removing barriers or using your position to help facilitate the process. Other times this may mean recognizing that a deadline needs to be extended or a project given more time to be done in the best way. It may mean providing more staffing. Sometimes it requires you taking the information you learn and thinking about solutions. You can then reach back out and offer coaching and advice on how to get it done.

Be Present to Give Feedback

When you go to visit your teams, the goal is not only to receive feedback (learn) but to give feedback. This could be giving feedback about the current situation or how current challenges are shaping the decision-making. Sometimes in-person transparency goes a long way toward helping the team understand why things are being done in a certain way. These meetings are an opportunity to address what the team is doing well, or maybe to talk about areas or things that could be improved. If you are never present and you decide to start visiting your teams, I would probably not make your first visit one where you tell them all the things they are doing wrong. The feedback you give can specifically reinforce your values as an organization and what you are grateful for.

Be Present to Emphasize Values and Purpose

We talked about this earlier in the book, but it is worth repeating here. In fact, emphasizing your values is something that needs to be done over and over. Spending the time as the leader to emphasize values with your team demonstrates their importance. The culture you want will not just magically happen; it has to be intentionally developed. These in-person meetings are great times to help instill the importance of your team values.

If caring is one of your personal values, showing up demonstrates you care about those you lead. You care about their opinions, care about their performance, and care about them and your organization being successful. If you care, you should use these times to say "thank you" in person!

Be Present to Demonstrate Gratitude

Gratitude is a force multiplier. People want to know their work is making a difference. They want to know their bosses recognize how hard they are working and that it is helping the organization be successful. We have an entire chapter dedicated to gratitude later in the book, but for now, I want to mention that when you as the leader thank people in person, it can have a dramatic impact.

You can thank people in a couple of ways. The first is to thank them in front of their peers. This does not have to be a big ceremony, just a simple recognition of what specifically they did well, and maybe the impact of how that supported a patient outcome or the success of the organization. The other way is to find them in their office and thank them personally without the fanfare. Some people don't like public recognition, and there is something more personal about thanking them alone—or maybe, if you are not their boss, you can take their boss with you.

Imagine if a charge nurse was working on a busy unit and the hospital CEO and the chief of nursing showed up at her office unannounced. "I have heard you are doing great things," they tell her. "I appreciate how you have adapted to the staffing shortage to keep things running smoothly. I know this was a big challenge and not optimal. Your leadership has made a tremendous difference. Thank you." Wow! Those leaders certainly just inspired that charge nurse! The leaders could also use the opportunity to ask what they can do to help and if there is anyone on her team that deserves special recognition as well.

Does this interaction sound unusual to you? Do you think this would drive performance and help prevent low morale and burnout? Do you think this would create more meaningful relationships and build trust for your organization? Gratitude is a powerful tool. You can start having these types of interactions in your organization today.

Presence When Not Physically Present

I know I have said you should not be an email warrior and that you need to physically go see your people, but this is not always possible. The higher up in a leadership position you are, the harder it is to see everyone all the time. You can communicate and be present in other ways, especially given how we have adapted to the virtual environment. Word of caution, though: don't get sucked into a virtual abyss. These should *augment* your in-person presence, not replace it.

Email used effectively can help you be present. This is especially true when your team is dispersed and you cannot be physically present with some of them. For example, many of us now have teams that are rotating at different hospitals or people who are working at different campuses. Some are working virtually. How do you connect with them and maintain your presence? Presence in email is harder to maintain, but think about the areas we covered above. How can you use email to listen, learn, provide help, coach, give feedback, and demonstrate gratitude?

Frequent contact is important as a leader. This demonstrates you care about those you lead and is your way to build culture and reinforce what is important. You can update them on where the organization stands and on key events. You should use this communication to point out and recognize team members who are modeling the behaviors you want to see. The most effective leaders I have worked with have used weekly emails to talk about key points, reinforce values, and thank people. These should be short and to the point. They can allow you to remain connected to the team.

Presence During Crisis

Bad things happen. It's inevitable. Dr. Chuck Callahan points out that in the military, we have a phrase: "People run to the sound of the guns." Having been in multiple leadership positions, I have seen just how many organizations and personal crises arise almost daily. Leaders need to be there when crises are occurring. COVID has taught us many lessons about leading during a crisis. For this chapter on presence, I just want to focus on the importance of being present as a leader during times of crisis.

During a crisis, it is even more critical to be present, because people will become anxious and start worrying about what will happen. They want direction and answers, or at least information about what is going on and whether someone is working diligently to solve the problems. Retired General Stanley McChrystal once said there are two things he keeps in mind when communicating in these situations: "What we don't know leaves a vacuum in our mind, and we fill it with the most terrifying ideas,"[6] and "Denying reality makes your people assume you're either lying or out of touch. Organizations can handle bad news and tough times if they feel their leaders are focused on solving the issues at hand."[7]

During a crisis, there is a continued need to learn and get the input of those you lead. If you don't communicate effectively during times of crisis, that lack of communication will be filled with rumors. Your job during times of crisis is to bring order to the chaos. You have to be present in order to effectively do that. The same is true in other times as well. Communicate, or people start telling their own stories about what is going on.

Dr. Chuck Callahan talked about a time when a young active-duty soldier died unexpectedly. He was at the code and then was calling the family of the service member to let them know what happened. While he was there doing this, he looked up from the chaos of the situation and across the room saw the medical center commander, Lieutenant General Eric Schoomaker (currently retired). Schoomaker would later serve as the 42nd Army Surgeon General. The commander was not only present to support but provided coaching on how to get through the situation. Twenty-plus years later, Dr. Callahan can still remember his eye contact from across the room in that moment and recounts this as an exemplar of being present as a leader. Those you lead remember if you were there, caring for them.

Even when things are going well in an organization, the people in your organization will be dealing with life events. While you may think it is not your job as a leader to help someone get through the death of their loved ones or a divorce, I would argue that it is your job. How do you show up as a leader when these events occur? Your actual job may not be to fix the situation, but make sure they know where and how to get resources. Make sure that, if they are not doing well, you facilitate a day off or longer if they need it. At a minimum, you should check in on them and inquire about how they are doing.

I wanted to end with a story that highlights the power of presence. My wife, Dr. Suzette Peng, is a badass. She is a former Army officer and now a captain in the U.S. Public Health Service (USPHS). She deployed to Iraq while she was in the Army and has had multiple deployments in the USPHS. In 2014, she was a member of the team of USPHS that deployed to Liberia. Yes, my wife, rheumatologist and USPHS officer, deployed to care for Ebola patients while her Army, Infectious Disease, husband stayed at home to take care of the kids. My colleagues find this funny and like to point it out to me. All that aside, during her deployment, President Obama called the Monrovia Medical Unit to check in with the team and thank them for what they did. He said, "I am personally and profoundly grateful for what you are doing."[8,9]

I was blown away by the President of the United States taking the time to call this team and let them know how important their work was and how much it was appreciated by him and Mrs. Obama. This was a demonstration of presence like nothing I had ever seen before. If the President has the time to make this call, we have the time to be present and support those we lead.

Prescription for Caring in Leadership

1. Work with your team. If you are in a position that allows you to, roll up your sleeves and work with your team. Cover a shift that no one else wants to (summer and holidays, at times). You need to think about your own well-being, but working on the front lines with those you lead builds trust and credibility.

2. Walk around to check in on how your folks are doing, and ask them, "How can I help?"

3. Check in on someone you have not seen or heard from recently.

   a. Go see someone face to face or set up a meeting.
   b. Connect virtually with someone whom you cannot meet with in person. People who work virtually still need to feel a connection. Be intentional about creating connections.
   c. Do this for a friend or family member as well!

4. When meeting with your people, use that time to reinforce the values of your organization. Remind people about what they do and its importance. Talk about the values that are important to your organization.

5. Make it a habit to check in on your people when something bad happens. Let them know you care by being there. You don't have to have answers or solutions all the time. Just be there and let them know you are thinking about them.

6. Check in on someone on your team and thank them for the work they do, emphasizing your organization's values.

CHAPTER 10

Care Enough to Set High Expectations

"High expectations equal high morale."
—Dr. Adam Barelski

How many of you look at where you work and say, "This place won't expect much of me, so I want to work there." I suspect none of you. We want to make a difference with our work and be able to feel like we are excelling in our jobs. Think of the best place you have ever worked. How much pride did you have working there? Did you wake up in the morning feeling energized about what you were going to accomplish each day? We don't need to be afraid about setting high expectations for people who work with and for us. It should be the expectation that we do. It's what most people want in their jobs. They want to feel valued and like their work matters. In healthcare, all our work matters! If each of us is not reaching our full potential, then what are we leaving unaccomplished as individuals and as teams and organizations? Whose lives could we more positively impact? It's exciting to know that every day, we have the opportunity to make someone else's life better, in big and small ways.

Dr. Amy Vertrees gives an example of how caring leaders set high standards for those they lead. She described her prior general surgery residency program director as a caring leader because of how he expected the best out of all of his residents. This allowed them to excel and become the best versions of themselves as surgeons:

> Colonel Shriver, who was our program director, probably led the most with caring. It's like, what does caring mean? I feel like caring means you see someone not just how they are but how they could be. They want the best for you, and that comes from a deep inner place of really wanting that person to be successful. He was always very stern and held high standards and things like that, but at the very depths of it, I really felt like he was the one who cared the most about the potential that I had—enough to make the hard decisions and push all the residents to the greatness that he saw within us...If someone demands something of you and you feel like you're not capable, it can come across as harsh. But if you believe that you have something to offer, and you have this person who pushes you from this position of "I know you are capable of more than what you think you are," that really speaks to an inner part of us. It really has to be a good match for that particular technique or that particular strategy to work. He really maximized the best of the people who were most receptive to it.

In the book *The Culture Code*, Daniel Coyle talks about how extremely successful groups and companies set high expectations.[1] He argues that people want to be part of these organizations because of their high expectations.[2] He uses the San Antonio Spurs, Pixar, and the Navy SEALs as examples.[3] People want to join these organizations because they are high-performing. Moreover, once in these organizations, they have high standards and expect the best of everyone.

How do your organization's history, culture, and values establish a sense of pride in being part of the organization? Do people in your organization feel motivated to do important work to further the legacy and reputation of where you work? I would argue that every organization involved in healthcare has the opportunity to establish a reputation of excellence. For example, Mayo Clinic has a reputation for outstanding patient care, education, and research. Building these reputations starts with setting high expectations for the organization and individuals within the organization.

If we care about people and want the best for them, then we must set high expectations and then hold them to those standards. At the same time, we cannot demand excellence without providing the support to reach it. The legendary football coach Vince Lombardi said, "*Perfection* is not attainable, but if we *chase perfection,* we can *catch excellence.*"[4] Our job as leaders is to inspire excellence. To help people become more than they thought they could become. If you want people on your teams and organizations to work hard, then set high expectations for them and then help them achieve them. Major General Jeffrey Clark said that leaders must "raise people up to the standard." Think about the best bosses you have worked for. I would guess that many of them challenged you while making you better at what you do. Consequently, you worked really hard because you didn't want to let them down!

Setting expectations has to be part of a process. Here are a few steps to help:

1. Set high standards—for the organization and for individuals.
2. Be as clear as possible about what is expected.
3. Provide the support to be successful.
4. Provide feedback on performance.

5. Recognize a job well done, including individual tasks as well as actions that support and build your culture.

We talk about each of these in this chapter briefly, but each of these steps is also addressed in much more detail later within individual chapters. We need to set high standards for our organizations and individuals. Then, we have to provide resources and support to enable people to meet or exceed those standards. We coach people and provide feedback on performance, and then we recognize a job well done. The support, coaching, feedback, and recognition cannot be overemphasized. This reinforces what is important by the investment in your time as a leader to ensure these standards are met.

Be Clear on Organizational Expectations

When thinking about expectations, it might be helpful to break them down into two specific categories. The first is organizational expectations. These are the expectations of what everyone does to support the culture of the organization. What is expected of each person to support a thriving culture? Remember that culture is ultimately about action and lack of action, so being very clear about what is expected and then holding people accountable is critical to establishing an effective culture. This starts with setting high standards for your organization and making sure everyone understands what is expected, followed by helping your people achieve those standards with support and feedback.

Major General Jeff Clark provides a story that emphasizes these points:

> General Steele was a compassionate individual. I worked for a good number of leaders who were compassionate and cared deeply about people, but you wouldn't call them soft because

they would hold you to a standard. They'd have expectations that we were going to accomplish each mission to a very high standard. We're going to do what needs to be done together. We will figure it out as a team.

I would walk around and check to see how our people are doing, but at the same time see how the mission is going. "How are things going?" And if we're not where we need to be, then we'll get back on course. That's part of the privilege of being a leader.

It doesn't mean you're easy on people, as I think General Steele summarized when he said, "If you're mediocre, you can do one or the other." You can be good to your people but let the mission not get accomplished; or you can be a hardass and push the mission while not taking care of your people, but then your people don't feel valued or know that you care about them. He said, "If you're good, you will do both." That's graduate-level leadership, and that's not easy. The best way I've heard it said is "Don't lower the standard to the individual; raise the individual up to the standard." Listen, understand, coach, support, improve the system and processes. You can do that for an individual. You can help them get to where they need to be. You can do it in the collective by having a high expectation for your team.

As you think about this, what are the standards that you want everyone in your organization to model and uphold? Some of these should be obvious, such as honesty and integrity—but that does not mean you should not be clear about them. Is it being civil and respectful? Is it supporting others on the team? Is it an expectation of delivering feedback to each other and having a growth mindset? Is it valuing diversity, equity, and inclusion? As a leader in your organization, develop a list of standards that will support your culture. Make sure these are communicated to your organization at the time of hiring and then reinforced periodically.

Individual Expectations—Roadmap to Personal Success

The second set of expectations are those for each individual based on their job or position. These are specific to the tasks that they need to accomplish. Often, we assume people know what is expected, which is true to some degree. For example, a charge nurse knows his or her role, but if new to an organization, the expectations may be different from their last role. Similarly, as conditions change, the expectations of individuals may need to adapt as well. As leaders, we need to make sure these expectations are communicated to those doing the work.

A friend and colleague, Dr. Adam Barelski, gives a great example of how we are not always clear about expectations. He was working as a faculty member supervising an inpatient medicine ward team. He was talking to a resident about how the interns on the team were performing. Interns are trainees one year out of medical school doing ongoing training in their specialty. The interns on the team were struggling, and the resident was talking about how he did not understand why they were not doing certain things. After listening, Dr. Barelski asked, "Do they know what they are supposed to be doing?" After reflecting, the resident was not sure, and it became clear that part of the reason the interns were struggling was because the expectations were not clear.

Setting clear expectations is a critical step for leaders and teachers. We set expectations so people know what is expected, but also to help them get better. When setting individual expectations, we should in part be setting them to help people improve at their jobs. Set expectations that allow them to grow and develop new skills. This way, the expectations are not just about the organization but an investment in the individual as well.

What exactly do we want those we lead to do? Ask yourself, "Do the people who work for me know what it is that I want and need them to do?" Do they understand the "why" of what you are asking them to do? It is important for people to know the impact of their work, as often this helps to motivate them. Help them see how their work makes a difference. How often do you review those expectations with them? Give them feedback on their performance, and recognize them for a job well done.

Challenge and Then Support the Heck out of People

Set high expectations and then support those you lead to reach them. Provide the opportunities, resources, and coaching for them to be successful. To develop high-performing organizations, we need to pair our high expectations with a high level of support. This could include resources like time, money, administrative support, etc. Whatever the task is, make sure that it is being appropriately resourced to be achieved. If I am a leader giving you a task, I know you can accomplish it. In fact, I know WE can accomplish it because I am going to have your back throughout the process to help you succeed. If it doesn't get done or done well, then I am also accountable for that.

Support involves giving feedback and coaching along the way. Our goal should not just be mission success but individual growth. As we meet the demands of our daily tasks, hopefully this is helping individuals and teams within our organizations to develop new skills or improve existing skills. The chapters on feedback later in the book should help provide guidance on providing feedback and the value of coaching.

Laurie Baedke illustrates the importance of having high standards, challenging others, and the impact of feedback. The story is also an amazing example of how when we invest in others, they improve and are incredibly grateful:

> I'll share an example of someone who cared deeply and how she showed up. I don't tell very many people the story of how I reached out to and introduced myself to Dr. Julie Silver[5] and had the courage to ask to join the faculty of the Women in Medicine CME course that she leads, and how generous she was. But suffice it to say that she cares deeply. She is a leader who cares, and she, of course, cares in part because she is a faculty member at Harvard Medical School and the standard of excellence in that institution is sky-high.
>
> She cares because if I am a contributing faculty member to her very highly regarded and extraordinarily popular course, how I show up reflects directly on her reputation. This will be my seventh year contributing to her course as a faculty in its eight-year history, and I am unbelievably honored and grateful. But what I'm going to say about Dr. Silver and how she cares and how much she cares is really rooted in the belief that I have—that I know that she shares—that leadership is a capacity. Some people think leadership is a title, or an appointment, or a rank, but leadership is a capacity.
>
> I was already, by the time I showed up at Julie's course, a very seasoned speaker. I'd been speaking professionally for over a decade, and I was an established faculty member at my current institution, Creighton University. My collaborations with Julie have taught me so much and expanded and bolstered my ability to teach to science. If you spend time going to academic symposiums, association conferences, or leadership development events, you know that you can go to some lectures that are steeped in evidence-based research and peer-reviewed literature, and someone's ability points to that. Then there are people who are inspiring and motivational, but there's really no evidence for what they're sharing.

I know that Julie has helped me to grow into the ability to far more effectively teach to science, something that was not a part of my background and is a lot more common in the training of a physician, scientist, or academic leader. How she demonstrated her care for me was to challenge me and to stretch me and to have an eye for my potential...leaning in to giving feedback, often tough feedback. As our "dear friend" (don't I wish that she was my real friend?) Brené Brown says, "Clear is kind."[6] If you're going to give feedback, you can just sugarcoat it. But that's not really kind. What Dr. Silver has done for me is to really have her leadership vision for my potential, an acknowledgment of where I was already solid but an eye for my capacity to become strong. That was only going to come from her really leaning into challenging me and giving it to me straight. I will tell you—and I say this very carefully, because this is not a complaint; this is me being deeply grateful for Julie and her generosity and her genuine caring—at the time of this conversation, I owe her my revised decks for this fall's course in a few weeks. I fully expect that she will spill red ink all over them...looking through every detail, scrutinizing [them], and pulling the very best measure of excellence out of me. It dings my ego every single time, but it continues to equip me to level up and improve, which I value immeasurably.

Recognize a Job Well Done

Recognizing a job well done is an important part of the expectation-setting process. If you set expectations but never follow up with feedback, coaching, and recognition, then it may give the impression that the expectations are not important. Recognition is a great way to reinforce what you value as a leader and organization. The more you point out the good things that people are doing, the more they will likely do those things—and the more others will want to do them as well. If we are setting high expectations for the people we work with and they achieve them, we should celebrate that! We celebrate when our sports teams win, sometimes in exuberant fashion. (Okay, yes, I have had two dogs named after a Pittsburgh Steeler player and a coach.) Why don't we celebrate successes at work that have an impact on the individual and the patients or their families with the same passion?[7]

High expectations are the road map to personal and organizational success. Hopefully this chapter inspires you to set high standards. The remaining lessons from this chapter provide some tangible ways to communicate those standards and help those you lead achieve them. This process allows each individual to become the best version of themselves—and when individuals are excelling, we excel as organizations. People want to be part of excellent organizations!

Prescription for Caring in Leadership

1. Reflect on your organization's culture. Is it clear what the standards are? If not, what do you need to clarify?

2. Identify two or three expectations (e.g., giving more feedback; modeling well-being; initiating diversity, equity, and inclusion efforts within your department; mentoring a junior staff member; etc.) you have for yourself that will allow you to lead more effectively.

3. Identify two or three items that you want to review and reinforce with your organization/team related to standards.

4. Identify areas where you can help people you lead reach higher expectations, then develop a plan to get them there.

5. Recognize someone on your team for living out your organization's high standards.

CHAPTER 11

Care Enough to Hold People Accountable

"There's a big misconception where people think winning or success comes from everybody putting their arms around each other and singing kumbaya and patting them on the back when they mess up, and that's just not reality. If you are going to be a leader, you are not going to please everybody. You have to hold people accountable. Even if you have that moment of being uncomfortable."
—Kobe Bryant[1]

HIGH STANDARDS NEED TO be paired with accountability. If we care about people and our missions, then we have to hold people accountable. Accountability is not about punishment and getting or forcing people to do things; accountability is about helping the people you lead reach their full potential and helping your organization be incredibly successful. If you have to force people to do things, then you are missing something as a leader. We should strive for commitment, not compliance. Leadership is about influence. Moreover, you don't want to live with the feeling of regret for not holding someone accountable and trying to help them or your organization become better.

Holding people accountable is a real challenge for many leaders. I have struggled with this. My own Leadership 360 feedback a few years ago pointed out that I don't always hold people accountable, and this impacts the way others see the culture and me as a leader. In the book *The Five Dysfunctions of a Team*, author Pat Lencioni talks about how leaders and others within organizations avoid conflict, which prevents teams from reaching their full potential.[2] The question is, how do we leaders and teams hold each other accountable to benefit the team and the individual? For homework, read Pat's book, because it is a classic and changed my life in terms of approaching conflict and leading teams.

I am a parent, and some of you are parents. If you are not a parent, all of you were kids at some point. My wife would argue I am still a kid at times—okay, maybe a lot of times. As an aside, my daughter frequently and unfortunately reminds me that I was a kid a *long* time ago. What do you do when your child misbehaves? Do you ignore that behavior? Do you discipline them so they change their behavior? We discipline and hold our children accountable because we care about them and want them to be successful. I don't want to say we need to treat the people who work for us like children, but we should similarly hold them accountable and discipline them when needed because of how much we care about their personal and professional success.

What happens when we do not hold people accountable? How does it impact their professional development and career? How does their professional development and career impact their personal life? Being successful at work dramatically impacts how one feels outside of work, and this can have a financial impact. If you don't perform well at work and lose your job, that impacts your family. Accountability keeps people on track and ideally prevents major life-changing events, such as being fired or missing out on a promotion. If we really care about people, then we need to hold them accountable to the high standards that we established the importance of in the last chapter.

Holding people accountable leads to better outcomes at work. Nate Regier, PhD is the CEO of a leadership consulting company called Next Element and author of the book *Compassionate Accountability: How Leaders Build Connection and Get Results*.[3] He calls compassionate accountability "the next leadership superpower" and cites research that cultures with compassionate accountability are rated "3.4x more likely to be rated as a best place to work" and "3.3x more likely to retain high-potential employees," as well as have better financial outcomes.[4]

Accountability starts with us as leaders. We are responsible for our actions, and we take responsibility for them. We don't blame others. As leaders, we recognize when people have not met expectations, and we address this with them. We hold ourselves and others accountable in order to improve.

Ellie Lindhjem, a licensed social worker, wrote a blog post titled "How to be a leader with an accountability mindset" for the American Association of Orthopaedic Executives.[5] She stated,

> Leaders who do not have an accountability mindset may try to blame other people or situations for their failures instead of taking responsibility for themselves. This kind of behavior is not just unhelpful; it also undermines trust in leadership because it shows that the leader does not care enough about their team members' opinions or ideas.[6]

If you are a leader, people are watching you. What lessons are you teaching? Are they the ones you *want* them to learn?

Major General Clark highlighted this point when talking about core values of an organization. He said as leaders, we should model core values: "Isn't that where people should look?"

We have to hold ourselves accountable before we can hold others accountable.

General and former Secretary of State Colin Powell famously said, "The most important thing I learned is that soldiers watch what their leaders do. You can give them classes and lecture them forever, but it is your personal example that they follow."[7] Holding people accountable starts with us as the leader. As leaders, we have to be the standard bearer and model these behaviors. If we do not uphold the standards and model the way, it becomes almost impossible to expect the same of others and hold them accountable. For the rest of the book, you need to look at each chapter and ask yourself, "How do I model this to those I lead? How am I being an example of a caring leader?" Don't feel bad if the answer is that you are not modeling these things. We all learn and grow, and this book can provide an impetus to start modeling more leadership behaviors.

As leaders, we often fall short even with our best intentions. Leaders will make mistakes, and, given we are human, there will be times when we mess up. When this happens, as a leader, we need to do three things.

First, we need to recognize that we screwed up—either we recognize it or we listen to someone who tells us. If someone told you, make sure you thank them for the gift of feedback for making you and the organization better.

Second, you need to own it as a leader. Take responsibility for the action.

Finally, change your behavior to move forward in a more productive manner. By doing this, we are demonstrating humility, a growth mindset, and exactly what we want everyone else to do when they mess up.

Let me give you an example. We had an expectation in our internal medicine residency training program that we were open to feedback and that feedback was critical to our growing as a team and individuals. My chief residents are junior military officers and physicians who help run the program. One day, we were having a debate about a particular topic. I did not handle the situation well. I blew off the feedback and was not receptive to it. This was exactly the opposite of what I wanted of others in the program. That night, I recognized I was not modeling what I wanted out of others. I had to apologize. I drafted and sent an email apology about what happened to all three chiefs immediately because I did not want to wait. I had to hold myself accountable to the behaviors I wanted from everyone else.

As mentioned above, if we care about others, we need to hold them accountable. Why is this so important? Well, if they are not held accountable and don't know what is wrong, they don't have the chance to improve. This hurts their individual performance and the organization. In healthcare, this also means we are not providing the best care. This means we need to embrace the discomfort and hold people accountable. If we are not clear with people on what they should do and how they are performing, then we are not caring about them.

Very often, when talking with a trainee who is struggling, a faculty member who is having a challenge, or an employee who is not meeting the standard, we will start the conversation with the following phrase: "We want you to know that we are giving you this feedback because we care about you and your personal and professional success."

Honestly, ask yourself how much easier it would be sometimes to just let certain things slide. Avoid confrontation with someone. You know the conversation is going to be challenging. It might get heated. It's not that big of a deal. Well, when you do this and "let it slide," you are missing opportunities to care about others as a leader. You are setting a new standard because you are not holding people accountable. More importantly, you are missing a chance to help them and the organization improve.

We had an intern who was nearing the end of his training but was struggling clinically. We could have just let him slide by. It would have been the easy thing to do, but it would not have been fair to him or his patients. He was going to be going out to take care of service members in his respective service. Interns from military programs can leave after one postgraduate year of medical education and be put in assignments where they take care of young active-duty Soldiers, Sailors, Airmen, and Marines.

We cared about him and his career. If we did not hold him to the standard, it would be possible for him to make a mistake in the future outside of training. He would be held responsible, and it could jeopardize his long-term career success. Making a mistake as a licensed provider could result in patient harm and him being placed on the national provider list. We stopped him from graduating literally weeks before he was supposed to and spent three more months getting him up to speed. He underwent remediation of some clinical skills and medical knowledge deficits. We worked on his communication and confidence.

He successfully completed internship and then went to his first assignment. He excelled in this role and was noted to be a servant leader and committed to excellence by his superiors. He was "dynamic," and he reorganized two departments and led a staff of thirty-seven people. He mentored those beneath him and ultimately was felt to exceed expectations. Would he have had the same success without us stopping his training? Maybe, but I don't think so. The extra time in training and dedication to his professional development paid off. He emailed me the following: "I wanted to thank you again for all the effort you put into helping me get through my intern year."

Not all stories end this way, but if we had not cared enough to hold him to the standard and to invest more training into him, then his success may not have occurred. His unit's success and the well-being of his patients may not have occurred. Accountability is a Caring Act of Leadership.

As we wrap up the chapter on accountability, I want to talk about group accountability. If leaders do an effective job of creating a positive work environment with psychological safety geared toward learning and improvement and not punishment, then the group will also hold each other accountable. In the book *Extreme Ownership: How U.S. Navy SEALs Lead and Win*, Jocko Willink and Leif Babin tell the story of how, during a chaotic battle in Ramadi, Iraq, there was an episode of fratricide.[8] Willink described fratricide as the "mortal sin of combat" in a TEDx Talk about the event.[9] This is when someone shoots someone on the same side instead of the enemy. An Iraqi soldier on the U.S. side had been shot and killed by the U.S. military, and another American, a Navy SEAL, had been wounded.[10]

In this particular situation, they recount how, during the debrief, rather than point fingers, each person wanted to accept the blame.[11] In the end, Jocko, the commander (leader) of the unit at the time, accepted the blame.[12] The important lesson in the title of the book is that we want to be part of organizations where everyone takes ownership. With this degree of accountability (extreme ownership) and commitment, teams learn, improve, and function more effectively. Willink points out during the end of a TEDx Talk on the event that "when a team takes ownership of its problems, the problems get solved."[13]

How is this type of environment created? Leaders must start by caring for everyone on the healthcare team. Through this caring, they develop trust over time. In her seminal work on psychological safety, Amy Edmondson, author and Novartis Professor of Leadership and Management at Harvard Business School, talks about creating workplace environments that create the conditions for anyone to speak up and hold each other accountable without fear of being punished or humiliated.[14] If you are not familiar with her work, I highly recommend it. In her book *The Fearless Organization: Creating Psychological Safety in the Workplace for Learning, Innovation, and Growth*, she gives examples of where organizations lacked psychological safety and how this "dangerous silence" leads to bad outcomes.[15] She then outlines a clear strategy to develop psychological safety in the workplace. Three of the most important steps are setting the stage, inviting input from everyone, and responding productively.[16]

We talk more about these throughout the following chapters, so I will not go into great detail here, but I will provide a brief synopsis. Leaders need to talk about how they develop this type of culture. They need to point out that failure will occur and that success and minimizing errors depends on communication between each other. Then they need to invite participation. They encourage this by demonstrating humility and the desire to learn from everyone on the team. If you are arrogant and dismissive, no one is going to feel safe bringing problems to you—especially if you are part of the problem. On the other hand, if you are humble and demonstrate a consistent desire to learn and grow and value every member of the team's input, then people will be willing to speak up. Don't just wait for them to speak up, but consistently remind them that you want—no, *need*—their input. The only way we all get better individually and as a team is if we can openly give feedback to each other.

The last step is to respond productively. When they give feedback, make sure to thank them! Even if you don't change anything because of it, let them know you appreciate their input and why or why not something was changed. Let others know about the feedback and how it was used. Make the exchange of feedback part of your culture.

Edmondson also highlights that this is not "all about being nice."[17] In fact, people avoid these challenging conversations because they don't want to upset anyone, resulting in a lack of change in behavior or process. That method can lead to detrimental effects for the person and organization. We will talk more about this during our chapters on feedback coming up next, but for now, understand that if we really care about people and our organizations, then we have to hold people accountable and give them feedback.

Prescription for Caring in Leadership

1. How are you not being accountable to those you lead? Think of a way you can improve your own accountability. Tell people about your goal and ask them for feedback.

2. Think of one person on your team who is not meeting the standard and have a discussion with them about their performance.

3. Talk with your team about how holding people accountable is a Caring Act of Leadership. Discuss why this is so important and how this could improve everyone's performance.

4. Read *The Five Dysfunctions of a Team*,[18] *Extreme Ownership*,[19] *The Fearless Organization*,[20] or *Compassionate Accountability*[21] by yourself, or read it with your direct reports and team and then discuss the ideas in the books.

CHAPTER 12

Care Enough to Give Feedback

"It's not personal, it is for personal development."
—Dr. George Ruiz

Giving Feedback—Feedback is a gift, and not just for holidays and birthdays!

GIVING FEEDBACK IS ONE of the most challenging things we do as leaders. It is also one of the most important, because it allows us to improve. If we care about the people we lead and the missions of our organizations, then we have to deliver effective feedback. Dr. Darilyn Moyer, CEO of the American College of Physicians, emphasized this:

> It means giving people crucial feedback. Giving them your honest opinion on things...if you're truly caring, you're gonna have the chutzpah to give people the crucial feedback that they need to grow. If I didn't care about you, I wouldn't be giving it. I wouldn't be talking to you now. I would just let you fall off the cliff on your own. But caring means stepping up to the plate and sometimes doing really tough things. Being caring means not just cheering them on; it also means giving them that crucial feedback and helping them in their pathway to leadership.

Retired Lieutenant General Mark Hertling also emphasized the importance of developing others through feedback:

> The ultimate act of caring, if that's your topic, is helping other people develop. In the civilian world, what I've learned…is the catchphrase for that is "coaching." I keep reminding people that it's more than coaching. True development comes from teaching, training, and personal counseling. Sometimes the tough-love mentoring and coaching, and each one of them have a different effect—but if you're truly caring for someone and you want your organization to be better, you have a certain set of standards you rely on, and you hold people to those standards, and you take different approaches to help them reach those standards in the best way possible. If you see they're not meeting them, you pull them aside and help them meet them.

If we think about feedback as the ultimate act of caring, how does this impact our motivation to deliver feedback? Look at it this way: if someone knew something that could make you a much better physician, leader, or person, and they failed to tell you—how would you feel? You might say, "I wish you had told me. That was not nice," or "That was mean of you for not telling me." This is the exact opposite of what we want. We have that same responsibility to give feedback to others.

> *"The ultimate act of caring, if that's your topic, is helping other people develop."*
>
> — Retired Lieutenant General Mark Hertling

> *Bottom line: If we care about people, then we have to embrace the discomfort of giving people feedback.*

Let me start with a story that I have heard similar versions of too many times to count in multiple teaching and clinical settings with trainees, faculty, and nurses. When teaching leadership, I ask students to tell me about leadership challenges they face and their strengths and weaknesses. One student was talking about his weaknesses and described that he had a really hard time giving feedback. He wanted to be "kind," so he would avoid the challenging discussions. He would even potentially talk about the person with others but would not specifically address the issues with the person who needed to change.

A person cannot improve if they don't know what they are doing wrong or how to improve it. In the field of medicine, this could mean that patient care suffers. This person's academic career may not reach their full potential because they don't know what they are missing. Obviously, these are important things to the individual and the organization. In this chapter, we are going to explore how caring impacts the feedback process to avoid this scenario and help each person and our organizations reach their full potential.

Giving and receiving effective feedback are critical to growth and development at every stage of our careers and lives. Author and leadership coach Laurie Baedke talks about feedback as the fuel for growth.[1] Despite how important giving effective feedback is, it remains one of the most challenging skills for leaders in every profession. I have seen this firsthand with many examples, from training medical students and residents to working with junior officers in the military. I have also observed this when working with my own kids and other kids on sports teams. Nothing says "I love and care about you" more than giving someone actionable feedback to improve. I can tell you how much I care, but how am I making you a better leader, teacher, physician, parent, or human? *That* shows you I care!

Mark Crowley, in *Lead From The Heart*, talks about how the millennial generation wants to be coached at work.[2] When interviewing Jim Harter from Gallup, he got this response: "This is a generation that comes into the workforce expecting to not just have a good boss but a boss who is a good coach too."[3] Our role as leaders is to help people reach their full potential, and coaching and feedback are essential in that process.

Let's start with these two premises: 1) Feedback is essential for personal and organizational improvement, and 2) if we care about someone, we have to give them feedback so they can improve. Reframing feedback in this way has been incredibly useful to me and to many others I have taught over the years. Once we start looking at giving feedback as a Caring Act of Leadership, it becomes much harder to avoid those conversations. Don't rob people of this potential professional or personal development.

We need to rethink the way we look at feedback. I don't like the term "negative feedback" because all feedback is valuable. We should use a different lens when thinking about feedback. Think about sports. My son and daughter both play basketball. Eleven-year-old girls and fourteen-year-old boys are bound to make mistakes. Even NBA and WNBA players make mistakes. When we talk about feedback about their playing, I constantly remind them that the feedback is not meant to be negative. They should not think less of themselves as players but rather understand that the feedback is given so they can get better. Without feedback, we fail to improve—whether it is in sports, music, public speaking, clinical practice, or leading. We need feedback to reach our full potential, making it a positive thing.

The feedback that we give or don't give impacts the lives of those we have the privilege to lead and teach. It impacts every life that they touch as well, so feedback is exponentially important. Many of you probably have examples of the power of feedback. Here is one example that I hope you keep in mind as you read the rest of the chapter—a text message I got from a former trainee, Dr. Phil Lindholm:

> I just wanted to reach out and say thank you for holding me accountable when I was a resident. I was a little bit hot-headed at times and appreciated your fortitude to tell me to knock it off. I don't know if you remember that or not, but it was a very important part in my development as a physician and adult.

When I asked Dr. Lindholm if I could use the quote for the book, he said yes and added, "You know what I feel strongly about is that medicine is losing the art of accountability. It's just like with my children. If I care about them, I will hold them accountable and show them compassion through discipline." I love this story and Dr. Lindholm's openness to sharing it as an example of the importance of feedback for growth. How would his career have been impacted had he never gotten the feedback?

My hope is that you will embrace the mindset of giving feedback as a Caring Act of Leadership. Sue Tetzlaff, RN and co-founder of Capstone Leadership Solutions, wrote a blog post on this topic titled "Healthcare Organization's 3-Point Pathway to Normalizing Feedback as an Act of Caring."[4] She emphasized the importance of caring related to feedback, stating, "Through frequent, well-timed, and well-intended feedback—offered up freely and welcomed graciously as an act of caring—healthcare organizations can supercharge their efforts to create a positive work environment where people feel appreciated, accountable, supported, cared for, and noticed."[5] I couldn't agree more!

Kim Scott's book *Radical Candor* is one of the most impactful books I have ever read; it changed the way I approach delivering feedback.[6] I would highly recommend reading *Radical Candor* and visiting the *Radical Candor* website, because there is a ton of useful information there on how to deliver feedback. Kim Scott emphasizes the point that we need to "care personally and challenge directly."[7] She breaks her feedback framework into four quadrants, including ruinous empathy, manipulative insecurity, obnoxious aggression, and radical candor.[8] Trust me when I say you need to take a deeper dive into this approach. The people you lead will thank you!

I would encourage you to take professional development courses on feedback and consider hiring a coach or asking a peer to coach you when delivering feedback. When you need to give someone feedback, invite a colleague or someone you consider effective at feedback and have them give you feedback on the feedback. If we want to get better, we need to practice and be intentional about it. If feedback is so important and a Caring Act of Leadership, then you will need some steps on how to deliver effective feedback. We will finish the chapter with a ten-step process to help you deliver feedback:

1. Establish trust and let people know you care about them

The most important part about feedback is not the feedback itself. Instead, the first step is to demonstrate that you care about your people. Invest in them every day. Anne Thompson highlighted the importance of investing in others when talking about a role model of a caring leader, saying, "It was clear that she was investing in you to help you get better."

How do you do this? How do you make it clear to those you lead that you want to invest in them? Well, this book is your guide. Each chapter outlines strategies to help those you lead know you care about them. If people know you care about them and have their best interests in mind, it is much easier (though still not easy) to give them even the most challenging feedback.

> *If people know you care about them and have their best interests in mind, it is much easier (though still not easy) to give them even the most challenging feedback.*

One thing I tell people whom I have not met before when I start working with them is "I care about your personal and professional development, so I am going to give you feedback. I want you to know that when I give you feedback, it comes from a place of me wanting to help you get better. Similarly, if you have feedback for me and how I can better support you or the team, please let me know."

A few other things can help build this relationship and trust. First, treat people kindly in every interaction. This seems simple, but kindness goes a long way. As alluded to earlier, this doesn't mean being soft or a pushover but simply treating people with respect. Also, invest in people with your teaching, mentoring, and coaching. If you are doing these things, feedback should become an expectation. Admit your own mistakes when you make them. Being humble and admitting mistakes as a leader helps create the mindset that we are all learning and growing.

Give positive feedback. This action step is discussed later, but I put it under this step because giving people positive feedback reinforces behaviors you want to be repeated and builds trust in the relationships with those you lead. Brad Johnson said, "Little micro-validations and micro-affirmations. They're not heavy lifts, but they do everything to change the culture and communicate to junior people that 'I'm valued here.'"

> *"Little micro-validations and micro-affirmations. They're not heavy lifts, but they do everything to change the culture and communicate to junior people that 'I'm valued here.'"*
> — *Brad Johnson, PhD*

People appreciate the feedback and that you notice and take the time to give them positive feedback. In the book *The New One Minute Manager,* Spencer Johnson and Ken Blanchard talk about "One Minute Praisings," which is when you "catch them doing something right." [9] This, like constructive feedback, which they call "One Minute Redirects," does not have to take long but can have a big impact.[10]

Giving positive feedback not only shows you value people, but it helps people know what right looks like. You should also consider that giving positive feedback is like putting money in the bank so that when it comes time to "make a withdrawal" (give constructive feedback), it is easier. You have already invested in their performance and what they do correctly.

One caveat I want to hit on: What if you are only working with a person for a short period, or only once? You might say, "I can't develop a relationship in that period." That's true. Can or should we give them feedback? Let's review the two feedback premises:

Feedback is required for personal and organizational growth, and if we care about people, we have to give them feedback. This is uncomfortable, but I would challenge you to give the feedback. You could say something like "We have only worked together for (insert time), but I have some feedback for you. I want you to know that I care about your development, so I did not want to miss a potential opportunity to help you. I observed..." You can include the other steps below.

Ultimately, it is up to them if they incorporate the feedback, but let me ask you this: Have you ever worked with someone for a short period of time who gave you feedback that changed the way you care for patients, teach, lead, or parent? I suspect the answer is yes, and that highlights what you need to do when you have the same opportunity to impact someone else.

2. Establish goals

Meet with each team member and establish goals. You want to help them know you care and want them to be successful in reaching their goals, which should align with the organization's goals. The important part here is to be specific about goals. I like the word "establish" rather than "set," because "establish" suggests a conversation between you and the person you are leading.

Goal establishing is important as it helps them focus on what they want to improve and allows you a much more concise lens through which to observe. Have them limit the number of goals to two or three, and make them be specific about their goals. For example, if someone is giving a presentation, they could say, "Can you give me feedback on my talk?" But it would be more effective to say, "I am working on my wait time when I ask questions and bouncing questions back to the audience before always answering them myself." You can see how the second goal will allow you to be much more focused as the person delivering the feedback. For many people you lead, establishing goals will be challenging at first because they are not used to getting this specific and being asked to give goals. The more you practice this, the more it becomes a habit and an expectation for your organization.

You should discuss your own goals if you have them. This models ongoing learning and the process of goal establishment. It is also how you continue to improve. One goal might be "I am working on giving more effective feedback."

3. *Observe and record*

Once you know what the goals are, you need to take the time to observe and record. This means direct observation. Showing up and observing takes time. It is an investment in the person you are giving feedback. It demonstrates caring.

Observe for specific actions and behaviors that you can provide feedback on. The more specific the action, the more valuable the feedback. Recording these actions is important because otherwise you will forget the details. I do this either by taking notes in a notebook that I carry with me or by dictating the events into my phone. I have started to use the latter more often because it is quick, and then I can email myself the notes to include in written feedback if that is needed.

An example might be "I noticed that you looked angry when they mentioned that topic in the meeting. They probably noticed your facial expressions as well. You may want to be more aware of your body language."

What my friend and colleague actually said to me was "Wow, you must have been really pissed off...it was all over your face." Yikes, I was totally unaware! I am, to this day, grateful that my friend gave me that feedback. I am much more aware of my body language and controlling it now. You might say that is harsh, but remember, we were friends and I knew he was looking out for my best interest. If he didn't care enough to give me the specific feedback, I would never have known. Not knowing impacts how others perceive us, as well as our relationships, influence, leadership, and outcomes!

What if I didn't observe the issue? What if someone else gives me information and I need to give feedback to someone based on it? This, of course, comes up a lot. You are the supervisor and maybe you get feedback about a subordinate's performance from someone else. First, I always ask the people giving me the feedback to deliver the feedback personally if they have not already. This is good practice for them; it helps them develop the skills, and it helps build trust in relationships rather than getting the feedback secondhand from their direct supervisor. If they do, then I usually follow up with a discussion and action plan, as outlined below.

Whether it is collective feedback or you have to do it secondhand, these steps will help. Gather as much information as possible from as many resources as possible. The more specific information you get from people, the easier it will be to deliver the feedback. Try to triangulate the information and look for a pattern. If the same feedback is coming from multiple sources, it is probably valid. If it is only from one person, it is still valuable but sometimes easier for the subordinate to discount as "just their opinion." If I get the sense someone has this attitude about the feedback, I say, "Could any of this be true? If it was true, how could this be hindering your performance? It's up to you what to do with the feedback."

4. Allow for self-assessment

Most of us already have an idea of how we perform. It is good practice to do a self-assessment of everything we do. Honestly, it is often the only feedback we get as we move on in our careers. After people read this book, hopefully there will be more feedback given!

Many educators recommend allowing learners to self-assess before delivering the feedback. This teaches them the self-assessment process and allows them to get a sense of how they think they are doing. Anecdotally, people usually have a general sense of how they are doing. Sometimes they know specific things they could do better, and at other times they know where they are struggling but don't know what to do to improve. This is a time for us to shine with our feedback, because we can provide specific advice to help people improve.

I find getting their self-assessment usually makes our jobs easier. When someone tells you they are struggling with something that you observed them struggling with, they just delivered the feedback you might have been worried about telling them. They already know! So now the two of you can focus on the action plan.

If you disagree with their self-assessment, you can give them feedback there as well. This is important for two reasons. The first is the individual who lacks insight. Here, your goal with your feedback is to help them see reality and where their deficiencies are so they can improve. This, as alluded to above, usually goes well, but sometimes (as mentioned, with people who lack insight) you may have to make your feedback crystal clear, be specific about examples, and give explicit goals for improvement. Follow-up with these learners is really important. If they are not engaging with the plan or trying to change, you—as mentioned above—may have to increase the stakes if they continue to fail to engage and improve.

The second individual is the one who lacks confidence. This is the learner or leader who always apologizes or always thinks they are performing below where they should be. In this scenario, your job is to correct that attitude and lack of confidence. You want your feedback to bolster their confidence and help them see they are meeting, or potentially even exceeding, expectations. This often takes considerable feedback over time to help them see themselves in a more confident manner. Helping them develop that confidence is critical in the practice of medicine and in leading.

5. Be kind with delivery and deliver specific feedback

How do you feel when you mess something up? Most of us feel like crap because we hold ourselves to such high standards. We are self-critical and at times even ashamed. This is why the delivery of feedback should be done with kindness. You usually recognize this because of the self-assessment of the individual. If so, tailor your feedback to the situation. You don't need to sugarcoat what went wrong. In fact, you need to dig into the events and observations as much as possible to learn from them. You also don't need to yell, ridicule, or belittle someone. Our job is to help them get better, not feel worse.

Since people can take feedback personally and be hard on themselves, Dr. Vertrees reminds us to address some of these issues upfront (I am paraphrasing some of her comments here):

- "I am not giving you this feedback because I think you are a terrible employee or student, but because this will make you better."

- "I don't want you to worry about your grade or failing, but I do want you to think about how this feedback might make you better."

Be clear with the goal of the feedback to prevent the receiver from thinking the worst.

When thinking about being kind, don't forget: we need to give positive feedback as much (if not more) than we give negative feedback. This positive feedback should be a habit and done consistently. Remember, you are making deposits for when you need to "withdraw" by delivering constructive feedback.

While we should give positive feedback, don't use the infamous "feedback sandwich": a positive comment, a negative comment, and then a positive comment. This just leaves people confused or thinking they are doing okay because the important feedback is lost. Rather than the feedback sandwich, skip the bread and just deliver the meat of the constructive feedback!

There are times when the feedback needs to be delivered in a stronger manner. I don't mean to be harsh. If someone lacks insight or is resistant to needed change, I link the feedback to clear expectations of what needs to be changed and the consequences of not changing. In twenty-plus years of service in military medicine, I rarely had to have this type of conversation because most people want to change and improve and have insights into their deficiencies. At times, though, you have to make it clear— and if something does not change, they may need to be fired or terminated from their position. In those cases, you may say something like this: "It doesn't seem like you understand or are willing to change based on the feedback we have been giving you. I want you to know that I still care about you and want you to be successful. You need to know, however, that if you do not improve or change your behavior, we will potentially have to terminate you."

Praise in public and criticize in private. You have probably heard this mantra thousands of times. While generally not a bad approach, I want to make three specific caveats I learned while taking the Stanford Clinical Teaching Program.[11] Feedback should be given publicly when there is a safety issue, there is a lapse in professionalism, and/or it is generalizable. The first point about safety issues seems obvious. You cannot wait to tell someone to fix something if it is going to cause patient harm or harm another individual. That feedback has to be delivered immediately. If someone does something unprofessional and it is not addressed publicly, the rest of the team and bystanders don't see the feedback. The team may take away that the behavior was okay and that it is accepted by the leadership. I will use my favorite example here: if someone criticizes another department when giving a talk to your department, you need to give feedback to them in front of the group. This tells everyone else those comments are not acceptable and reinforces your values and culture.

The point about generalizability is a little more nuanced. Setting the stage for this is important. If you develop a culture of feedback and learning, this is easier. If you create that culture, then everyone recognizes the feedback is about growing and getting better, and it becomes less about the person getting the feedback. In many situations, someone does something and it is something the entire group can learn from. For example, let's say you are rounding in the intensive care unit, and you notice that the intensive care unit fellow who is running rounds doesn't ask for pharmacy input at the end of each presentation. You could give this feedback to her later, but instead, you might give it in front of the group. What are the advantages of that? Seriously, think about this before reading on.

If you give the feedback to the group, you can not only help the fellow learn, but you can teach the same skills to the interns and residents who are on the team. You are teaching them about team-based care and how each member plays an important role. You are reinforcing your organization's values of respect and teamwork. Rather than just the one fellow getting that feedback, now the entire eight- to twelve-member ICU team has gotten that feedback. More importantly, that feedback is fostering a positive interprofessional work environment. Will this make the fellow uncomfortable getting the feedback in the group? Maybe, but are there not many more positives to giving it in the group?

6. Discuss reaction to the feedback

Feedback should be a conversation. Talk to the learner about their thoughts about the feedback. Do they agree or disagree? Work through the differences. Were you missing something about the situation? The goal is to come to a consensus about what happened and what needs to be improved. This discussion can help lead to the next step or a plan for improvement.

7. Give an action plan for improvement

There is data suggesting feedback is rarely paired with an action plan for improvement. One study reported only 8 percent of faculty gave an action plan with their feedback.[12] How does one improve without a plan on how to get better? Remember the goal to change behavior! Work with the person to develop a specific action plan on how to improve. This could be providing them with resources to learn more about a topic, opportunities for practice, and ongoing coaching related to real-life situations.

Let's say you wanted to help someone become more effective at feedback. You could have them read this chapter or the references I provide below. You could deliver a talk on feedback or have them attend a faculty development session on feedback. You could use simulation and role-play to have them go through some challenging feedback scenarios in which they would have to practice these skills. Finally, you could observe them giving feedback in real time to a trainee or subordinate, depending on their position, and give them feedback on their feedback.

8. Follow up, if you can

Once you have an action plan, you need to follow through with it. If you care about them developing, you won't just give them a plan and send them on their way! Make a point to follow up on the action plan. You may want to keep a log of this or a tracker to remind you. As you follow up, continue to coach them to improve. Your coaching and feedback are investments in them and your organization.

If you only work with someone once, this may not be possible, but you could email or text them. You might also link them up with someone else whom they will be working with who can continue to help them. Following up shows you care.

9. Make it a habit, not an event

Move from specific, time-based feedback (quarterly, midyear, yearly, or the middle or end of rotation) to ongoing, frequent, on-the-spot feedback. Feedback should occur on a daily basis. This is the ideal end state. Habits are built by repetition, so the more you give feedback and the more those you lead give feedback, the more you become a person who gives feedback.

One way to facilitate this is by building reminders, like feedback cards. Develop cards that are used as a prompt to deliver feedback. The card can be written on and then handed to the person who is getting the feedback. These can be as simple as a 3x5 notecard with strengths and areas for improvement. You could be more elaborate if you want to and add other prompts. An example might be to add the values of your organization and use the card to emphasize which value you are giving feedback on.

The second example is an act called "Feedback Friday," used in our internal medicine residency program. This was developed by two former internal medicine chief residents, Dr. Adam Barelski and Dr. Ben Vipler. They made every Friday a time to give feedback, and they would walk around and talk to all the inpatient medicine teams and remind them to give feedback to residents and rotating medical students. You might argue this *is* an event, but every Friday is still more often than only at the end of rotation!

10. Develop a culture of feedback

Did the leaders who you think cared about you the most invest in your professional development? Do people and organizations thrive if they can learn and grow? Feedback needs to be an essential part of your culture.

Make it an expectation that everyone is giving and receiving feedback. You can include feedback as part of mentoring discussions. Specifically talk to those you mentor and lead about how they are fostering feedback among their team. Celebrate people who are effective at giving feedback, and thank people for being open to feedback. Model giving and receiving feedback as a leader.

No feedback is still feedback!

One final thing to think about: If you observe someone doing something wrong—such as an unprofessional act, like yelling at another team member—what feedback are you giving if you *don't* give feedback? Think about this and ask yourself, "What does this tell that person?" They walk away from the situation thinking, "It must have been okay, since no one said anything." Not giving feedback is taken as "I'm doing okay." This is crazy scary and a stark reminder of why, if you care, you have to give feedback.

Be a leader who invests in others through feedback! Giving others feedback can change their lives and change the function and effectiveness of our organizations. Recognize that giving feedback is a true Caring Act of Leadership in the workplace and at home. Go forth and create a better tomorrow through your feedback!

Prescription for Caring in Leadership

1. Give someone positive feedback each day this week.

2. Make it a point to give someone specific feedback this week to improve their performance. Note: If you have been avoiding giving someone feedback, this is the person you need to deliver the feedback to.

3. Meet with your direct reports and talk to them about your approach to feedback and how you can improve as a team with giving and receiving feedback.

4. Ask someone to observe you giving feedback and to give you feedback on it.

5. Develop a pattern of giving feedback where you work—like Feedback Friday.

6. Read the book *Radical Candor* by Kim Scott, or go to her website, read her blog posts, or watch her videos on feedback.[13]

7. Read *The New One Minute Manager* by Ken Blanchard and Spencer Johnson.[14]

8. Read the 1984 reference by Dr. Jack Ende that I am including in the notes, which is a timeless class on feedback.[15]

CHAPTER 13

Care Enough to Receive Feedback

*"Feedback is a free education to excellence. Seek
it with sincerity and receive it with grace."*
—Ann Marie Houghtailing[1]

WHEN TALKING ABOUT FEEDBACK, we tend to focus on the delivery. While this is important, it neglects the importance of *receiving* feedback. We can deliver the most eloquent and detailed feedback in the world, but if the person we are giving the feedback to does not receive it and implement it, then it is worthless. If we really care about getting better for ourselves, our teams, our organizations, and our families, then we must learn to properly accept feedback. We should crave feedback and work to be better at receiving and applying it. Most of us have never been taught how to approach feedback. This chapter will outline a process to help you receive feedback and coach those you lead on it as well.

Atul Gawande is a world-renowned surgeon who works at Harvard. He is also an author who has published multiple books. He wrote an article for *The New Yorker* called "Personal Best: Top athletes and singers have coaches. Should you?" The article talks about the importance of coaching, which of course is centered around the idea that the only way we improve is with observation and feedback.[2] Gawande talks about how his surgical skills plateaued after having completed well over 2,000 operations.[3] He was a very accomplished surgeon, but he did not feel like he was getting better. He was worried he would get worse. At the same time, he was a tennis player and had hired a coach to help improve his tennis serve. It led him to ask the question of why athletes have coaches, yet physicians do not:

> Nearly every elite tennis player in the world [has a coach]. Professional athletes use coaches to make sure they are as good as they can be. But doctors don't. I'd paid to have a kid just out of college look at my serve. So why did I find it inconceivable to pay someone to come into my operating room and coach me on my surgical technique?[4]

The rest of the article talks about the importance of coaching and how physicians should consider coaching for professional development.[5] Gawande chronicles the specific feedback he got from a coach. He asked a former professor and surgeon he worked with to observe him in the operating room. He was able to get very specific feedback that improved his skills. Was the feedback valuable? Gawande described it as follows: "That one twenty-minute discussion gave me more to consider and work on than I'd had in the past five years." If an accomplished Harvard surgeon can benefit from feedback after years of practice, it is fair to say that we can all benefit from feedback.[6]

The point of sharing this story is not that everyone should go out and hire a coach. The point is coaching is all about feedback. Most of us have experienced coaching and were used to getting feedback that made us better. Athletes, singers, and musicians all have coaches. As we moved away from these activities to work activities, the coaching and feedback decreased, and so did our opportunities for maximizing our professional and personal growth. Moreover, our sensitivity and how we take the feedback changed as well. Without the frequent stream and expected nature of feedback, now when we receive feedback, many of us become defensive. It's a hit to our egos. We think, "Maybe I am not as good as I thought I was." The problem with this response is that it does exactly the opposite of what we want, which is to get better.

Dr. Jeff Hutchinson talked about how he coaches leaders to receive feedback: "How do I get leaders to [accept] the bad news and go forward? It's the reminder of what their goal is. Reminding them that you can't do this alone. That feedback really is not criticism, but it's the idea of how you make it back on the path and to the goal that you're working toward."

He added that we need to separate our emotions from the feedback. We need to think about it logically. "What was actually said, and how might that allow me to lead more effectively or our organization to improve?" Remember, feedback is given because people want you and your organization to get better. The other point he emphasized that we should all remember is "that bad things don't get better by ignoring them."

Your struggling employee or student is unlikely to just figure it out on their own. They need your feedback.

Since being defensive about feedback is a common issue, I thought it would be worth mentioning a few strategies here that might be helpful when receiving feedback. These are useful for us and helpful to teach and talk about with those we lead. Dr. Ali Algiraigri, a medical educator from the University of Calgary, published a paper in *Medical Education Online* in 2014 titled "Ten

Tips For Receiving Feedback Effectively in Clinical Practice."[7] Table 1 from that paper is included here, and some of those tips are discussed in more detail below.[8]

	Point of emphasis	How to deal with it?
1	Self-assessment	Break down the task into different components rather than looking at the global picture.
2	Do I really need feedback?	Everyone has a blind spot, which prevents us from reaching the next stage of growth, so go and discover it.
3	Your preceptor(s)	Connect well with your teacher and build up the bridge of success.
4	Little or no feedback	Take initiative and ask for the feedback.
5	Positive feedback	Thank your instructor and appear confident. Take that task to the proficient level.
6	Your emotion	You are expected to make mistakes. It is normal to receive constructive feedback. Feedback is an opportunity for improvement. Be a good listener.
7	Your turn! What after the feedback?	Here is what really matters, be part of the constructive action plan and follow that up.
8	Generation differences	Acknowledging this will help you to better understand your preceptors.
9	General, non-specific feedback	Probe and ask questions to figure out what exactly is the point.
10	Be ready for it	Situations matter, feedback can happen at any time and in any form.

Reference: Ali H. Algiraigri (2014) Ten tips for receiving feedback effectively in clinical practice, Medical Education Online, 19:1, DOI: 10.3402/meo.v19.25141, copyright © Taylor & Francis Ltd (2014), reprinted by permission of the publisher.

A *Harvard Business Review* article by Sheila Heen and Douglas Stone, "Finding the Coaching in Criticism," provides six practical tips as well.[9] We review several of these below. Of note, the article also states that "55% of employees said their most recent performance review had been unfair or inaccurate" and that "When senior HR executives were asked about their biggest performance management challenge, 63% cited managers' inability or unwillingness to have difficult feedback discussions."[10]

Hence, we definitely have some work to do on giving and receiving feedback.

Here are five steps to foster receiving feedback:

1. Feedback is required for improvement; always have a growth mindset.

If we care about ourselves and our professional development, then we have to have a growth mindset. Feedback, as alluded to earlier, is the fuel for growth. That being said, we have to be open to feedback. Feedback should stoke our fires of ongoing personal and professional development. The term "growth mindset" comes from the work of Carol Dweck, PhD.[11] When an individual has a growth mindset, they believe skills can be developed and see failure as a path to growth and learning. Rather than shying away from challenging situations, individuals with a growth mindset seek them out as opportunities, recognizing that with effort and feedback, they will grow and improve.

2. Start with self-assessment.

The process of self-assessment is important in our learning. In many situations, our self-assessment is all we have to base future performance or actions on. Ideally, we marry our self-assessment with external feedback. This calibrates our self-assessment and gives us a (hopefully) less biased assessment of how we are doing. Does the feedback align with your self-assessment? The difference is often the performance gap that we need to fill.

3. Seek specific feedback, and thank people for helping you get better.

People tend to be reluctant to give feedback. Let's be honest, our first reaction to getting feedback is typically a defensive one. We try to avoid it or push it away. We put up our feedback shields. While these shields may protect us at times, we can learn from almost all feedback, so we are preventing ourselves from benefiting from feedback. We have to avoid blocking potentially valuable feedback that will help us grow and potentially set our careers on fire—in a good way!

We need to lower our shields and make it as easy as possible for people to give us feedback. Sheen and Stone recommend that you just "ask for one thing," as this makes it easier for the person giving the feedback and you are not surprised but actually excited when you get it.[12] They go on to say, "Research has shown that those who explicitly seek critical feedback (that is, who are not just fishing for praise) tend to get higher performance ratings."[13] Seeking feedback helps us get better and leads to improved evaluations. Seems like a no-brainer that we should want to do this!

Laurie Baedke gives a great example of how to solicit feedback:

> I always lead with my objective, which is I want to grow and improve. To that end, I would welcome your candid feedback. That's my ask. And then the next statement is..."I will do my best to receive it gracefully." My saying that to you hopefully sets a table of psychological safety that lets you go, "Okay, Laurie's serious. I can actually tell her this thing that she probably doesn't want to hear." It also is a verbal cue for me that I must do my best to receive it gracefully. That's the cue for me to shut my mouth and open my ears and not react and defend it or justify it, but rather just receive it, sleep on it perhaps, and consider what merit it has—or [what] morsel of truth exists for productive application.

It starts before the activity you are doing. Ask people for specific feedback, not a general response. What areas do you need or want feedback on? For example, if you want feedback on your public speaking, ask someone to observe you beforehand and tell them you want specific feedback. This allows them to observe more carefully and sets up an expectation that they will give you feedback. Rather than feeling awkward about giving you feedback, they will feel bad if they *don't* give you feedback. Once they give you feedback, be sure to praise and thank them. You want to encourage them to do it again. Hopefully others observe that you really do want feedback.

4. Find the gold in the feedback.

Once we receive feedback, we need to make sense of it. Sheen and Stone emphasize that "Your growth depends on your ability to pull value from criticism in spite of your natural responses."[14] The key is to unpack the feedback and determine what the lesson is from it. All feedback is useful. Let me say that again: all feedback is useful. If nothing else, it reinforces what we already know and supports a culture of giving feedback. Both are important to individual and organizational improvement. When you get feedback, try to separate the feedback from the individual, especially if you have had conflicts with that person. Sheen and Stone describe this as trying to "disentangle the 'what' from the 'who.'"[15] Look specifically at what behavior is described. If it is unclear, ask the person for more details, and don't be afraid to ask others if they observed the same thing. Remember, the goal is improvement and not just to make ourselves feel good.

5. Develop an action plan to improve.

Once you have the feedback, develop a plan on how to improve. Ideally, this is developed in discussion with the person who gave you the feedback. If not, work on it by yourself or seek advice from someone you know is better in that particular area. This is a great opportunity for coaching, as we discuss later. Don't be afraid to test out the feedback. Too often, we are so concerned with outcomes that we don't experiment enough. One of my favorite lessons I learned from Elizabeth Armstrong, PhD—the founder of the Harvard Macy Institute—was that we should be running educational experiments every day. Obviously, we need to consider the stakes and context, but sometimes we need to test new skills and strategies as leaders. We put in the effort trying them out, knowing that we will learn about ourselves in the process. Sound familiar? It's a growth mindset! Don't be afraid to run experiments as a leader and encourage those you lead to do the same—and give them feedback so they can improve.

A critical part of leaders seeking feedback and receiving it well is that it models it for those we lead. The humility to continue to learn fosters a learning environment for others. It is much easier for people we lead to admit mistakes and be open to feedback when we model that behavior for them.

Prescription for Caring in Leadership

1. Reflect on the last time you received feedback. How long ago was it? How did it change your behavior?

2. Ask yourself how open you are to feedback. Are you willing to put down your shield to become better at what you do? To become a more effective leader?

3. Identify one area that you need feedback in and find someone who can observe you and give you feedback.

4. Talk to your team or an individual you lead about how each of you needs feedback to improve and how to be more open to feedback. Consider sending the team the Sheen and Stone *Harvard Business Review* article.[16]

5. Read the book *Thanks for the Feedback: The Science and Art of Receiving Feedback Well* by Sheila Sheen and Douglas Stone.[17]

CHAPTER 14

Care Enough to Seek and Value Feedback from the Team

*"A leader should encourage the members
of his staff to speak up if they think the
commander is wrong. He should invite
criticism. It is a grave error for the leader
to surround himself with yes-men."* [1]
—General Omar Bradley

WHAT I AM ABOUT to say may be a big challenge for you. It has been for me, at times, but I think it is critically important if we want to get effective feedback from our teams. A *Harvard Business Review* article by Bill Taylor captures the idea in the title: "True Leaders Believe Dissent is an Obligation." He states, "Put simply, you can't be an effective leader in business, politics, or society unless you encourage those around you to speak their minds, to bring attention to hypocrisy and misbehavior, and to be as direct and strong-willed in their evaluations of you as you are in your strategies and plans for them."[2]

We may perceive dissent or feedback as people "complaining to us." We may even have the urge to tell people to be more positive.

Before you do this, remember that people aren't complaining—they are caring. As my former department chair in internal medicine, Dr. Louis Pangaro, used to say, "If people are taking the time to give you feedback, then you should be grateful. It still means they really care about the organization and want it to improve."[3]

Complaining (Feedback) = Caring

Let me give you an example of what this might look like. I was in a meeting once about feedback we had received in response to a survey. Someone responded with about a solid page of feedback. They were blunt and to the point, and frankly pretty harsh about how we were doing and what we needed to fix. In full disclosure, my initial response was that this person was just complaining. Dr. Pangaro pointed out that we should be grateful that they spent the time to give us the feedback. This moment was a game changer for me in how I receive feedback as a leader. I no longer looked at it as them unloading on me or just complaining but as a true act of them caring enough to try to help us get better.

The worst thing that can happen as a leader is to get to a point where people are so uninvested or angry that they stop giving feedback. Secretary of State and General Colin Powell famously said, "The day the soldiers stop bringing you their problems is the day you have stopped leading them. They have either lost confidence that you can help them or concluded that you do not care. Either case is a failure of leadership."[4] We need to make giving feedback an expectation. Make it clear that as a leader, you need and expect them to provide feedback and dissent when necessary. We want those we lead to feel like they are letting the team down if they are not giving feedback and voicing dissent at times.

Dr. Argyros provides an example by talking to his team and ensuring they speak up and provide their expertise. He shared this story of how he communicated this message with his team:

> If you are our subject matter expert, if you're at the table, my expectation is you are going to represent us—and how is this going to impact us?...When I started my fellowship, Yancy [Phillips, our former Army colleague] said to the fellows, "I want no silent nonconcurrence." You might think, "What the hell does that mean?" There's like three negatives in there, and in a short sentence. What he said was this, and I use that term with my team all the time.
>
> Getting that team together, trying to understand the perspective of whatever the issue is we're discussing from everyone's perspective. If you are concerned about something we are talking about, don't sit there silently so you're nonconcurring with what we're talking about. If you don't say anything about it and we make a decision based on the available information and we move forward—if there's a problem down the road, you give up your ability to say "I told you so" if you didn't tell me so.

Dr. Argyros's lesson is a valuable example of how we can communicate this expectation to those we lead. We expect you to speak up. We need you to speak up. You can choose this approach or word it differently, but make sure your team understands the expectation is for them to provide input and shape both the discussion and decision—then thank them when they do.

> *"I want no silent nonconcurrence."*
> —Dr. Greg Argyros

There is a mantra that says, "Don't just bring problems—bring solutions." We should, without question, be asking people to bring us problems and potential fixes. Often, frontline workers already know how to fix the problem and just need our support as leaders to implement the solution. This could mean resources or removing potential barriers. However, there are times when there are complex problems and there may not be a clear solution. We need people to bring these problems forward even when they cannot offer a solution. I think it's fair to ask people to think about and recommend solutions when they may have them. This empowers them and demonstrates their leadership ability. That said, make it clear that you want to know about *all* problems, even if they can't bring you a solution. Those are the problems likely needing your eyes the most.

To illustrate some of these points, let's look at an example from Dr. Greg Argyros. He highlights the importance of being present, listening, and how to respond to feedback:

> When I took over as chief medical officer, the morale of the medical staff was awful. There had not been effective engagement with the medical staff in any measurable way. I started to do town hall meetings. I had a quality manager with me whose sole job was to write down every issue that was brought up in these town hall meetings and ensure that we followed up on them. My communications person also attended and just listened so that she could shape the communication that was going to come from me and my office. I had to wear Kevlar to some of those; I would just get blasted.

> We did eighty town hall meetings that first year, and my quality manager tracked 700 items that were brought up...The three of us did eighty town hall meetings every year, and the number of items identified for action decreased from seventy to seventeen that last year when I was CMO.

> You might say, "Well, did people just [say], 'You know, we brought these things up, nothing happened, and we're just going to stop'?" No, it was that so many items had been

resolved. You get to the point where you can say no as a leader. It doesn't always have to be yes, but it has to be yes enough so that when you do say no, the answer isn't "Well, you're just a bean counter," "You don't know what you're talking about," etc. When the announcement went out that I was going to be the president, the first couple texts that I got were from position leaders, and they said, "Congratulations, but are we still going to have access to you?" or "We're still going to be able to get things done." That's a win. That's a win a hundred times in a row, and that's what you need. You need that, not just in the leader but the leadership team.

Leaders must work intentionally to create an environment where the people we lead are willing to bring us their feedback. Just like feedback for us as individuals, feedback to us as leaders for our teams is a gift. You can see from Dr. Argyros's example that people valued his leadership because they knew he would listen and take action to fix things.

We all want leaders who will listen to our feedback and make changes. This is how we get better. What are some ways we can promote this feedback? How do we foster an environment where everyone is willing to speak up? To close this chapter, here are some tactical steps you can use as a leader to create this type of culture.

Steps to Promoting Dissent and Embracing Feedback

1. Set the expectation with your teams for dissent.
2. Model humility and listen.
3. Point out dissent when it happens in a meeting or other setting.
4. Thank people for their dissent and feedback.

5. Close the loop by providing feedback to the group about changes implemented based on the feedback.

When I work with new teams, I tell them explicitly that I want their feedback, especially if they disagree with me. I remind them intermittently before we start our meetings. It is important, so we have to say it more than once. An article by Ron Friedman, PhD on physicianleaders.org says that instead of asking for feedback, ask those you lead, "What are you stuck on?" Similarly, I like the phrase "How can I help?"

We want to make it clear that some opinions are dissenting opinions and that's a good thing. We want to be intentional about our gratitude. I might say something like "Great, thank you for being willing to give us a different perspective. This is how we get better. I want to remind everyone that this is the expectation for all of us so we can ultimately get to the best solution." One great example of these steps was when we had a meeting and were discussing a particular issue. Everyone around the table was agreeing, and then someone disagreed. Dr. Pangaro listened and then said something to the effect of "I want to thank you for that. I appreciate the different perspective." This created the space for more divergent opinions.

The last step is critical. What do you do with feedback? You need to close the loop. Sometimes this is obvious because a decision is made in a meeting and everyone knows. That is not always the case. Sometimes it takes time to get to solutions. Sometimes no solution can be found. Make it a habit of communicating back to your team what you have done with the feedback. You can do this in person or via email. Remember, you want them to know their feedback was valued and made a difference. Explain why a decision was not made, if possible. The whole goal is to foster more feedback so you can improve as an organization. Closing the loop on feedback may look like this:

We received some feedback about the lack of places for women to breastfeed. This feedback was really important to us, and we were able to work with hospital leadership to identify several areas closer to clinical care that could be designated for breastfeeding. We were able to procure refrigerators for those areas to store breast milk. Thank you for your feedback, as it allows us to better support you!

Leaders need to make giving and receiving feedback for organizational improvement a priority. The steps and ideas laid out in this chapter are tactical ways to improve the flow of feedback. Let's commit to giving more feedback and working to get more feedback for ourselves and our organizations.

Prescription for Caring in Leadership

1. Ask those you work with for feedback so you can improve. You might just ask, "How can I help?" or use one of the following questions:
   a. "What could I do to make your job easier?"
   b. "What am I doing that makes your job harder?"
   c. "How could I be more supportive of your work?"
   d. "What is the one thing you really wish I would stop doing?"
   e. "How could I help you with this project?"
   f. "How could I be a more effective teacher, manager, etc.?"

2. Thank your team for their feedback when they bring you issues to fix.

3. Begin each meeting with a statement about the importance of dissent, then point out dissent and thank people when it occurs during the meeting.

4. Give feedback to your team on what was done with the feedback you received. This can be in person or via a summary email. Do it every time you get feedback.

5. Read *The Five Dysfunctions of a Team* by Pat Lencioni.[5]

CHAPTER 15

Care Enough to Be Humble

"You can do what I cannot do. I can do what you cannot do. Together we can do great things."[1]
—Mother Teresa

HUMILITY IS ESSENTIAL FOR leaders and impacts everything we do. Being humble demonstrates to those we lead that we care about them. We are humble enough to continue to learn, humble enough to respect and value their opinions and feedback, and humble enough to let them get the credit for success. In medicine and life, if you are not humble, you are on the road to being humbled.

Humility is defined, according to the Oxford Dictionary, as "the quality of not thinking that you are better than other people."[2]

Below, we talk about the value of humility, but before we do, let's address a common misconception. Too often, people confuse being humble with being weak. On the contrary, being humble requires even more confidence in one's own ability.

Retired Lieutenant General Mark Hertling highlights the importance of confidence and humility in healthcare, especially how it impacts individual patients, but also our ability to improve the system as we work with each other in optimal ways:

> Confidence is usually quiet, and so is humility. Cockiness is usually trying to make up for something that you're not. It reflects insecurity in your true approach or your competence. If you're confident, you are usually pretty humble because you know there's always something more to learn. If you're cocky, you think you know it all and you don't have to listen to anybody else. You know the confident leader...in an interprofessional environment, where you're dealing with a surgeon talking to a hospitalist or talking to an anesthesiologist. They all know that they are competent in their specific skill set, but they should be humble in taking advice from each other. A surgeon taking advice from an anesthesiologist on something that person sees that the surgeon doesn't, or something that the hospitalist picks up on during the treatment before passing over to a specialist—it all gets to the competence in (or the confidence in) your competency and your skill set and how it's reflected in dealing with others. By the way, based on my research for my dissertation, that's the biggest challenge between physicians and administrators and physicians and nurses. From what I've seen, [the biggest challenge] is the inability to be humble enough to listen to other specialties. And research has shown there's huge tensions in most healthcare organizations between those three things. That's why I think it's important.

> *"That's the biggest challenge between physicians and administrators and physicians and nurses. From what I've seen, [the biggest challenge] is the inability to be humble enough to listen to other specialties."*
> *— Retired Lieutenant General Mark Hertling*

In medicine, it is impossible for us to know and do everything. Charlotte Flood-Stith, a program coordinator for the Department of Psychiatry and Behavioral Health Science at Oklahoma State University, captured this in an editorial in the *Family Practice Management* journal, stating, "In health care, the ongoing evolution toward team-based care and quality measurement calls for leaders who can attract and inspire followers, but a big, self-confident personality is not always a sign of real leadership. Sometimes a dose of humility is what's needed most."

We want confident leaders, but not overconfident leaders. Humility requires the ability to be vulnerable with the team/followers. The most confident leaders are okay asking for help because they are confident in their own abilities and put the goals of the patient/ organization above themselves. They are not just okay with it but fully recognize that it is essential for them and those they lead. They are confident in what they know and just as confident in what they don't know. They recognize that they need others to fill in those gaps and point out errors in their judgment when they occur.

Role/Title Does Not Equal Impact

Angela Costa, RN, BSN, MPM talked about how while we may have different roles, we need to remind ourselves that everyone matters. Each of us brings immense value and impacts others. Despite different roles, we should not think of ourselves as above others:

> I sit in a different role than you sit. I have different responsibilities, but don't put me above you because we're all equal. I may have some harder decisions to make than you do on a daily basis, but it's because I have a different role. I don't see myself as better than or above anyone. I have a job, just

like everyone else. We're all here for a reason. Everyone has value, and when you treat people like that, life just gets easier.

Given the complexity of medicine and the need to rely on each other's expertise, we have to work to foster teamwork. This requires each of us to be humble. Atul Gawande, surgeon and author, wrote about this in an article titled "Cowboys and Pit Crews" in *The New Yorker*.[4] It was originally a commencement speech at Harvard Medical School. He argues that doctors can no longer be cowboys who practice independently, but rather that medicine needs pit crews—teams that work together and support each other. Gawande said this will require new skills, including

> ...humility, an understanding that no matter who you are, how experienced or smart, you will fail. They include discipline, the belief that standardization, doing certain things the same way every time, can reduce your failures. And they include teamwork, the recognition that others can save you from failure, no matter who they are in the hierarchy.[5]

Dr. Argyros gives an example of how we all have a role in medicine and we need to be humble and listen to and value the roles of team members as leaders:

> I only know as much as I know, so I have to bring my leaders in regularly so that we can be true to our commitment to quality, safety, and patient experience. The rules and regulations that apply to medicine can be complex and are ever-changing. It is not uncommon for me to bring my regulatory experts, general counsel, and compliance leadership in to provide subject matter expertise. Every leader must fully embrace the responsibility they have and not be hesitant to ensure that they are advising me and the rest of the team to the best of their abilities.

> When we don't value the members or our team, we risk losing their input and expertise. This results in decreased

performance by the team. We are also losing out on innovative ideas. Often, we can become burned out because we are doing too much and not working as a team. If we care about our organizations and their impacts on patients and trainees, then we have to care enough to be humble.

Brené Brown has made a career out of the idea that vulnerability is a key element in leadership and life.[6] Why would so many people be drawn to her work if the idea of vulnerability and how it improves leadership did not have credence? People resonate with leaders who are humble because they can relate to them, and they feel more valued because their contributions are recognized in helping the organization. Humility and vulnerability foster a psychologically safe workplace, which further supports ongoing learning, innovation, and creativity.

Humble leaders and organizations create effective learning environments. They create a safe space where people don't need to have all the answers. It is expected to say, "I don't know." It is less about "I" and "me" and more about "us" and "we."

Psychological safety, which has grown in popularity with the work of Amy Edmondson, is the idea that people "feel comfortable sharing concerns and mistakes without fear of embarrassment or retribution. They are confident that they can speak up and won't be humiliated, ignored, or blamed. They know they can ask questions when they are unsure about something. They know and trust their colleagues."[7] There is no way that psychological safety exists at work or in other relationships without humility. Edmondson includes humility as one of the elements in her "Leader's Toolkit for Building Psychological Safety."[8]

Teamwork, as we have discussed, is essential in medicine. Humility and psychological safety are key elements for effective teams and organizations. So, how do we foster the conditions to allow these to occur? What steps can we take as leaders to be humble and create cultural humility? The good news is that we can be intentional about developing these behaviors as leaders and encouraging them within our organizations.

Before we move on, I suspect there may be some of you who are still questioning the importance of humility or saying, "Yes, this is needed for patient care, but in business—and, at times, medicine is a business—humility is just not as effective." However, the evidence would support that the most effective leaders (and organizations) are humble.

There are several ways we could look at how humility impacts the bottom line. A study published by researcher Dr. Peter Ruberton et al. in 2016 concluded that humble physicians have better patient communication and improve patient outcomes.[9] Amy Edmondson outlines the importance of humility on psychological safety and patient outcomes in her book *The Fearless Organization*.[10] You can read her book for examples and all the data, but here is a takeaway: "Twenty years of research on psychological safety finds positive benefits for learning, engagement, and performance in a wide range of organizations."[11] Her research includes medicine, and given the complexity and interdependency of people working in teams, medicine is especially influenced by psychological safety— which is, in large part, driven by humility.[12]

"Do Humble CEOs Matter?" This was the title of a research paper published in *The Journal of Management* by Amy Ou, David Waldman, and Suzanne Peterson in 2018.[13] They hypothesized that humble CEOs would result in top management that was "more likely to collaborate, share information, jointly make decisions, and possess a shared vision."[14] They examined 105 small- to medium-sized computer software and hardware firms in the United States. They surveyed chief executive officers and chief financial officers. The CFOs were given a validated scale to assess CEO humility. They found that humble CEOs contributed indirectly to firm performance and were more likely to have pay equality.[15]

Brunzel and Ebsen published a paper titled "The Role of Humility in Chief Officers, a Review" in the journal *Review of Management* in 2023.[16] Their systematic review of seventeen papers published in *Elsevier Scopus* highlighted many benefits of humility.[17] These included increased sharing of information among teams, improved psychological safety among workers, and "significant positive correlation with team contribution" ($r = 0.31$, $p < 0.01$).[18] The data supports the importance of humility and shows more research is needed.

Jim Collins, in his legendary book *Good To Great,* studied what makes companies excel over the long term.[19] He identified five levels of leadership, with Level 5 Leaders being at the top.[20] These were the types of leaders who led the companies that performed the best. He defined a Level 5 Leader as a leader who "builds enduring greatness through a paradoxical blend of personal humility and professional will."[21] He went on to say that Level 5 Leaders are "...incredibly ambitious—but their ambition is first and foremost for the institution, not themselves."[22]

Sound like someone you want to work for? Sound like the type of leader you want to be? Collins points out at the end of the chapter on Level 5 Leaders that the ability to be a Level 5 Leader exists in most people, and it just needs to be developed.[23] Being a caring leader and following the lessons in this chapter and book can help you evolve into a Level 5 Leader. I hope that excites you as you think about how to more effectively lead others.

While humility is considered important, an online survey of over 1,200 global respondents by McKinsey & Company in 2020 reported that only "36 percent of respondents say their organizations...[teach] leaders how to develop a personal-growth mindset and curiosity."[24]

Organizations need to make a concerted effort to teach about humility in order to support psychological safety. The last part of this chapter offers you some tangible ways to become more humble and foster humility among those you lead.

Strategies for Being Humble and Teaching Humility

The first thing to remember is that we set the tone as leaders. A leader demonstrates what they consider important by how and where they spend their time. A leader shapes the tone of their organization through what they do and don't do. Everyone is watching their leader. The leader should model what "right" looks like. What type of role model you are will shape the expectations for those you are privileged to lead.

Humble leaders are aware of their actions and that those actions set the standard for those they lead. If you want a culture of humility, then be humble in thought, word, and deed. Do you truly listen and consider input? How do you respond when things don't go well or mistakes are made? Do you demonstrate a continual desire to grow and improve? Do you take credit or reward others? Do you admit when you are wrong? Do you use first person plural pronouns (we, our) or first person singular (I, me, my)? Do you consistently demonstrate that you care, personally and professionally, about your people because you know that by taking care of them the organization is better? You are the flag bearer for your organization.

Let me give you one of the best examples of humility I have seen. Major General Jeff Clark was at an intern ice cream social. This was an event to welcome new interns to our hospital. He was the director (CEO) of Walter Reed National Military Medical Center at the time. He and his wife, Mrs. Sue Clark (also an exemplar of a caring and humble leader), hosted the event. There was lots of free ice cream for the new interns and nurses and their families. Major General Clark stayed for well over an hour, and at the end of the event, there was a young junior enlisted service member picking up trash and putting away tables. She was struggling with something. He walked over and helped her finish what she was doing. When I asked him about it during our interview, he said the following:

> I was raised that if somebody is working, you don't walk by. You see what you can do to help. That's just how I was raised. There is a story about George Washington at Valley Forge. The troops were trying to put together some little cabin or something to, you know, get away from the cold, and he was riding by on his horse. He got down off his horse and helped them. He helped them put up the top beam on the little shack they were putting together...I just think it's a natural thing to do. I don't think you should walk by if there's work being done, right? It's your team; you should be part of it. I think I did it because it was just the right thing to do. You just don't let somebody stack tables, or whatever that individual is doing, by themselves if you can help them.

The next time you are thinking about humility and jobs you should or shouldn't do as a leader, I hope you remember this example of General Clark. If an Army general can pick up trash and stack tables, then many of us probably need to think about how we embrace humility.

One of the things as a leader that demonstrates humility is how you demonstrate your caring toward those you lead. We obviously have to accomplish the mission, but how do we go about that? Do you show that you care for the people you lead? This entire book gives you Caring Acts of Leadership, but I will highlight one here that can demonstrate humility. We are humble by giving up opportunities for ourselves so that others can shine.

Dr. Darilyn Moyer, the CEO of the American College of Physicians, gave a great example of this when talking about sponsoring people for career opportunities:

> I mean, how else are they going to gain the same skills, experiences, and leadership trajectory that you've had if you don't afford them the opportunity? We need to be egalitarian in this. I think it requires, though, a level of confidence in yourself to be able to do that and to say. "I'm not diluting my brand [and] everything that I've worked so hard [for]... by offering this opportunity or sharing this opportunity with someone else."

> How do you respond to mistakes? How do we embrace failure? Do we cast blame? Do we approach these as learning opportunities? Do we cover up our own mistakes or talk about them openly so others can learn? By being vulnerable, do we create the space for others to do the same?

One of the most effective ways to demonstrate humility is by being open about our own failures and supporting others through theirs. We spend a lot of time focused on success and less talking about where we failed as leaders. We need to approach failure and mistakes as learning moments. This is easier said than done in the high-stakes business of medicine, but if we don't, we risk losing psychological safety, thus having worse outcomes and losing out on the innovative ideas that people might be willing to bring to the table if they felt safe.

This starts with us admitting when we are wrong. As leaders, if we cannot admit when we are wrong, then what message are we sending to those we lead? By being vulnerable and admitting our mistakes, we allow others to do the same. It makes you more approachable as a leader and creates a culture where it is encouraged to admit and take ownership of mistakes.

The good news is when you do this, if you have earned their respect over time, it actually rallies the troops. They want to support you and see you succeed. When you succeed, they succeed. Chelsea Hayes said on this subject,

> People will generally give you a second chance if you come from a place of humility. People are very responsive when one human says, "Hey, I messed up. I need help." People are like, "I got you. We'll fix it." That doesn't happen very often, because most often, people struggle to admit they made a mistake or they try to fix it on their own to no avail. They try to make it seem like "No, I didn't do all that," and that is when we see deep conflict and things that people cannot recover from. But when you find these leaders who are like, "I messed this up! I tried to fix it, but it's not working. Help!" We want to pick them up and help. I encourage my leaders to practice and model that, especially for their more junior teammates.

To emphasize the point about failure as a leader and being humble, let's look at a few more examples that illustrate the value of humility for building relationships, learning as individuals and organizations, and fostering change. Dr. Darilyn Moyer, CEO of the American College of Physicians, gave these remarks:

We need to have the courage to make it personal and to tell people our personal anecdotes from when we fell flat on our faces, when we fell into holes, and [when we] tripped up, because they seem to think that our journeys were seamless and never had any rocks in the roll. Meanwhile, there were boulders everywhere. Didn't you feel like Sisyphus…pushing that rock up the mountain at times in your career? I think it's the ability to humanize ourselves to people, to tell them to learn from our stories where things didn't turn out so well… You need to learn how to differentiate between responsibility and authority. That's something I did not do early in my career. I was given the responsibility to do X, Y, and Z, but I had no resources. I had no power on the organizational chart. I truly had no control. So, you know, teaching folks about those times that you stumbled and fell, and letting them know that it wasn't all smooth sailing and that your leadership, at the end of the day, doesn't come from when things are handed to you on a silver platter and things go smoothly. It is from hitting those bumps and those boulders and those landmines of life that… truly your inner leader emerges. You've got to humanize yourself. These younger folks think you're some kind of superhuman, and [that is] not at all [true]. I mean, we all have tons of battle scars. As you get more comfortable, more confident in your own leadership ability, you're able to open up and talk about those failures, and you know the lesson is to fail forward. To take those lessons learned and

> *"Teaching folks about those times that you stumbled and fell, and letting them know that it wasn't all smooth sailing and that your leadership, at the end of the day, doesn't come from when things are handed to you on a silver platter and things go smoothly. It is from hitting those bumps and those boulders and those landmines of life that…truly your inner leader emerges."*
> —Dr. Darilyn Moyer

incorporate them subsequently so you don't repeat the patterns of the past. That's the most important thing, where no one's going to be 100 percent successful, even though it looks so easy...when you talk to people not just about the successes but the failures.

Dr. Amy Oxentenko provided another example of how a humble and caring leader supports the individual and fosters creativity in an organization:

If you're not willing to admit your mistakes and take ownership of them, then that's just problematic. Then, it's just a defensiveness that is not well received. I think we all know, in medicine, that we're going to have errors. You wish there were none, but there are errors that do happen. We have an idea that when we push forward through our mistakes without reflecting on them, it doesn't work out so well. Taking ownership through the good—but more importantly, the bad—creates an environment where people will want to continue to follow someone like that, someone who isn't trying to create a false perception that they're always perfect and flawless. Everybody has flaws. Everyone makes mistakes. In a way, let's normalize them, because it allows other people to be willing to take risks, knowing that when they fail, they're not going to be humiliated. I think it depends on the environment you're in. If you want to get the most out of the people that you're leading, creating that kind of environment is key, especially if you're trying to think of great innovative ideas. If you want to be bold in your thinking and [want] others around you to do the same, then you need to be open to failure.

Normalizing upfront that you know that half of these ideas may not come to fruition, but we're never going to make big inroads (and the things we're looking to achieve) if we aren't willing to take some risk—I think having that expectation upfront [makes it so] that risk is okay. You know, failures are okay...Sasha Shillcutt[25] is kind of infamous for this—failing forward. I mean that when we fail, we probably learn the most. I think being open about that...is probably one thing leaders could do more. I mean, you really think about it: How many leaders, whether it's at your institution or whatnot, have you ever heard of reflecting on a failure? Not very often, right? We don't hear that all that often, at meetings or whatnot. But boy, the ones who have an openness and a willingness to talk about those things—suddenly, they just become more relatable, because we've all been through those experiences. Trying to find a way to make a positive out of a potentially nonideal situation, I think, is something that people will respect and admire.

Humility fosters innovation and creativity. People need a safe place to be able to throw out ideas that may seem a "little out there," and people need to be able to make mistakes. This requires humility among leaders. Dr. Caroline Blackie, head of medical and scientific operations at Johnson and Johnson Vision, talked about this:

> We work in the business of innovation, and innovation is like fruit. You can go buy innovation, but that means somebody else created the environment where they can grow the fruit and then you buy the fruit. But if we're going to create an environment where *we* can innovate, that context needs to be very nurturing. You've got to feel safe and like you belong. You can't just inform people they feel safe and belong and require them to believe it. Feelings of safety and belonging are a matter of the heart, earned through trustworthy behavior, demonstrated over time. Of course, like any healthy relationship, we experience rupture (I make mistakes all the time), but as a team, we commit to repairing what has been ruptured and we get back on track. Some of my epic fails are hilarious, and some of them make me want to hide under the couch interminably. Thankfully, my team also has a phenomenal sense of humor.

Why is my dad so impactful for me? His parents and upbringing were quite harsh. He was sent off to boarding school as a tiny little kid. He was very courageous. He achieved incredible things in his life. He endured tremendous hardship, even in his later years, and yet, he always looked forward. I've got a sign on my wall; it says, "Don't look back. You're not going that way." It is helpful to me, because when I make mistakes, my natural tendency is to dive down into the pit of despair and marinate in a self-loathing, tortured eternity until I or somebody else drags me out. I have learned, through the observation of Dad, that while we all fall, getting up is a critical next step. Just get up! Take your learnings, make apologies, be real about failure, but leave the shame and the emotional baggage in the pit of despair and keep moving forward.

Dr. Blackie's response highlights how failure impacts people psychologically. Do we ramp up their feelings of despair, or do we support them? Our response can impact their psychological well-being. Our goal is for them to learn and get back to doing great work. We want them to know that when they mess up, we are there for them.

What does an effective response look like? When someone messes up, do you get angry? Do you cast blame? Do you make it a learning opportunity for them and the organization? Accountability is important, but we can hold people accountable in a compassionate way. There are two important things to consider in your response, as illustrated by the next two stories.

The first is what a positive response to failure looks like. Dr. David Smith, coauthor of *Athena Rising*[26] and *Good Guys*,[27] talked about this when describing an example of an ideal caring leader. When describing his first commanding officer in the Navy, he said the following:

In my first squadron, I remember the first time flying with my new commanding officer. As a rising junior officer and pilot in the squadron, I was definitely looking to make a good impression. I remember having the worst training flight of my life—and I still look back on it. I saved the hard copy evaluation notes from that flight. I remember because it was one that always stood out and reminds me that you're going to have a bad day. Everybody has a bad day. You can learn something from that. The thing that really spoke to me and set the stage in my relationship with that commanding officer—that started there and continues to this day—was he looked at me afterward in the debrief and said, "Dave, do you play golf?"

And I said, "Yes, sir, I do."

"So do you know what a 'mulligan' is?"

And I said, "Yes, sir, I do."

He goes, "Well, Dave, today was a mulligan."

For the people who don't know what a mulligan is, your golf partner can grant you a "mulligan," and in the game and the round of golf, it's a do-over—it's basically a freebie. In other words, what happened before didn't count, and we're moving forward from here at this point. He could certainly see that I was probably trying very hard—probably to impress, probably too hard—and because of it was making mistakes. He could see past that and see there was more to me than just that. He cared about me as one of his junior officers, but also as a person, and how I took that and what I was going to do with it moving forward. There was a certain amount of care and compassion. That set the stage for me in the rest of my career and thinking about [questions like] "How do I approach leadership?" "What does good leadership look like from a 'caring for your people' perspective, both professionally and personally?" "How [do] people respond to the host of different situations that you know we all encounter?"

Think about how you would feel about receiving this response versus someone who cast blame on or belittled you. This interaction changed the way he led throughout his career. Think of the impact we have on others as leaders by how we respond when they mess up. Not only does it impact that individual, but— as pointed out by Dr. Smith—it potentially impacts those they lead throughout their careers as well. Our actions as leaders are teaching moments for those we lead. What lessons do you want to leave about how to respond to failure?

The second story focuses on who takes the credit for success and the blame for messing up. According to Dr. Greg Argyros, "I will not take credit for anything. I will take the blame for everything. I will take the blame publicly, even if you didn't tell me. I will take the blame, but we will have a conversation after that happens. You'll lose your team right away if you take all the credit for something or you push the blame off onto somebody else."

In medicine, there are times when we will be responsible for clinical decisions. If I prescribe the wrong antibiotic, that is my mistake. That said, there are also times when, as a leader, you can choose to cast blame or take blame. For example, if your department is working on a new process for lab processing and it leads to a mistake, do you take the blame as the department chair, explaining that your team is working on the process? Do you blame the team lead? If we are asking people to fix problems and then blame them when things go wrong, it is going to significantly limit creativity and people being willing to lead these initiatives. Let them know you have their back as they work for solutions or as they lead in other ways. Just as importantly, when they are successful, this is *their* success, not your success. Don't take credit for the work your people do, even if you set the conditions for them to be successful. People want to feel valued, and if you take credit, you are stealing that from them. Taking credit for the work of those you lead is a clear message that "I am the important one here." Model humility and shine the light on them.

We have covered a lot in this chapter on the importance of humility. To end, here is a list of ten steps that you can implement to demonstrate humility. These steps are Caring Acts of Leadership that you can do or teach others in your organization to do.

10 Steps for Fostering Humility

1. Show concern for and invest in others.

When we show our concern for others and invest in them, it demonstrates not only that we care but our humility. By spending time with them and helping them, we are saying with our actions, "I care about you. I need you. I want you to be successful as much as or more than I care about my own success. I am not treating you like a widget or a number but as a person I value." There are so many ways to care, as outlined in this book. Recognize that every time you demonstrate caring, you are being humble.

2. Use the Humble Nine.

Nine words that demonstrate humility are

"I don't know,"

"I was wrong,"

"I am sorry."

These words say a lot about your humility and the culture you are creating. "I don't know" illustrates how you are humble enough to know you are not the smartest person in the room. In fact, if you are the smartest person in the room, you need to recruit more talented people.

"I was wrong" and "I am sorry" demonstrate humility in admitting mistakes.

"We all screw up" helps you build trust and credibility and foster relationships. If you are only out for yourself, people will know that. I am definitely not saying people should sabotage their leaders, but when leaders are humble, they are supported by their followers in much stronger ways.

3. Promote a growth mindset.

One of the best ways to model humility is to be open to new information and seeking to learn. This mindset demonstrates that we don't know it all and that we are constantly trying to improve. It creates an environment where we can innovate, as both Dr. Blackie and Dr. Oxentenko pointed out. These are the types of leaders we want to follow. One way to do this is to frequently talk about what you are learning. Share what you are reading or listening to with them. When you mess up, talk about the lessons you took away from the experience. If someone on your team gives you feedback, thank them and tell them what you learned and what you plan to do differently. Ask them about their job so you can learn more about what they do and how they do it. Sometimes we are disconnected from the front lines, but we leaders can learn from those doing the work. It demonstrates humility, allows us to learn, and demonstrates our appreciation for their work. Those are all leadership wins!

4. Value each team member's role and expertise.

Medicine is complicated, and each team member brings unique expertise to the team. One way of demonstrating humility is listening to your team, really getting their input, empowering them, and utilizing each team member's expertise. Make it a habit to seek out the ideas of those you lead. Let others lead initiatives based on their expertise. We often feel like we need to be in charge, but we should be empowering others to lead. It helps them feel valued. It develops their leadership skills. Consider coaching them if they need it, or if they don't, get out of their way and let them shine.

5. Embrace failure as a learning opportunity.

Leaders are responsible for the failures of their teams and should take responsibility rather than cast blame. If your team fails, own it and support them. They already feel bad about it. Your response will impact how badly they feel, and maybe how they respond or act in the future. Help them recognize it is a growth opportunity. Failure is only failure if we stop trying. Each failure is a building block to your monument of success. Think of times when you have not succeeded. I would bet my favorite Pittsburgh Steelers jersey that these are some of the most valuable learning experiences in your life. Share these experiences with those you lead and mentor. Tell them about when you failed and what you learned from it. These lessons are helpful to them, and sharing them allows your team to be more vulnerable with you. It creates the psychological safety needed to admit mistakes or concerns and learn together.

6. Give credit for success and take responsibility for failures.

Seems unfair? Welcome to leadership! That's right—when things go well, make sure you give the credit to the team and recognize their value and input. Thank them for their work. Think creatively about how to do this. Conversely, when things go south, as the leader, you should take the blame. Ultimately, you are in charge and responsible, and by taking blame publicly, you are demonstrating to your team that you care about them and are willing to stick up for them. This builds trust for you as the leader. Taking the blame or not reveling in the team's success could be a blow to your ego publicly, but the impact on your team will pay massive dividends.

7. Listen to others.

If we actively listen to others and value their input, it helps them feel good about themselves and it demonstrates that we are humble. Make listening to others and seeking others' input for decisions a priority. If you don't, you may make the wrong decisions, as Angela Costa, RN, BSN, MPM points out:

> You cannot go in thinking that you're better than others. The decisions I make are based on what I am hearing. What's the right thing to do? What are you hearing from around the hospital to guide that final decision? You must know what's happening. I can't be out there on that platform on my own just deciding things, because I will make wrong decisions. Things will run amok when you don't stay in tune with your front line. If you are the manager of a unit and you don't know what's going on in your unit, it will snowball into bigger problems, such as retention problems and patient complaints.

8. Make it about "us" and "we," and not "I" and "me."

Language is important, so when talking about things, focus on the team and organization. Try to avoid using the word "I" as much as possible, in both written and verbal communication. Using "us" and "we" suggests you are working together rather than people working for you. You can also use "you" or "the team." When writing emails, review them and look for the word "I" or "me," then see if you can reword it to be more focused on the team. Try to connect with those you lead and be part of them rather than coming off as above them. Everyone knows you are the leader. You don't have to emphasize it.

What you say communicates to your team how you value and appreciate them. Make it about them, not about you!

Here is an example:

I am proud of the access to care metrics from this past quarter.

versus

You should all be incredibly proud of the access to care metrics you achieved this past quarter.

Steffens and Haslam studied the use of "us" and "we" in Australian political elections: the winners "made 61% more references to 'we' and 'us' and used these once every 79 words versus every 136 words for losers."[28] The winning language of leadership is "us" and "we," so be intentional about this and avoid "I" and "me."

9. Decrease your psychological size.

Each of us has a psychological "size" based on our position. Whether we like it or not, based on our position, rank, or title, people are going to view us a certain way. If I am a charge nurse, the nursing assistant is going to view me differently than how he or she views a floor nurse or a physician. When I was an internal medicine residency program director and Colonel in the Army, no matter what I did, I was going to have a large psychological size compared to new interns who had just entered the military. I may not have viewed myself as that far removed from being a resident, but the fact was it was a fifteen-year difference in our careers.

Psychological size can create a barrier between leaders and followers. This can result in the follower not being as comfortable talking to or bringing up important points. The classic example is a surgical tech noticing something wrong in the operating room but being afraid to say something to the surgeon. If they don't say something, something bad can happen. How do we decrease psychological size? Many of the same things discussed throughout this chapter and related to psychological safety will decrease the psychological size difference.

A few other points: First, make it clear that you value everyone's input. Be explicit about this and tell people you want and need their input. Tell them you make mistakes and will need their help. Acknowledge that medicine is hard, and everyone—regardless of position—needs input from others. Admit that you don't know, and can't see, everything, so you are relying on them. Thank them profusely when they do offer suggestions (see point 8!).

10. Be kind!

Treat people with kindness. We are taught to do this as kids, and it is the foundation of this book. We interact with lots of people each day, and they have lots of things going on in their lives. This includes people of varying positions at work and in society. The people we work with and those in our communities don't need or want people to treat them poorly. Make every interaction a positive one.

Bad things happen, in medicine and in life. People screw up. We can point these things out and discuss them without berating and belittling people. We can hold people accountable in a compassionate way, as we discussed earlier in the book. If you are a Level 5 Leader with humility, when the people you lead screw up, you will need to console them and not berate them, because they will feel terrible about letting you down. Being kind builds leadership capital.

If you implement the practices listed above, you will foster an environment for learning, innovation, and wellness. This will pay off for you as a leader, your organization, and the people you lead. Everyone wins!

Prescription for Caring in Leadership

1. Make a list of times you have failed as a reminder to keep you humble and to use as examples when mentoring others.

2. Talk to your team about failure and how you view it.

3. Talk to a mentee about failure when you meet.

4. Invite a speaker to your organization and have them talk about humility or how they have learned from failures.

5. Pick one of the tips for being humble above and make it a point to perform that behavior this week.

6. Read *Humble Inquiry* by Edgar Schein.[29]

CHAPTER 16

Care Enough to Listen

"I remind myself every morning: Nothing I
say this day will teach me anything. So if I'm
going to learn, I must do it by listening."[1]
—Larry King, CNN

W E ALL KNOW LISTENING is important, yet many of us struggle with being effective listeners. We have many distractions and often lack the patience it takes to really listen. The fact is that listening is critical to almost every other chapter in this book—not to mention our relationships at home. It is hard to give and receive effective feedback if you don't listen. How do you mentor, coach, and sponsor if you don't take the time to learn what the person you are investing in needs? How do you learn as an organization if you don't listen to the people you lead? How do you tackle issues related to diversity, equity, and inclusion if you don't hear the voices of the people in your organization?

According to Dr. Jeff Hutchinson during our interview, "The biggest tool to show that you are a caring leader is your ability to listen to people and actually hear them...That's a skill that makes a difference between someone who is just trying to check a box and someone who really wants to make an organization or an individual better." Just to hammer that point home, we listen because we care deeply about the organization and the individual. I would add we listen because we value their input in helping us get better.

Would you describe your listening as aggressive? Are you an effective listener? What would those you work with say? What would your family say? I love the phrase "Listen aggressively,"[2] because I think it speaks to listening with a passion and purpose. I was introduced to the phrase by my chief of medical residents, Dr. Melanie Wiseman, who was reading the book *It's Your Ship: Management Techniques from the Best Damn Ship in the Navy*.[3]

The book, written by Navy Captain D. Michael Abrashoff, is excellent. I recommend it as a foundational book for leadership skills. Chapter 4 is titled "Listen Aggressively."[4] He described his evolution in becoming an effective listener while working with then Secretary of Defense William Perry in Washington, D.C. He admired Perry and learned from him about how to listen.[5] He said when people were talking to Perry, they had his "complete, undivided attention" and "everyone blossomed in his presence because he was so respectful."[6] Abrashoff wanted to be like Perry, but it took him time to get there. Abrashoff said that at times, he "pretended to hear people...barely glanced up from my work when a subordinate came into my office...I was marking time until it was my time to give orders."[7]

Does this sound familiar? Listening or partly listening just until it's your time to talk?

It was when Abrashoff took command of the USS Benfold that he learned how to make listening a real skill and priority.[8] Abrashoff recognized the need to be a better listener and set out to "treat every encounter with every person on the ship as the most important thing at that moment."[9] Wow, think about how you would feel if someone was giving you this degree of attention. What could you learn from others by listening in this way? The listening paid off for Abrashoff, as he learned a ton from his crew, and it resulted in his ship becoming "the best damn ship in the Navy!"[10]

Listening is an act of caring. If we care about those we lead, then we all need to listen aggressively. If you don't like the word "aggressive," maybe you would prefer "generous listening." Brad Johnson, author of *Athena Rising*[11] and *Good Guys,*[12] in our interview stated,

> David and I often talk about generous listening, spacious listening. This just relates to, do you actually make the time? Do you set the time aside? Do you block out competing obligations? Do you make the space just to listen and be present, even for somebody who's [a] junior? Even when you are really busy—do you make that time? I think that suggests care more than almost anything else.

David Smith added, "Being heard in the organization is something that everybody wants. Every human being wants to be heard. I want you to not just hear me but also react or do something with it."

Listening is your bridge to growth as an individual and as an organization. We must continue to evolve, especially in healthcare. We all have blind spots. What happens when you ignore the sensors on your car? If you don't listen, you rob yourself of an opportunity to make change and better support your patients, colleagues, and families. Many times, listening can prevent the bad stuff from happening.

Listening demonstrates humility. It says, "I don't know everything, so I want your help." We listen because we respect those we work with. We value their ideas and input. To be frank, the frontline workers are the ones whose input we need most. Abrashoff listened and used the input from over 300 Sailors to improve his ship.[13] Listening can foster a psychologically safe work environment. Amy Edmondson, in *The Fearless Organization: Creating Psychological Safety in the Workplace for Learning, Innovation, and Growth,* describes the importance of modeling "intense listening" to build a culture of psychological safety.[14] How much personal and organizational learning and improvement are you leaving on the table if you aren't listening effectively ? Create a culture of listening in your organization to continually foster ongoing improvement.

> *How much personal and organizational learning and improvement are you leaving on the table if you aren't listening effectively?*

Dr. Greg Argyros gives an example of how to demonstrate humility, listen, and empower those you lead. It is important to get input from everyone, or at least as many people as possible, when making decisions:

> You know, when you go into a situation and try to identify... everyone who could be potentially impacted by what you are talking about, sometimes you invite people unnecessarily. At the first meeting, I tell those who feel that they may have been invited and don't have anything to contribute that they do not need to come to subsequent meetings. I also ask the group if we have missed someone who should be at the table. That way, everyone feels like their perspective is considered—that is how you positively engage and influence people.

A quote by Professor Deborah Tannen in the Department of Linguistics at Georgetown University highlights this point:

> *"To say that a person feels 'listened to' means a lot more than just 'their ideas get heard.' It's a sign of respect. It makes people feel valued."* [15]

Sometimes, the act of listening is all we need to do. People might just need someone to talk to. They don't want or need advice, but rather just to be heard. They want to know if people value their opinion or need to tell someone about something going on. Dr. Jeff Hutchinson shared that he learned this as part of his clinical practice, and it applies to leadership as well:

> My experience through adolescent medicine and leadership—and everything there too—is sometimes just [that] the act of listening is therapeutic. To be able to sit back and reflect [on] people's comments to show that you're really listening to what they say—that is often all that they need. They don't want a solution. They don't need a solution. They want to feel heard. So, listening is a critical point in having people feel heard.

Listening is a leadership superpower. Not listening is kryptonite for leaders and organizations. There are multiple books, articles, and podcasts on how to effectively listen. To end this chapter, I am providing a list of seven steps to help you become a more effective listener. It starts with creating a mindset of caring about the person you are listening to and what they have to offer.

Steps to Building Your Listening Leadership Superpower

1. Be humble and curious.

Approach each conversation with the intent to learn.[16] Be open to new ideas and recognize that you have the opportunity to learn from everyone in your organization. Take advantage of your team's wisdom and experience. We often listen to solve problems rather than listening to learn. Go into meetings with the intent of listening first. Being more patient while listening and not just waiting for your turn to talk and offer advice is a mind shift for many of us. Dr. Darilyn Moyer highlighted this point:

> Caring means being there for people. Listening in an open way, not jumping to judgments...Whenever I go into something new, I'm very quiet, which for people who know me, they know I'm not usually that quiet, but I really want to listen and learn and understand the culture. I certainly did this when I started at the college in 2016 because I didn't want to make conclusions where I shouldn't be drawing conclusions, making snap judgments; [I wanted to be] understanding [of] where people have come from, where organizations have come from, to know why we are where we are and where we're going.

Think about ways to create times for listening. This might be walking around and talking to people with the intent of just listening, or it might be setting up meetings where you just want to listen and learn about your people and what they are doing. When I was the internal medicine residency program director, I would host fireside chats at my house to just get people together. We would have dinner and drinks outside and just talk. When you start a new job, make it a point to meet the people you work with and let them tell you about their experiences.

2. Set the agenda.

The agenda setting depends on if this is an individual or group meeting. Sometimes it can be helpful to ask what they are looking for from the conversation. Are they looking for input? Do they want you to know what is happening? Do they just need someone safe to confide in? Are you walking around and talking to people to learn more about your organization? Having prompts in these situations can facilitate discussion. Depending on the context of the situation, I might ask a particular question.

Conversation Catalysts

- "How do you think I can help today?"
- "Before we start, is there something you are looking for from me?"
- "As I listen, do you have a particular goal in mind for this conversation?"
- "What could I do to better support you?"
- "What do you need that would make your job easier?"
- "What are we missing to be more successful?"
- "What bugs you the most about our organization?"
- "If you could fix one thing, what would it be?"
- "How are we doing as a team related to [insert what you want to know more about]?"

3. Be present.

Create an environment where the person you are listening to feels like they are the most important person at that time, that you value them and their ideas. You cannot listen if you are not focused.

- Move away from the computer. I use the lock screen feature so I don't see anything popping up, and I do it to intentionally show the person that they have my attention.
- Put your phone down.
- Make eye contact.
- Don't interrupt.
- Nod or acknowledge their comments.
- Be okay with silence. You do not have to fill silence with your voice. Sometimes silence allows others time to think, process, or regain their composure. Let silence be your friend when listening. It is amazing what people will tell you when you are not talking.

4. Take notes.

I can't remember everything, so I take notes. I use paper (notebook or notecard) to avoid my computer being a distraction.

5. Ask clarifying questions and rephrase what they said.

Once they are done speaking, ask questions if you don't understand or need to clarify something. Rephrase what they said so they can verify you heard correctly and to show you were listening. Rephrasing can make sure you got the story right before you launch into further discussions or offer advice about how to approach a particular situation.

6. Provide support and advice if desired—in that order.

Before you jump into your solutions, offer compassion and acknowledge the challenging situation they are going through. Recognize the impact whatever they are facing has on their life.

This step is critical. It demonstrates that you listened and, more importantly, shows that you care about what they are facing. Once you have done this, you can provide input, if they want it. The acknowledgment of the challenge is sometimes missed, so let me give you an example.

A subordinate comes to you and reports that he is trying to figure out his work schedule. His two-year-old son had a seizure this past week and has a neurology appointment this week he wants to go to. Rather than jumping right into how you adjust his schedule, hit the pause button. Say, "This sounds scary. How is your son? How are you and your wife holding up?"

Then, after he answers, respond with, "Look, we will work on the schedule for the appointment, but I want you to know we are here to support you and your family. Please don't hesitate to come back if you need coverage or more time to deal with your son's medical issues. We are here for you."

Don't get so focused on solving the problem that you don't take the time to show compassion.

7. Thank people for the input or for sharing with you.

Be grateful when people bring you problems and potential solutions or simply come to you as a source of support. Thank them for their feedback or for the opportunity to share something personal with them. Leadership is about relationships, and listening to and supporting those you lead fosters relationships and builds trust.

What Is Your Talk/Listen Ratio?

One last point before we close the chapter: If you are talking, then you are not listening. Some people love the sound of their own voice. They feel like they have to provide input into every discussion. If they don't get to add a point or make a comment, they get uncomfortable. In fact, there is a term to describe this, which is called "Talkaholism."[17] I learned this from the book *STFU: The Power of Keeping Your Mouth Shut in an Endlessly Noisy World* by Dan Lyons.[18] Certainly a catchy title!

Lyons, a self-professed talkaholic, dives into the data behind talking, why we may talk too much, and ultimately strategies to talk less.[19] He provides data and argues that people who talk less are "more likely to get promoted at work and more likely to prevail in negotiations" and that talking less "improves our relationships, makes us better parents, and can boost our psychological and even physical well-being."[20] The data is convincing enough for me. Think about the people you have observed who don't say that much and spend the most time listening. Then they seem to make a comment or ask a question that is like a heat-seeking missile— right on target! The lesson is that it's not how much we say but the impact of what we say.

Dr. Darilyn Moyer gave an example of this when talking about Dr. Molly Cooke, former president of the ACP, who was an excellent listener: "You weren't really sure. Was she really paying attention? [In the end, she] would just have this amazing ability to sort of sum up the points that had just been made and take it to the next level."

Dr. Moyer also pointed out the differences and risks in talking and listening between men and women. Unfortunately, women's comments are at times overlooked, or the credit is given to a man who speaks after her. Men and women should be aware of this and take into account what is said, not just how much is said. Men and women should also think about how to amplify the voices of women and other underrepresented voices, as illustrated in this example:

> Sometimes people say to me, "You were really quiet during that meeting." I say, "I was just listening and learning." And that's okay, to be listening and learning, but you also need to pepper it with speaking up when necessary. I have found that for women, it can be challenging to be at leadership tables and have your voice heard and your points be impactful…We're not going to let others appropriate our comments. We're going to give shout-outs when someone says something. That's impactful and meaningful and strategic. We are going to not allow it to be appropriated by others, because we have been observing that phenomenon of appropriation of comments and not crediting the appropriate people with those thoughts and concepts. I think you know the term "bropropriate," when men do it to women.
>
> I'll never forget sitting at another organization's board. I was at their strategic planning retreat. There was a woman from another organization sitting next to me. She spoke, and everybody said, "Thank you for that comment." Then the guy sitting next to me essentially said the same thing but paraphrased what she said—and everybody's like, "Oh, that is the best idea ever." The woman leaned over to me and she said, "Can you believe that just happened?" I said, "Oh, yeah, I believe it." I went, "You know, I'd love to build on the idea that Doctor X (the woman) brought to this group, and that Doctor Y (the man) expounded upon, and add this." To be a caring leader, it takes kindness and openness and listening, but it also takes speaking up when you need to speak up.

Dr. Moyer illustrates many strong points in this story. The first is that listening is okay. The second is that as you listen, you need to strategically give input as well. We also should be aware of what others are saying and look out for people taking credit for others' comments—in particular when it happens to women. We can point this out when it happens. We can also proactively amplify voices and ideas to help prevent it from happening.

Leaders have to consider that when we are talking, it influences what others might say. I find it helpful to not say too much too early to avoid impacting free discussion of those I lead. The thoughts of those we lead can and should frame our decisions. We need to listen to get there. If you struggle with this, you could consider making it a point that you will not say anything until a certain number of people have offered ideas. This will give you a goal—be sure to stick to it. Depending on how much you struggle with this, you may want to start with three and then work to five or ten as you become more patient. Silence is not bad and does not need to be filled. Make silence your friend in fostering creative dialogue.

Liz Wiseman in *Impact Players* suggests considering talking like playing poker chips.[21] She says you should go into each meeting or conversation with a certain number of chips and that "each chip represents a comment or contribution to the meeting and is worth a specific number of seconds of talking time. Use your chips sparingly, weighing in when you have an insight that is... relevant...evidence-based...unique...succinct."[22]

Being succinct is often an overlooked skill in both written and verbal communication. A colleague of mine, Dr. George Ruiz, worked with Dr. Anthony Fauci long before Dr. Fauci became famous. At the time, he had still advised many presidents, and Dr. Ruiz asked him how he approached it. Dr. Fauci responded, "Precision of thought, economy of words." This is brilliant and useful. Say what you have to say in the most succinct and simple way possible. The Gettysburg Address, one of the most impactful speeches of all time, was only two minutes—272 words. When making your point, the longer you ramble, the less impactful it will be. Make the precision strike with your point, then stop. This includes written communication. When writing emails or giving talks, once I am finished drafting, I will go back and look specifically to see how I can shorten each sentence and remove unnecessary filler words or lines. People are busy. Communicating in a succinct manner helps them get the message in a clearer way and saves them time.

Listening does not occur in a vacuum. We listen in multiple environments, and the principles above apply to any setting. We need to be acutely aware as leaders that people are watching how we listen. Being an effective listener unlocks ideas and creativity on your team and shows that we respect the team. When we are not listening, we are not learning. If you want to have a culture of listening in your organization, model it. Set the standard and the expectation that everyone listens.

Prescription for Caring in Leadership

1. Practice listening aggressively by creating opportunities to listen in one-on-one meetings, while walking around, or during conferences.

2. Make an intentional effort to listen to learn and with curiosity—not to solve problems.

3. Listen with gratitude. Thank people for bringing potential ideas and solutions.

4. Practice writing emails that are as succinct as possible. Ask a colleague for feedback on this.

5. Make an intentional effort to talk less in meetings. Play your chips wisely!

6. Be on the lookout for "bropropriation"—try to avoid it, and point it out when you see it.

7. Amplify a colleague's point if they are not given credit for it, or simply to amplify it.

8. Read a blog or listen to a podcast on listening, or read Dan Lyons' *STFU: The Power of Keeping Your Mouth Shut in an Endlessly Noisy World.*[23]

CHAPTER 17

Care Enough to Delegate

"I get anaphylaxis from micromanagement."
—Dr. Rohul Amin
Lieutenant Colonel, U.S. Army

IMAGINE AN ENVIRONMENT WHERE team members are given tasks to execute commensurate with their roles, but they *know* if they start to struggle, they'll get a little help re-engaging with professional growth and development! Imagine leaders explicitly thinking about delegating tasks and opportunities that would allow people to grow and evolve as clinicians and leaders. Imagine a leader who recognizes people for the innovative and excellent work that they do, a leader who feels like they have more time to do their work because they are not doing the work of those they lead. Would you like to work at that place?

Now imagine the opposite: a leader who fails to delegate and is often overwhelmed and burned out. A leader who delegates tasks but specifically tells people how they must be done. The leader who delegates but, at the slightest sign of struggle, de-delegates and completes the task themselves. The leader who does not recognize people for their ideas and the work that they do. What would it feel like to work in a place like that?

If you struggle with the topic of delegation, you are not alone. If you don't think you struggle with this topic, you should check with those you lead.

Every spring, I teach a leadership workshop to the Infectious Diseases Society of America Leadership Institute. As part of their training, they complete leadership 360-degree evaluations. Delegation and micromanagement are always the most frequently cited areas of struggle from the leader and those who complete the evaluation on them. How can we delegate and avoid micromanaging more effectively?

Caring leaders delegate because they value their team members' expertise and experience. They value their contributions to the mission. They want to invest in those they lead to grow and develop new skills. They care about the time of those they lead, as well as their own time. They know that effective delegation is a force multiplier and a Caring Act of Leadership. They know effective delegation is about more than just an individual leader and an individual follower. It is about how people within the organization work together and support each other. It is about a culture where people know their roles but understand that the organization thrives when each member functions at their highest level. They do their work *and* jump in to help when the need arises.

One common rationale for not using delegation as a tool is concern that delegation is perceived as "dumping work" on another person. I would argue the extreme opposite! The downsides to not using delegation are that your team thinks you don't trust them with important tasks and that you don't value their work, you take away potential growth opportunities from team members, underperformers skate by because it's easier to let someone else do the work, and you are stuck in the weeds, preventing you from doing work that only you, as the leader, can do. All of these can lead to an incredibly heavy workload, frustration, and burnout.

Suzanna Fitzpatrick, DNP, CRNP raised a really important point when talking about delegation and the idea that you are being dumped on. Delegation of tasks should be a discussion if there are concerns about the work from the leader or follower perspective. We need to create environments where we can have these discussions. The work has to get done, but how and by whom are the business of leadership:

Most of the time when you feel like you're getting dumped on, pause for a minute to the person who talked to you and dumped it on you. Are they hearing you? Are you getting your point of view across in a clear and concise way? Are they going to hear your words like "I cannot do this for the following reasons," "I can do this tomorrow because of these reasons," or "I cannot do this ever, because in my workflow, this is the amount of time and energy and resources I have"?

> People are bad at [saying things like] that, and because of the burnout and the resilience and the fatigue that you know we have in healthcare, they just say, "Nope, I can't do it" and walk away, as opposed to going, "I can't do it, but let's think about it thoughtfully, because it still has to get done."

She goes on to point out that having discussions around delegation is not easy, but we need to have them all the same. We need to teach people how to have them:

> I try to tell people the only person looking out for you is you. It's not a selfish thing, and it's not an inconsiderate thing. It's

just the thing. If you're feeling unheard or undervalued, you need to say to that person, "I'm hearing you. This needs to get done right now. I can put it as a priority," and then, "I'd like to have a discussion about how to move forward." That's a grown-up thing to say. People are not good at that, so you just have to learn how to do that. Teach people how to do that.

As leaders, we need to create a culture where it is safe to have these discussions around delegation and other issues. Make it clear that you always want feedback from those you lead about the tasks they have to do. Ask them, "Do you have time to do this? What are the barriers? What can I do to help if needed?" If we have more of these discussions, it should facilitate delegation for us as leaders and for our followers.

The Monkeys

Everyone needs to read the *Harvard Business Review* article "Management Time: Who's Got the Monkey?" which highlights how managers take on tasks (monkeys) that should be done by someone else.[1] It features some great insights into delegating and task management. Delegation is part of every profession and, without question, one of the most important skills for leaders. Effective delegation helps others grow and develop, and it allows the leader to spend their time on tasks that only they can do. Let's look at an example.

Think about a senior resident physician, or maybe a charge nurse. Sometimes, when in these positions, it is easier to do the work yourself. A resident could go see the patient in the emergency room and put in all the admission orders to "help" the new intern rather than send the intern to see the patient. The charge nurse might decide she will put in an intravenous (IV) catheter on a patient who is a difficult stick. The problem with this is that the junior nurse and intern just missed out on an opportunity to get better. They want to do these things, and they should be doing these things. How do we expect either of these folks to improve when they aren't given the opportunities to do so? Plus, what could the resident and nurse be doing with this time? Maybe they could work on a different, more challenging task since they are freed up? Maybe they could observe and coach? Failing to delegate can lead to frustration on both sides. The leader gets frustrated because they are doing all the work; the followers get frustrated because they don't feel valued and trusted or they feel like they are missing out on learning opportunities.

Delegation is ultimately about leveraging every member of the team. We all have roles and responsibilities. It is about getting every member of the team to function to their highest level, about valuing the work of every member. If we value them in their role and they recognize their importance to the mission and team, then delegation becomes easier. This is why it is critical to help everyone feel valued on your teams (more on this later). It is about trusting people to do their job. If you are doing the work that should belong to someone else, you are telling them that they are not doing the work correctly or you don't trust them to do it.

Giving people opportunities to learn new skills through delegated tasks and coaching people when they miss the mark or need help is vital. We must create time for leaders to focus on their essential tasks instead of doing others' work. Delegation is not easy. It requires leaders

> *Delegation is not easy. It requires leaders and followers to effectively work together, but when done well, it unleashes the power of the whole team.*

and followers to effectively work together, but when done well, it unleashes the power of the whole team.

We cannot cover everything related to effective delegation in this book, but I want to point out a few key elements with some examples. These tips should help you as a leader establish when and when not to delegate and how to delegate more effectively. The most important thing to keep in mind when delegating is what needs to be done (mission accomplishment), who should be doing it, and how we can use the work to help the team (every individual) learn and grow. Believe it or not, these don't always have to be competing ideas, and in many situations, you'll find that you can balance both so you achieve the dual purpose of mission (or task) accomplishment and subordinate growth.

How to Delegate

The first things to think about when delegating are role and task. What is the task that needs to be done, and who is most suited to do the task? You can also ask yourself, "Is this *goal-oriented delegation* or *growth-oriented delegation*?" Many times, there are very clear delineations of who should do the task. For example, if developing a budget for your department, there is likely an administrator on your team who is right for the task. Matching task to role is an easy litmus test on who should do what and demonstrates value and respect to the person who is doing "their" work. Medicine, for better or worse, tends to be hierarchical, and tasks are laid out by position. In some ways, this makes delegating easier—but we should also consider how delegation is a learning opportunity.

We need to be cautious about saturating the same people with tasks. We all have high performers who we know can get things done. We should not delegate to them just because we know they will do great work. If we continually do this, we run the risk of burning them out, and they may start to develop resentment toward others on the team—or you—for carrying a heavier load. Think about the whole team and who should be doing it. Who can do it? Who could learn from it?

The second thing to consider when delegating is "What does this person need to learn in order to be able to do my job or to be able to step into another job? How can they learn from the tasks that need to be done?" This may include tasks that we could do ourselves and tasks which might be easier to do ourselves. We are not helping them get better if we are doing the work for them. By giving them an opportunity and then coaching them on it, we increase their skill set. We delegate because we care about their professional development. Don't be afraid to make this an explicit part of the discussion. Say something like "I would like you to do this task because in doing so, you can learn these skills."

Delegate the Task—Don't Dictate the Execution

Once we have made the decision to delegate, we should let the person do the work. One of my favorite quotes on this is from General George Patton. Interestingly, Patton was known as a very strict leader who had no problem telling people what to do or how to do it. Yet, he recognized that in commanding thousands of troops, he could not be involved in every single decision and certainly could not do all the work. Sound like a department chief, program director, or hospital CEO you know? General Patton famously said, "Never tell people how to do things. Tell them what to do, and they will surprise you with their ingenuity."[2]

Here is a news flash: The frontline workers and leaders likely have more effective ways to solve the problem than you do. I have seen over the years that the best ideas in medicine come from the front lines. This could be an operating room tech, a bedside nurse, a resident or intern physician, a physical therapist, a pharmacist, etc. The people on the ground know what works and what doesn't. We talked about this earlier, but it is worth repeating here: we need to listen and learn from them. We need to have them provide solutions and do the work to fix things.

Captain David Marquet emphasizes this point in his book *Turn the Ship Around! A True Story of Turning Followers Into Leaders*.[3] It pains me a little to point out how right a Navy Officer is as an Army guy, but I have to in this circumstance. The whole premise of his book is that leaders are responsible for developing other leaders.[4] We do this by giving up control as a leader and allowing our followers to find solutions and lead in their space. That's right, a captain of a Navy nuclear submarine is telling us that as leaders, we need to give up control![5] This part of his book captures some of the essence of why this is important for organizations:

> People are frustrated. Most of us are ready to give it our all when we start a job. We are usually full of ideas for ways to do things better. We eagerly offer our whole intellectual capacity only to be told that it's not our job. That it's been tried before, or that we shouldn't rock the boat. Our suggestions are ignored. We are told to follow instructions. Our work is reduced to following a set of prescriptions. Our creativity and innovations go unappreciated. Eventually, we stop trying and just toe the line.[6]

Delegating is not only a learning opportunity for the individual, but it is leveraging the full brain power of our teams. Don't miss out on that! Dr. Cristin Mount, a retired Army Colonel and critical care physician, captured this point when I was asking her about delegating as a leader, stating, "Delegation is the perfect tool to support innovation within teams and organizations."

For example, if you are trying to improve the process for checking in patients for your clinic to improve the flow, instead of giving the plan, you could put your clinic nurse or lead administrator in charge and let them develop a plan based on their expertise. Then, you could potentially provide guidance or input based on what they tell you. This is in contrast to you outlining a new plan for them and telling them to implement it. This also allows them to grow as leaders and feel more valued. You can capitalize on their success by recognizing and thanking them for making the team better.

> *"Delegation is the perfect tool to support innovation within teams and organizations."*
> — *Dr. Cristin Mount*

Delegation is a way to develop the leadership skills of those you lead. The Army has a term called "Mission Command," which encapsulates decentralized command and the leader's intent.[7] These work synchronously. Mission Command is a philosophy that involves "exercise of authority and direction by the commander using mission orders to enable disciplined initiative within the commander's intent to empower agile and adaptive leaders."[8] The guiding principles are building cohesive teams through mutual trust, creating shared understanding, providing clear commander's intent, exercising disciplined initiative, giving general orders/guidance, and accepting prudent risk.[9]

The leader establishes his or her intent and ensures a shared understanding with the team. This is the vision of where they want to go and general guidance about how to get there. Using decentralized command, the leader then delegates authority for decision-making and action to lower echelons of leadership.[10] This allows leaders closer to the problem to solve it based on their expertise and to act more rapidly, as they do not have to continually wait for guidance or approval from above. In doing this, the leader accepts risk, but accepts it as the Mission Command approach empowers other leaders, making the organization more agile as a whole.[11] Allowing these leaders to make these decisions helps them feel valued and respected, and it develops their leadership ability.

When I was the program director of our over seventy-member residency, we would often have last-minute schedule changes or need to make decisions about providing coverage or not. I could have asked that each of these decisions be brought to me, but instead, I exercised Mission Command. My chief residents and I met at the beginning of the year and talked about our approach as a program. They would then handle these issues on a daily basis. They would bring me major issues or decisions, but generally, the decision was made at their level. I supported their decisions if anyone questioned why a resident was or was not present for a particular rotation or shift. We can use the Mission Command approach for our teams and organizations in healthcare.

Part of this process and delegating in general is providing guardrails. We should not tell people how to do the work, but we should set up a timeline and clear expectations of what we want done. What does "right" look like, and by when? It might be worth determining when you will check in on progress. Let the person you delegated work to know that you are always available if they have questions, but you trust them to get the work done on their own. When done, give them feedback on their work and let them know how they can improve. Remember, we are using delegation as a tool for growth and development. Finally, make sure they understand how much you appreciate and value their work.

Help Move the Patient

We have been talking about delegating, but we need to recognize that there are times when we need to step in to help. Even when it's not our job, we recognize that the team or individual just needs help getting the task done. Don't rescue people from a learning opportunity—but don't be afraid to get your hands dirty when it's clear helping is the right thing to do. A colleague, Dr. Kasi Chu, phrased this beautifully, saying, "Do we as leaders pitch in or position out?"[12] She further writes that by helping, "it seems as though there is the potential for unquantifiable impact in these moments."[13] The balance of helping or not was captured by Lieutenant General Hertling when talking about a former colleague: "He was always in the middle of things. He extricated himself when he knew that his team had it and they could do it without him." The key is to help out when needed, and then step out and get back to our role.

Frequently, when seeing patients on morning rounds, the patient will be all twisted in bed. It is actually at times surprising and impressive how some patients get so twisted. No question the patient is uncomfortable. At other times, we will come into a room on rounds, and it is clear that a patient has had a bowel movement. Medicine can be a smelly business. In these times, physicians could easily just leave and let the nursing staff and techs move or clean up the patients. That said, if physicians are there, we can and should help. If there is a team of three or four of us on rounds with one nurse, we can move the patient without delay and without needing to call other people into the room. The work gets done quicker, and it demonstrates we care about the patient and care about our colleagues. Think about this when delegating—when do you need to step in to help because somebody needs it? As an aside from the topic of delegation, imagine the impact on the culture of your organization if everyone was doing these small acts of helping each other.

See the Big Picture!

A final point about delegating: If you've successfully delegated to your team, you get to reap the benefits of the time you've put back into your schedule. One of my favorite phrases related to leadership is from Jocko Willink, a retired Navy SEAL and now author and speaker who runs a leadership company. He talks about detachment being a leadership superpower.[14] This is similar to Ron Heifetz and Martin Linsky, who, in their book *Leadership on the Line*, emphasized the importance of getting "on the balcony," because in order to effectively lead, we have to be able to see the big picture.[15] In combat, when people are shooting at you, there is chaos often referred to as the "fog of war," and in order to determine the next step to survive, the most important thing, sometimes, is to detach for a moment to think about what you need to do.[16] To be an effective leader in any situation, to take care of the people we lead, and to accomplish the mission, we cannot be stuck in the weeds. If we don't delegate effectively, we are always stuck in the weeds. The best example that is familiar to us in medicine is running a code blue. The person running the code is supposed to be at the head of the bed. You can't run the code if you are doing chest compressions, putting in medications, or placing a central venous catheter.

As leaders and healthcare providers in general, we have to detach and be able to see the big picture. We need to be able to see what is going on in the moment and adjust fire. We quite simply need time to pause and think. Delegation affords us more time to detach. While we can always make the choice to detach in any given situation (and we should more than we do), the less we are doing as leaders, the more we are naturally in a position to see and focus on the big picture. Leaders at all levels need to think strategically and plan. If we are always doing tactical work, then we don't have the ability to plan and improve.

We often don't have the time to take care of ourselves. Delegating effectively is also a wellness issue for leaders. The more effectively we delegate, the more control we have over our time and how we potentially use that time. Aside from thinking and planning, some of that time can be put into taking care of yourself as a leader.

If you are a leader in charge of a group, by effectively delegating, you can carve out time to think about the big picture. As a department chair, this might be the time to think about your research agenda for the future or how you plan to reshape your approach to academic promotions. As a charge nurse, you might use the time to think about how to more effectively schedule your team or communicate changes that are passed on from hospital leadership. As an educational leader, you might use this time to think about a curriculum that needs to be implemented or adjusted.

Delegation as a Leadership Superpower

This chapter provided reasons why delegation is important and how it can be beneficial to you as a leader. Delegation is not "dumping" work, but rather aligning goal-oriented and growth-oriented tasks with the right people. It is about trusting the people you work with and valuing their work and expertise. It is about creating opportunities for growth and recognizing people for jobs well done. It is about creating a culture where everyone excels at their roles and jumps in to help others when needed. It's about creating time and space for leaders to think, do *their* work, and take care of themselves.

Prescription for Caring in Leadership

1. Talk to your team about delegation and the concepts in this chapter. Ask them for their input about how you could delegate more effectively.

2. Identify one task you should no longer be doing based on your role and give that task to someone else whose role is more in line with the task.

3. Identify one task you can delegate and use as a learning opportunity for someone on your team. As you think about what you are delegating, ask yourself, "Is this a growth-oriented task or a goal-oriented task?" You can potentially discuss these differences with those you lead.

4. Block at least one hour per week on your calendar to "get on the balcony" and think about the big picture for you and your organization. Where are you? Where do you want to go? If you are stuck in the weeds all the time, it's hard to see where you want to go and what you need to do.

5. Step away from the chaos and day to day tasks—dedicate some time to think about the big picture for your team. Consider having a meeting with your leadership team to brainstorm the areas that need the most attention. Hold a strategic retreat to spend longer time on planning.

6. Read "Management Time: Who's Got the Monkey?" in *Harvard Business Review.*[17]

CHAPTER 18

Care Enough to Invest in Those You Lead: Mentoring, Coaching, and Sponsorship

"I tell her that working for her was like hitting the lottery, because as the Chief Diversity Officer and President of the GE Foundation, she was on the front lines of one of the largest companies in the world. She was constantly traveling globally, yet she always made time for me, taught me to trust my own instincts, and exposed me to so much. I KNEW she cared for me because she constantly gave me the one thing she could never get more of—time. Her leadership style remains the blueprint for me and so many others."
—Chelsea Hayes

I F YOU CARE ABOUT those you lead, take the time and put in the effort to find ways to make them better, both personally and professionally. When I think of the leaders I admire most, they are the ones who invested in me. They took a personal interest in my career and helped me to become more effective at my job or provided me with opportunities to succeed. David

Smith highlighted this, saying, "Two things scream 'care' louder than anything else, if we are talking about junior people and developmental relationships. That is when a senior person or mentor makes time...Do you make the space to listen and be present?"

Are you investing in their careers and lives? Leaders are responsible for developing new leaders. We need to continually replenish the leadership pool in order for our teams and organizations to thrive.

Chelsea Hayes talked about how working for her initial boss, Deb Grant, was like hitting the career lottery! Imagine the impact a person must have had on someone's career for them to talk about working with them like hitting the lottery. Be intentional about investing in those you lead, and try to leave a legacy of career lottery winners! In this chapter, we will talk about some tangible ways to invest in your people.

Dr. Alex Niven, a superior mentor and sponsor (as we will see below), talked about how Dr. Lisa Moores always invested in him. It is a great example of what being a caring leader looks like and how when you invest in one person, that person often leads in a similar way in the future. Dr. Niven described Dr. Moores in an article about her for *CHEST*:[1]

> ...when they were collecting a bunch of leadership articles a few years ago that I titled unconditional support and that's how I've always felt about Lisa. Because she cares enough about me and my professional development that if I reach out to her for something, she's always going to make the time. She's always going to listen. She's always going to give advice when asked, but she's also always going to challenge me. You know, the things that she thinks I can think through and for my own personal development, and that takes obviously

extra time. She's willing to spend that time and share herself so that I can get a little bit better and take that problem off my plate. It depends what you really mean by caring. I think unconditional support would be one way to describe it.

The impact Dr. Moores had on Dr. Niven is captured by this quote:

> *"I think that one of the most important things that you can do, as a leader and a mentor, is to challenge the people that you're working with to think about what their passion is, what they care about, and then help them to develop a thoughtful timeline and process for success."*

We can invest in others in this way.

Make investing in others' development a part of what you do—and if you are in charge of a department, hospital, school, etc., make it an expectation of those you lead. Leaders should be evaluated on how we are developing other leaders. This is not a one-person job. It is not someone else's role. We are all responsible for developing future leaders. There should be a cascading effect from the top down, with each level working hard to promote the professional development and personal well-being of those below us. Leaders should be recognized for this just as much as someone is recognized for outstanding patient care, teaching, or research.

Are you giving people tangible feedback to help them improve? Who was the last person you mentored? Who are you coaching to get better at their job or improve in work-life balance? Who was the last person you sponsored for a role or other opportunity? How many people have you mentored, coached, or sponsored? If you can't think of someone, then I would argue that you're missing opportunities for impact as a leader. Maybe you need to think more about how you can proactively mentor, coach, and sponsor those you lead. Don't wait for people to reach out to you. As a leader, make this part of who you are. I will challenge you at the end of this chapter to track your investments. We track our investments in the stock market—isn't our investment in the people we lead just as or more important?

Who are you investing in? Chelsea Hayes makes a great point:

> It is important to distribute caring equally. If you don't know how to distribute it equally, you need to ask for help, because it can get individuals and companies in a lot of trouble. It's natural for us to care. It's natural for us to work with people who remind us of our uncle whom we love and want to see at Thanksgiving. That's natural—but favoritism is a real thing. Bias is a real thing, and the outcomes for all of the above can be severe.

Within your own organization, are you investing in just your direct reports? What about people one level below you? What about people five levels below you? Even if you are not investing in them directly, how are you encouraging those you lead to invest in them? Does everyone you invest in look like you? Are you investing in men, women, underrepresented minorities, LGBTQ+ employees, and whoever else I am missing? The point of this paragraph is that we need to think about diversity, equity, and inclusion. This has to be part of the equation or lens we look through when we are picking who we invest in. Keep this in mind for each of the sections below.

> *We track our investments in the stock market—isn't our investment in the people we lead just as or more important?*

Mentoring

Mentoring has been an incredibly important part of my career. I have had many formal and informal mentors over my career. We can be mentored by people we don't even know these days (see Mentoring Pyramid).

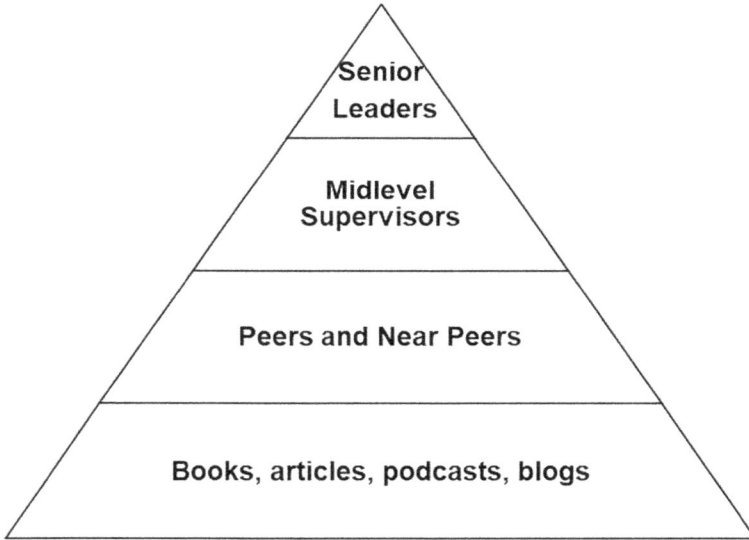

Mentoring Pyramid: Consider mentors from each level and from within and outside your organization for both personal and professional development and well-being.

Major General Jeff Clark pointed out that "some of the best mentors I have ever had have been leaders I met via books." For a mere twenty dollars—or even a free library card—we can get access to some of the greatest leaders of all time.

Mentors I have met through books have changed the way I lead and the lives of those I lead. They have influenced how I teach about leadership. I interviewed Brad Johnson and Dave Smith for this book because their book *Athena Rising*[2] was so impactful to me. It led me and a colleague, Dr. Jessica Servey, to teach hundreds of healthcare leaders nationally and across the military healthcare system about how men can more effectively mentor women. Books are available 24/7 to provide advice for your problems, so take advantage of that.

We can learn from voices we would not otherwise have access to through blogs and videos as well. Take advantage of these resources. When you find ones that are particularly useful, keep track of them, and then use those same books, blogs, or videos to help mentor and coach those you lead. Make it a habit to share these resources with your team. When I read an article or book that I find particularly useful, I will send a link or even buy a copy for someone whom it will help. This is a great way to proactively mentor and invest in others.

Mentoring is a team sport. Some people will refer to their "mentoring board of directors" or their "panel of mentors." Some will just call it their mentoring team. Laurie Baedke, leadership consultant and the author of *Mentor, Coach, Lead to Peak Professional Performance*, writes, "Enlisting a single career mentor is less career-enhancing than building robust networks or constellations of mentors, allies, and advocates."[3]

The bottom line is you need to have multiple mentors for different areas in your life.

As a leader, this should take the pressure or expectation off you that you need to mentor everyone. As I advanced in my career and made more connections, I became much more of a mentoring matchmaker. I try to help people find the right mentors rather than mentoring everyone myself. This is important because it's impossible for one leader to mentor everyone. One leader will not be the right mentor for all mentees. Helping mentees find other mentors opens them up to new ideas, new connections, and possibly new sponsors in the future.

Who should be on your mentoring team? I already mentioned the first level of the pyramid, which is made up of books, blogs, and videos. Mentoring often comes from our peers as well. We can learn a lot by talking to each other, sharing struggles and solutions. Work and life are not meant to be traveled alone, so create a network of peers who can support you and whom you can support. This does not need to be a formal process and can often be a simple phone call or meeting about a problem you are experiencing or about how to move forward with an idea. These relationships also enhance collegiality and respect at work.

Your mentoring team may or may not include your supervisor. This can be tricky at times given supervisors are often the ones making high-stakes decisions about a subordinate's career. Let me be clear: you should 100 percent be mentoring those you supervise. If you want them to trust you and work hard for you, then mentoring and investing in them is an effective way to get there. That said, your subordinates may not feel comfortable telling you *everything*, just like you do not feel comfortable telling your boss or supervisor everything. This is why it is important to have mentors outside your rating chain (supervisors), and at times outside your institution. It can be incredibly helpful to have mentors outside your institution. Outside mentors have different lenses. They see things differently than we do in our own organizations, and their perspective can be powerful.

Don't be afraid to ask for mentoring advice. The American College of Physicians Chief Executive Officer, Dr. Darilyn Moyer, said,

Catalyze people to feel comfortable, to reach out to others, and [to] ask them to tell them their stories. I encourage folks to do this all the time...people are really generous with their time and their stories. You shouldn't, quote, "wait for the tiara," wait for it to show up on your doorstep. Sometimes you just need to go after it. I think that so many people that you would have thought are not approachable are just incredibly approachable and want to share their experiences and their lessons learned. Don't be afraid to approach people and ask them about their leadership journey or other things.

Stretch Mentors

One of the most impactful things in my career has been having stretch mentors, which I define as senior leaders who invest in you. These can be long-term relationships or a brief mentoring encounter. I was selected to be an Alpha Omega Alpha Fellow in Leadership, and this led to me being mentored by the then dean of our medical school, Dr. Art Kellermann, and a former U.S. Army Surgeon General, Eric Schoomaker. Both leaders provided me with insights into leadership that I had not considered and shared with me many lessons. Most importantly, they both invested in me and gave me the confidence—and, at times, connections—to build on ideas or get opportunities. In other words, they sponsored me. Stretch mentors, if you can find one, are an incredibly valuable resource.

Depending on your level, be a stretch mentor for someone else. If you are senior in position, consider mentoring someone whom you would not normally mentor. You will learn from them as well. One great example of this is Army Brigadier General Clint Murray, who mentors people of all ranks in the military. He graciously, as a general officer, agreed to meet with an internal medicine resident and talk to her about a career in military infectious diseases. He is famous for investing in the careers of people within military medicine, and because of that, people appreciate his leadership. They know from the fact that he takes the time to mentor them that he cares about them. Being a stretch mentor is a powerful investment in the people you lead and is therefore a Caring Act of Leadership.

Mentoring won't look the same for everyone, and it is not the process of cloning people to be like you. Find out what drives them, and then help guide them and lift them up. This is why being a mentoring matchmaker is important, because as you explore a mentee's goals and dreams, you may realize they would best be mentored by someone else. One of my favorite things to do when mentoring is make connections like this.

I had an internal medicine resident who was interested in healthcare advocacy and policy, of which I know very little. I am fortunate, however, to know an expert in the field: Dr. Tracey Henry, an associate professor of medicine at Emory Medical School and former Presidential Leadership Scholar. She was kind enough to spend some time talking to my resident, and it was incredibly impactful for his learning and professional development.

Mentees don't belong to you or your organization. This is important to remember. If we care about those we mentor and sponsor, then we have to understand that they may leave our organizations. For many of us, our mentoring directly helps them with these goals. We should celebrate their success and, if and when possible, continue to invest in their careers. This builds your influence as a leader. Other people see this and will want to work for you. They will recognize that you care about people and their success. This influence will attract talented people. Some leaders get frustrated by this process, as they are always "losing good people." They are not losing good people; they are *propelling* leaders forward, making us all better.

Mentorship is about helping people solve problems, helping them to identify tangible areas for career growth, and guiding their journey. There are many times when, as a mentor, you might be aware of something that a more junior person does not know exists. This could be a clinical opportunity, research, a professional development course, etc. For example, I met with a junior trainee who had a significant interest in infectious disease. We talked about potential career options and pathways that would be typical of a career meeting. Knowing how impressive this trainee was, I wanted to provide him with some areas for growth that would support his career. I connected him with two senior leaders who both were willing to meet with him and provide more guidance. I had a specific ask for one of the leaders, which was to help get the resident a position on a national committee, recognizing that this would be beneficial to his career. My colleague was able to make this happen. The trainee was extremely grateful for the opportunity and investment in his career. Our job as leaders is to invest in those we lead!

Reverse Mentoring

The idea of reverse mentoring has been gaining traction. Laurie Baedke called the concept "mind blowing" in her book.[4] The concept is this: Rather than the flow of advice solely going in the direction of from mentor to mentee, there is a reciprocal exchange of knowledge and advice. The more senior mentor actively seeks to learn from the more junior mentee. Those who are more junior often have a lot to offer, whether it be skill-related (many times, more junior generations are noted to have superior social media skills) or about insights into how to best lead other junior employees. In an article in *Fast Company* in November 2022, Sarah Grimstead pointed out that through reverse mentoring, "mentors can gain as much as they give, if they listen well, forge a personal connection, and seek out new skills."[5]

When interviewing Dr. Jeff Hutchinson, he pointed to an example of one of his caring leaders, Dr. Chuck Callahan. More than once, Dr. Callahan had told Dr. Hutchinson that he had "mentored his mentor" on issues concerning diversity, equity, and inclusion. I asked Dr. Callahan about this and was told that he speaks frequently, often weekly, on the impact of racism on health outcomes in Baltimore—and in nearly every talk, Dr. Callahan uses examples and ideas that he learned from Dr. Hutchinson.

The higher up you go as a leader, the less connected you are to the people who do the work. As a department chair, you spend less time teaching and less time in the wards or clinics. As a hospital-level leader as a physician, charge nurse, or administrator, you simply have less contact with more junior people and those who work on the front lines. Reverse mentoring gives you the opportunity to meet with a junior nurse or an intern physician. You can learn about the problems they are facing, what they need for career development, and how you might better be able to support them. Let's be frank: as senior leaders, we could discuss these issues amongst ourselves, but if we are humble, we recognize that we really don't understand what is going on at their levels. If we care about them, we should learn and support them.

Reverse mentoring is important beyond just what a mentor can learn from his or her mentee. This should be reason enough, as there is a lot all of us can learn from each other no matter what stage our career is at. That said, reverse mentoring demonstrates several of the actions of caring leaders that we have talked about already. The mentor is taking the time to listen and learn from someone more junior. This demonstrates humility and models the growth mindset. In some ways, it models how to effectively solicit and receive feedback. Maybe most importantly, reverse mentoring should improve the relationship and build trust. Better relationships result in more effective teams and organizations.

For example, let's say you are a senior surgeon and have been out of training for several years, maybe a decade or more. You recruit a junior faculty member to join your practice or your team—this person has learned a new technique or approach. This is an opportunity for you, as the more senior faculty member, to learn from them. This might fall into the coaching category, but as alluded to earlier, mentoring often can lead to identifying areas for coaching.

Mentoring provides opportunities to give career and personal advice. It allows you to learn from those you mentor. You can be a mentoring matchmaker and identify other potential mentors for mentees. Often, when mentoring, you can identify areas where your mentee may benefit from coaching and sponsorship, which we talk about next.

Coaching

You were introduced to the idea when we talked about Dr. Atul Gawande and his article related to coaching.[6] There is a growing recognition that coaching can be an effective form of ongoing professional development and can fill many gaps that exist among healthcare providers who have completed their training. Over the course of my career, I have recognized that I have deficits or areas that I need to improve on. Once we are done with our formal training, ongoing professional development is left to us as healthcare professionals. Sure, there are continuing education courses we can take, but these often fail to provide the kind of longitudinal development that coaching can. The goal of this section is to get you to think about how you can benefit from coaching and how you can use coaching to support those you lead.

Dr. Jeff Hutchinson works as a consultant and coach and added this important point:

> Leaders need coaches. Everyone needs someone else outside the organization they can bounce ideas off of. I think that's critical because it is hard to see things when you're in the middle of it...It at least can give you another perspective. And you know the whole story about the blind men and the elephant. If you only have one perspective, you only see one thing. So you need multiple perspectives.

Coaching is not only valuable when you are in the storms of life; it can also be used to improve at any time. Ideally, you use coaching in some instances to prevent the storms. How many of you have stayed through a terrible meeting wondering when it would end—or worse yet, wondering why it was ever held in the first place? Wouldn't it be great if more people had coaching on how to run an effective meeting? Ever watch a presentation and think that the presenter could use some pointers with their slides—or, uh, ah, hmmm, avoiding filler words? Why not have a coach for developing more effective and inspiring presentations? Did you take over as a charge nurse and struggle with how to delegate and give effective feedback? Did you leave academic medicine and now are running a private practice but need help with understanding how to manage the business aspects? Coaching can help with all of these!

To get you started, here is a list of areas in which you may consider receiving coaching or offering to coach someone else.

Potential Areas For Coaching to Excellence
Business of medicine: hiring, firing, budgeting
Change Management
Communication: listening, strategic communication, email management, public speaking
Conflict Management
Developing personal values and purpose
Emotional intelligence: Manage your emotions and social interactions
Giving and Receiving Feedback
Gratitude: develop ways to recognize others
Mentoring, Coaching and Sponsorship: how to do these more effectively
Running meetings
Teaching skills
Time management
Well-being – how to take care of yourself

Sponsorship

One of the most powerful tools we have as leaders is using sponsorship to promote people and advance their careers. Sponsorship uses your influence as a leader to create opportunities or recognize someone you lead. Given what we know about the power of sponsorship for career advancement, we should do our best as leaders to support those we lead. If you're a leader mentoring someone and you're telling them about an opportunity they should take, the question you need to be asking yourself is "Can I help them get that opportunity? Can I make this a reality for them? Can I sponsor them, rather than just telling people about opportunities?" That is your job as a leader. As author David Smith, PhD puts it, be a "raving fan" for those you lead. This means we amplify their work, publicly promote their expertise, and sponsor them for career-advancing opportunities.

There are a few key things to keep in mind with sponsorship. First, if we care about the people we lead, we should sponsor them. Second, we should make it an expectation that those we lead sponsor others. Third, it is our responsibility to make sure that we sponsor people who deserve it and be aware of issues related to diversity when choosing who we sponsor. Finally, we should set up systems within our organizations to foster sponsorship on a macro level.

Laurie Baedke outlines eight key steps for leaders to consider when sponsoring others.[7] These are outlined in the table below and useful for how we as leaders can best support those we sponsor. The eight steps go from start to finish in regards to sponsoring someone. This is the sponsorship playbook, so keep it handy!

Sponsorship Best Practices

Identify talent	Proactively identify talent – ensure you are supporting a diverse network of talent
Identify the best "stretch role	Identify and match roles to talents to help people advance
Tee up the role	Help the person see why they are qualified (fight off impostor syndrome if it is present) and do what is necessary to prep them for the role
Support development	Continue to support with mentoring and coaching. Provide budgeting and resources as needed.

Sponsorship Best Practices

Leverage your network	Use your connections to foster their ongoing success in the role or other roles
Provide quality feedback	Coach for success. Provide ongoing feedback to help them continue to grow and improve in the role.
Bolster resiliency	Provide support when setbacks occur, talk about your own failures, provide advice as needed to get things back on track
Promote and recognize high achievers	Raise visibility of protégé's success and continue to sponsor and recognize excellent performance. Advocate for raises and promotions.

Adapted from Mentor, Coach, Lead to Peak Performance by Laurie Baedke, original source: "How to Be an Effective Sponsor by Elizabeth McDaid published in The Council of Insurance Agents and Brokers Leaders' Edge.

Let's circle back to Dr. Alex Niven and see how he mentors and sponsors as an example. Speaking about a pulmonary critical care fellow he works with, he gave this example:

> ...a couple folks I was really close to graduated this year, and they spent a lot of time telling me just how much that I did for them—when it just didn't seem like that much. I had a frank conversation with somebody about how to look for jobs and the things to think about in that setting. Then I had a frank follow-up conversation with her to say that she was just like me. She had a million different interests, but if she wanted an academic position in the major medical center, she needed to focus and be able to tell a concise story, and [to] build a succession of projects that demonstrated she was serious [about] progressing toward the goal. She did that. Then she wanted to go to Atlanta because she had family there. She was frustrated that nobody was picking up the phone. So, I sent a message to a friend of mine there, and she got an interview, and she ended up getting the job. Those are just such simple things, but she looks back and thinks that those are some of

the most important points in her fellowship. I think it just highlights the fact that being a mentor, being a coach, or just simply sponsoring someone is part of being a leader.

While Dr. Niven thinks these are simple things, they are not. They are also not actions that all leaders think about doing, intentionally, to support those they lead. Giving feedback, coaching, mentoring, and sponsoring have life-changing impacts, as illustrated. What can you do more of as a caring leader?

One of the best examples of individual sponsorship that can be emulated was my program director, who is now the chief of infectious diseases at Washington Hospital Center in Washington, D.C., Dr. Glenn Wortmann. When I was a junior faculty member just out of fellowship, Dr. Wortmann made it a point to help me and my colleagues get invited to presentations. He would get invited to give a talk, and then he would either say that he was unavailable or simply recommend me or another junior colleague in his stead. This opened doors for us to speak at institutions early in our careers that we would not have otherwise, helping to advance our academic careers. When he left the Army and went to another local hospital, he made it a point to invite speakers every year. This is a great example of sponsoring others by giving up talks or creating opportunities for giving talks. He would do similar things with publications, inviting more junior faculty to coauthor them with him.

If you are a senior leader or a full professor, how do you share publishing and presenting opportunities? Ask yourself these questions: "Could I do this presentation with a more junior colleague? Could they do it alone with my coaching? Could someone I lead do this news interview? Who could I invite to coauthor this paper with me?" Senior leaders are often asked to write editorials or have the ability, based on their professional stature, to have editorials published. If you are one of these people and publishing papers by yourself, you are missing an opportunity to coach and sponsor someone who works for you. Yes, they work hard for you and your organization, so consider investing in them by sponsoring them. This means you as the leader are giving up the spotlight to shine that light on someone else—not to take away from whatever paper or presentation you give, as your work is important. But in all reality, the exact work for most of what we do will not be remembered for years to come. I promise you that if you give the opportunity to someone else, *they* will remember it forever.

Dr. Darilyn Moyer is a role model who illustrates how, as a leader, to think about sponsorship:

> When I get asked to do something—get asked to speak, get asked to write an article—I frequently think, "Who can I bring along this path?" "Can you work with me on this?" or "Is there someone who's better suited to do this than I am?" I do more and more of that, as I try to lift up the others who are walking by my side or our folks who are in younger stages of their professional development. I think that has become naturally incorporated into my style because I saw it in others, emulated it, and put it into practice.

> I think about who I am representing and what is best for the organization that I'm representing. Am I the best person to sit at that table, or are there other people? Ninety-nine percent of the time, the answer is there are other people who are better qualified, more worthy, and [more in] need [of] those opportunities as they develop along their own leadership trajectories. I think being generous is really important. I have seen way too many people suck up all the oxygen in the room—[these are] self-aggrandizing, narcissistic behaviors.

> Are you building your CV or building up others'? You can do both. What would it do for the career trajectory and well-being

of junior healthcare professionals if more senior leaders took this approach to invest in those they lead? Those who do are investing in the future and building their legacy as leaders, as we will see at the end of the book.

Establishing a system of sponsorship is a terrific way to amplify many careers. This can take many forms, but the idea is that your organization makes it a habit to sponsor people. Over the course of my career in academic and military medicine, we looked for specific recurring events that we might be able to sponsor people for—then, every year, we sponsored people for those things. These included recurring awards, conferences for professional development we could send people to, and other career-advancing events.

An example of a system of sponsorship was by Dr. Jennifer Koch, the vice chair of academic and faculty affairs in the Department of Medicine, University of Louisville. When she was the program director for the internal medicine residency program, she created a network to facilitate sponsorship. Her sponsorship resulted in six women being invited to speak at her institution. This means six women had their careers impacted by her sponsorship just with this one initiative. The speaker's bureau she created had over 172 people registered as potential speakers, creating the opportunity for many others to pick from the list and sponsor others.

One final point I want to make about sponsorship. Once we sponsor someone, our work is not done. We need to help make sure they are successful in their role. The term "spentor" was developed by Dr. Julie Silver to capture the need for ongoing mentoring and supporting of those whom you have sponsored into a particular position.[8] She defines **spentorship** as "the act of sponsoring someone and then mentoring them through the process to build their confidence and ensure their success."[9] If you sponsor someone for a leadership role, make sure they have ongoing mentorship and coaching to help them do well in that role. If they perform well, it makes you shine and builds your influence, allowing you to sponsor others in the future. Plus, this level of investment in someone's career is a remarkable demonstration of being a caring leader!

Keep Score—Measure the Impact of Mentoring, Coaching, and Sponsorship

One last point on mentoring, coaching and sponsorship: This is about how to scale your impact as you become a senior leader and the importance of measuring outcomes. What we measure matters. The quote "If we can't measure it, we can't improve it," attributed to management guru Peter Drucker, is important for us leaders when we think about mentoring, coaching, and sponsorship.[10] If we care about others and invest in them personally and professionally, then we should be tracking our impact. We should make it an expectation for those we lead that they mentor, coach, and sponsor. We should hold them accountable. For each level of leadership, those we lead should be able to provide examples of who they are mentoring, coaching, and sponsoring. This helps to identify people on your team who are consistently investing in others and not just their own careers. Developing this type of tiered system demonstrates the importance to those we lead and allows us to reach the most people in our organizations. If we mentor, coach, and sponsor in this way, not only does it make our people feel valued and supported, but it ensures we are developing and creating more leaders.

Prescription for Caring in Leadership

1. Review who you are mentoring and think about who you could reach out to and mentor. Send them an invite to meet, or ask them in person if you can help them in any way with their career.

2. Make sure those you mentor don't all look like you. Seek out people from underrepresented groups in medicine and junior people to mentor.

3. Be a mentoring matchmaker by connecting someone on your team with a mentor who you think would be a good fit for them within or outside your organization.

4. Identify a skill that you will ask someone to coach you on from the list provided above.

5. Agree to coach someone you lead on a skill, or find them a coach to help them.

6. Review your sponsorship scorecard in Appendix C. Who could you sponsor and how? Make a list of opportunities that you could routinely sponsor people for. Here are a few examples to get you started:

   a. Invite someone junior from an underrepresented group to give a talk or grand rounds for your service, department, or hospital.
   b. Sponsor someone to get a position on a hospital or national committee, depending on your position.
   c. Invite someone more junior to participate in research, coauthor a paper, or help rewrite a hospital policy.
   d. Nominate someone for an award that will further their career and—as we will talk about later—make them feel valued.

7. If you are in a leadership position, start asking each of your direct reports to identify who they are mentoring, coaching, and sponsoring.

8. Recognize people who work for you when they mentor, coach, and sponsor others. Consider creating awards in your organization to highlight people's efforts in these areas and to reinforce that you think this is an important part of your culture.

9. Read the book *Mentor, Coach, Lead to Peak Professional Performance*[11] by Laurie Baedke, *How Women Rise: Break the 12 Habits Holding You Back*[12] by Sally Helgesen and Marshall Goldsmith, or *Athena Rising: How and Why Men Should Mentor Women*[13] by Brad Johnson and David Smith.

CHAPTER 19

Care Enough to Advocate

"Advocacy is not a part-time or side gig. In the words of the Mandalorian, 'this is the way.'"
—Vineet Arora, MD, MAPP, MACP
Dean for Medical Education, University of
Chicago, Pritzker School of Medicine

I F WE CARE ABOUT those we lead, then we will have to advocate for things that are important to us and to our teams, families, and communities. The ability to advocate is critical. It is a Caring Act of Leadership. Advocating for others shows that you are willing to fight for them. Think of a leader whom you respect and admire, and ask yourself, "Did they advocate for me? Did they advocate for my team and our mission? Did they stand up to power and protect our well-being? Did they advocate for resources? Did they advocate for recognition?" I suspect the answer to most of these will be yes.

Dr. Greg Argyros emphasized the importance of the people who work for him knowing that he has their back and will advocate for them:

The hospital center leaders, starting with me, are known to speak out professionally. We have worked hard on improving operations in the operating room. I brought in a VP of perioperative services five or six years ago—very experienced and knows how to run things. Beyond that, he has excellent interpersonal skills. He spends time with the surgeons and anesthesiologists. Everyone in and around the operating rooms. He knows everybody and people trust him. Similar to being part of a higher-level command in the military, my hospital is part of a healthcare system and—for quality, safety, and financial reasons—it is important to have standard work processes. Each hospital is different in size and scope, and as the largest facility by far in the system, it is important that decisions that are made to standardize things take into account our differences. The VP of perioperative services represents our facility in many of these discussions, and I have had frequent discussions with him about the importance of him professionally and collaboratively representing the needs of our institution. This is a very fine line to walk. My message to him is that if he disagrees with something, the answer can't just be no. It can be "No, and here is why it is no, and here are some alternatives we might look at." He is not just sitting there quietly but providing necessary feedback for the issue being discussed. Sometimes giving this feedback upsets others. My team knows that if they are being professional and giving our reasons, I will always have their back.

As healthcare leaders, advocacy is often multidirectional. To advocate effectively, you must have the courage to speak truth to power. You will need to rely on influence and persuasion to push things forward.

To get us started, here is an example from Dr. Chuck Callahan about a time he had to advocate for his people. He recounted a story of one of many visits by President Bush to Walter Reed Army Medical Center:

> President Bush came at the end of the *Washington Post* articles about lapses in care coordination at Walter Reed (February 2007). The articles had a devastating national effect, and the place was already hurting. The White House staff had scheduled an ambitious agenda: they were planning to visit the hospital, visit the barracks, tour the hospital, meet the staff, and then hold a press conference in the old Red Cross building on the campus.
>
> We staged it all for them. We were planning a meeting with the President for seventy-five people. In the next call, the White House staff told me, "Oh that's too many. It should be more like fifty people." We begrudgingly agreed, selected a couple dozen people from the list, and then I called them and had to disappoint them.
>
> A day or so later, the White House staff called back and said, "We need to get the number down to twenty-five." That was it. I had to call them out. So I told the staffers, "Let's be honest with each other. You're treating our people like potted plants. You just want them standing around the President for photos or something, and we're not having it. So, the number is fifty staff members or we're not doing it." They responded, "Oh no, that's not it at all," and provided lots of other explanations. After they finished, I told them, "So then it's fifty." They came back to me and agreed that they would make fifty work.
>
> A week or so later, the President visited, and at the last stop met with the staff before the press conference. As he wrapped up the staff visit and headed out to the press, the President walked over to me, put his arm around my shoulder, and said, "Okay. Let's go out there with the potted plants." I'm sure I turned bright red. He had a kind of whimsical smile on his face, and he knew he had a joke on me. It was worth it. For

those people who got to meet the President, I know they will talk about that visit for the rest of their lives.

We won't all be advocating to the President, but regardless, advocacy for our people matters. The goal of this chapter is twofold. The first is to convince you that advocating for those you lead and for important missions is a Caring Act of Leadership. We need more caring leaders to advocate at work, in our communities, and for our nation. Once you make the decision to advocate, the question becomes "How can I be more effective at advocating?"

This chapter provides practical steps you can take, as a leader, to advocate. When going through this chapter, think about it from the lens of the boss and the lens of the person advocating or leading up. Being aware of this perspective has helped me recognize when others are leading up. In fact, understanding the need of those below you to lead up to help support you as a leader is critical. That said, it is a skill that is not often taught or always considered by those in the higher leadership positions.

Leading Up

The most common situation requiring advocating at work is that of leading up. This is when you as a leader have to go to your supervisor to get support for those you lead. The question you have to ask yourself is related to if and how you are advocating for your people.

Are you standing up for your people, or sucking up to your boss? Your job as a leader is

Are you standing up for your people, or sucking up to your boss? Your job as a leader is to help advocate for the people that you lead and get them the resources and support they need to complete the mission.

to help advocate for the people that you lead and get them the resources and support they need to complete the mission. At the same time, you need to advocate for their well-being, protect their time, and make sure they're rewarded for the things that they do well. These are not at odds with your boss's goals. You should have the same goals. In fact, your job is to make your boss as successful as possible. You both ultimately care about the success of the organization and the well-being of the team.

Some of you might be asking, "But don't I answer to my boss? If I don't do what they want, then won't my own job be at risk?" Possibly, but if you are doing what is best for your team and the organization, then this should be less of a concern. Your goal is to help your boss see things from your perspective to help him or her and your organization be successful. If you develop your relationship with your boss, then he or she will understand your motives are for the benefit of those you lead and the organization.

In an ideal world, you, your boss, and your team are all aligned and there is no difference of opinion or conflict. Of course, that is not always the case. There are multiple reasons for this, including the lens through which we look at the issues at hand. That said, we need to avoid as much as possible falling into the "Us versus Them" trap that exists in many organizations. We are on the same team! Teams need to support each other and care about each other. This means you as a leader need to care about leading up and recognize and support those below you as they lead up. We are all in one of these dyads throughout our careers no matter how high we rise. Even chief executive officers have boards of directors to answer to. We need to be able to lead up and down the chain of command.

Given the natural conflict that arises between more senior leaders (any level leader above you) and those below them, it is the job of the senior leader to listen and learn. They need to understand how to support and help those they lead to be successful. This was discussed in the chapter on delegation and will be hit on again when we talk about developing your people as a leader.

The role of the mid-level manager or leader is to advocate for their people and to help their supervisor understand the situation more clearly to support those being led. Sometimes your boss may not have the information they need to make the best decisions. Your job is to inform them and ensure that you get what you need so your team can complete their work. If we see things differently than they do, then we need to ask ourselves why. Sometimes your boss's information will shift your stance on an issue, and then you will need to convey that to your team.

To help you lead more effectively, here are **Six Steps for Leading Up**. These steps are effective when advocating with peers or others.

1. Demonstrate excellence and commitment to the team.

Demonstrating excellence and a commitment to the organization are the foundations for advocating for yourself and others. If you want to influence your boss or colleagues, then you have to work hard. Be excellent at your job. People recognize those who work hard and support others and the mission. This means you need to do the tasks assigned to you well. It means helping out the team. If you see someone needs support, step in and help without being asked. If you know your boss has something that needs to be done, volunteer to take it off his or her plate.

You need to balance your own well-being and your team's well-being! You cannot overcommit your team to gain favor, as this will backfire. Before you take on a new task, pause and ask yourself if it is really mission-essential. Ask what it will require of your team in terms of people and time. Ask what the deadline is and if that is realistic. Can the deadline be moved if needed? Are there things that could be deprioritized for your team? Are there things your team can stop doing?

2. Build the relationship.

Leadership is about relationships. If you want to advocate effectively, you need to invest in building relationships. People know when you care about them and when you care about the organization. You want to take time to get to know those you lead, your boss, and others you work with. The time invested in these relationships builds trust and understanding.

It is important to remember that this is not about you or your boss. As a leader, this is where humility is key. We are much more willing to lead up when we know that a boss is going to be receptive. This is about the success of your organization. You will both be better off when egos are left at the door and you both come to the table with open minds. The more we learn from each other, the better we are as an organization. These same relationship ideas apply to peers that we may be working with and need to advocate to at times, as we discuss later in this chapter.

3. Understand the big picture.

We see things from our own foxholes, and we can only see so far— so we don't see the entire picture. This means that we want to help ourselves and those we lead. We tend to focus on what is in front of us. While this is important, *we need to understand the big picture.*

We are all supporting a larger organization in some manner. The more you understand the big picture and strategy of your organization, the easier it will be to advocate for what you want. When they align, you can pair your advocacy with how it supports the larger mission or vision. For example, you may want to hire a new nurse case manager. You can point out how having a new case manager will support access to care, patient satisfaction, and physician well-being. Ideally, every time you advocate, you link it to your organization's purpose, mission, vision, and/or values.

When something does not align with the larger strategic mission, you need to ask yourself, "Is this really needed?" If it is, why? If it is not, should you be doing it? Can you communicate the reason why to your boss and other stakeholders, given the potential scarcity of resources? Recognize that you may still need to advocate, but put it in the context of how it supports the mission.

4. Be a problem-solver.

If you consistently help solve problems, this builds influence with your leadership. The more you are positive and see opportunity within challenges, the more your boss will look to you, listen to you, and use your input. We live in an environment where many people focus on the negative. If you are someone who focuses on the positive and creates forward momentum, it will allow you the opportunity to advocate and speak frankly when you need to.

5. Communication is a leadership love language.

Communicating with your leadership is essential. This needs to be an ongoing process and not just a tactic for when you need something. Remember, your goal is to build trusting relationships. Some leaders will establish how they like communication to work, including when to check in or when there will be meetings. Others may let you work independently.

Leaders hate surprises. Keep your boss informed of the work you are doing and what you need in order to be successful. If there is something you think they need to know about, they probably do. Bosses can always delete emails they don't want to read in detail or may already know, so don't assume they know everything you email them.

Use your communication to highlight the great work of your team. You can demonstrate your ability to develop leaders and support your team by letting your leadership know when people are doing great work. This is about recognition, as we discuss later—but it also allows your boss to thank people and start to get a sense of who the top performers are in the organization.

6. You are support staff.

In the military, there is only one commander. This is true in other organizations as well. Ultimately, there is someone in charge who makes the decision and has authority and responsibility. The rest of us are support staff. The reality is, at times, we are all in a supporting role. While we should all take ownership of our organization's success and/or failure, ultimately, the leader is responsible.

It is our job to make sure our leader is as informed as possible. If something is important and we feel they are missing something and going to make the wrong decision, then we have to continue to ask questions, talk about our concerns, find more data to support our position, or enlist the support of others who may have influence. We all want the right decision, so if you feel like the wrong decision is going to be made, you have to lead up until the decision is final.

Once the final decision is made, everyone needs to move forward as a unified front to help the plan be successful. Unless the plan is immoral, unethical, or illegal, your job is to support it. If you care about your boss and your organization, you don't want them to fail.

Protect Your People

One last point about leading up is about protecting those below you. This means pushing back against your leadership. You may be tasked with something that is unreasonable or not resourced appropriately. You may be asked to do something on a timeline that you know will not work for your team. When you are confronted with what seems unreasonable, your job as a leader is to push back. You need to convey to your leadership why this is not a good idea. If they still want to pursue that course, then march on. Let your team know that this is the plan and that you all need to support the boss. Getting the work done builds trusting relationships and influence.

If this does not change over time, then you may have to have another discussion: "Hey, boss, we are trying to be supportive and get stuff done. We have been able to do these things you asked us to do, but this is not going to be sustainable." If your leader does not change, then he or she has to understand that people may vote against this decision by leaving—or, at a minimum, by stopping putting in extra work because they don't see it ever letting up.

> *Leaders, beware that this type of behavior of "doing more with less" will drive results in the short term but erode culture, well-being, and long-term organizational success. Do you really want to trade in today's victory only to lose the war?*

Advocating Across and Sideways

Much of what we do in healthcare requires interprofessional and interdisciplinary teamwork. This includes not only those delivering the care but also educators, human resources, and facility management. We have to work with many different groups to optimize healthcare and medical education. This requires the ability to advocate for your interests. If you care about your team, you will advocate for them. When those we lead see us advocating for them, it builds trust and makes them think we care about them, their opinions, and their work.

The same steps we discussed above are critical when developing the influence to help you advocate outside your direct chain of command. These relationships are critical. Hospitals, schools, or practices that have employees who have been together for a long time have the potential to excel. These relationships foster the ability to have frank discussions, because everyone knows that you are on the same team.

The more respect we show, the more we build relationships. We need to value every member of the healthcare team. This means we leverage expertise. We value opinions. We let others lead when they should be leading.

Here is a great story by Angela Costa, RN, BSN, MPM about how to advocate laterally, set standards, and hold people accountable:

> There was an environmental services manager on my floor who had a tough time in his leadership role. One day, I saw the manager outside of work and he came up to my then-twenty-one-year-old son. He said, "Your mom made me the person that I am today by giving me feedback about the importance of my role and advocating for her patients." He said that by advocating for my patients, I was helping him understand the impact his team had on patient care. In a hospital setting, we all impact patient care. When the environmental services team does its job well, the rooms are always clean, the patients are safer, and their families are happier. By tying the cleaning to patient care, I was able to allow the manager to enhance his team's performance and hold them accountable to their roles. I was able to help the manager realize the impact the environmental services team has on patients.

This act of advocacy for her patients had a lasting impact not only on the patients but on the career of the person she advocated to. Advocating for what is important and holding people accountable changes lives. As caring leaders, we have to advocate for what is important on a personal and organizational level.

Advocating for a Bigger Cause

There is a leadership gap in the world. Healthcare professionals have knowledge, skills, and leadership abilities that can help fill that gap and make the world better. We are starting to see physicians, nurses, and other healthcare professionals taking on more prominent roles in advocating for important issues. Yet, others remain hesitant to advocate and even consider it "dirty," as a group of doctors from Indiana pointed out in a recent editorial.[2] They emphasized advocacy is an "ethical obligation."[3]

One example is the #ThisIsOurLane movement and physician involvement in gun control advocacy. Numerous physicians speak out about gun violence. Dr. Joseph Sakran is a trauma surgeon who works at Johns Hopkins Hospital in Baltimore, and he is the founder of the #ThisIsOurLane movement.[4,5] Dr. Sakran is a survivor of gun violence, having been shot in the throat as a high school student while he was hanging out with friends at a playground.[6] Fortunately, he survived and, as he said, was "given a second chance."[7] In an interview for a Hopkins publication, he stated, "As I went down the path of becoming a surgeon, I quickly came to realize both the power of my own story and the importance of working beyond our operating rooms...Because there's only so much that you can do once someone's been shot in the head. We know how high the case fatality rate is for that. We have to think about preventing these incidents from happening in the first place."[8]

We have seen healthcare leaders speak out about other issues and even step up to run for public office. Advocating and leading in the public arena requires leaders who are courageous. If we care about our communities and nation, some of us may have to answer that call. Even if we are not running for office, we can use our talents to support important issues. We can support organizations that support these issues, write letters to Congress, and join advocacy events sponsored by professional medical societies. At a minimum, we can vote.

Healthcare providers' lives are dedicated to caring for patients. We can no longer only care inside the walls of a hospital, clinic, or exam room. The issues that are impacting our patients are happening in our communities, streets, and homes. If we care about our patients, we have to engage and lead in new arenas.

Advocating is a Caring Act of Leadership and takes many forms. We advocate up, down, and across the organization. We can advocate for public health outside of our jobs. Ultimately, we advocate because we want better lives for our patients, our colleagues, and ourselves.

Prescription for Caring in Leadership

1. Reflect on leaders you know who are advocates for your team or for some cause. What drives them? What makes them impactful? What strategies do they use? How could you use those to improve your leadership?

2. Ask your team what you can do to better support them. "What do you need to be successful? What are the barriers to your success?" The answers to these questions could be things that you need to advocate for.

3. Think about the **Six Steps for Leading Up** and work on one or all of those steps to allow you to more effectively support your boss and the people you lead.

4. Invite speakers to your organization to talk about important topics related to advocacy, or invite speakers to talk about how to more effectively advocate.

5. Consider trying to become a member of your hospital or school's advisory board. Become an advisor or advocate for something in your community outside work (e.g., a school board, parent-teacher association, or community/national organization that is important to you).

6. Think about a cause that is important to you, either at work or outside of work. Step into that space and advocate for positive change.

7. Make it a point to vote every year. We can complain about politicians and our public leaders, but if we are not voting, then we are part of the problem.

8. Consider reading the book *Mountains Beyond Mountains* to see the work of Paul Farmer.[9] It is an inspiring story of leadership and advocacy. I sometimes give this to new medical students to help inspire them to think about the impact they can have on the world.

9. Read the book *Leading Up: How to Lead Your Boss So You Both Win* by Michael Useem.[10] This book has some great tactical strategies based on examples from history and the business world about how to lead up.

CHAPTER 20

Care About Diversity, Equity, and Inclusion

"None of this is new. This has been going on.
There have been decades of people talking
about this stuff. So, it's really a matter of
leadership's desire to change something."
—Dr. Jeff Hutchinson

To BE FULLY TRANSPARENT, I completely missed the boat in regards to the content of this chapter until 2020. It is not that I did not care about underrepresented groups of people who have fewer advantages in society—I always considered myself a proponent for diversity. It's just that everything changed one day when I had a discussion with one of the physicians and junior military officers that I was training to be an internal medicine physician.

In 2020, after the death of George Floyd at the hands of Minneapolis police officers, there was a clear impetus for social change. I met with some of our Black residents to make sure they were okay. When I met with Isaiah Horton, we talked about the events and about how the residency program could respond in a positive way.

We wanted our residency training program to help foster change within our program, in the hospital, and across military medicine.

Isaiah told me he had always felt supported as a resident. He appreciated the dedication to his education and professional development opportunities. Then, he dropped a bomb on me. He said that while he appreciated all we had done, he never felt supported as a Black man in medicine. My heart sank. I realized this was not something I had ever considered for any of the underrepresented minority residents we had in our program over the years. He went on to tell me that no matter what he did when he left base, despite being an Army officer, without his Army uniform and white coat, most of society would see him as a Black man with all the stereotypes and biases that exist. Isaiah is one of the kindest and most caring people I know, yet to a stranger on the street, they may see him as a threat.

While this is beyond disappointing, it is also a reality of where we still stand as a society. For example, one study showed that Black Chicagoans are 650 times more likely to be killed by police than white Chicagoans.[1] This conversation forever changed who I am as a leader and as a person. It has motivated me to learn and, even more importantly, take action so we can help fight the racism that still exists within medicine. This is incredibly important for our colleagues and our patients.

Isaiah's story is unfortunately not unique. We had completely missed what was a vital part of their professional identity formation. They were not just physicians but Black physicians. I did not consider the potential implications of this, that people may feel threatened by him or certainly not look at him as the Army physician officer he was to us.

Another colleague of mine, Dr. Erika Walker—a successful Black female physician—talked about how when she was with her kids at an airport, someone gave them money. The story is an example of how even with good intentions, false assumptions and stereotypes can lead to harm. Dr. Walker was concerned about her children's safety as a stranger was giving them money, and she was baffled as to why her kids were chosen out of a crowd:

While returning home from a ski vacation in Montana, my husband and I were separated at the connecting leg of our return flight back to Washington, D.C. We were in Salt Lake City, Utah, and as usual, my three kids were clamoring for food when they saw their favorite Asian fast-food restaurant. After receiving our food, I seated the kids at a table and instructed them to be still while I got utensils and napkins. When I returned two minutes later, they were waving a five-dollar bill. I was shocked and worried that they picked it up after someone unknowingly dropped it. We have a rule that they are not allowed to [take] money [they find] without making every effort to return it to its owner. I asked sternly where they got the money, and they said, "That lady gave it to us," pointing at an older woman. When I turned to look at her, she said, "They wanted fortune cookies and I just wanted to bless them." She seemed very satisfied with herself and her actions. I politely declined and returned the money to her.

I was horrified that she chose to approach my children and offer them money while they were unattended and not ask my permission. I was less than ten feet away; she waited until my back was turned to make her move. There was a young couple next to us with their infant—why didn't she choose to bless them? This was during the government shutdown, when TSA workers were furloughed and working without pay— why didn't she choose to bless them? She was an older white woman, and we are Black, and I couldn't help but think that this factored into this scenario and why she felt empowered to do this without my consent. Did she think I was poor? Did she think I was a single mother? Why, as another woman (and possibly mother), did she not feel it was important to protect their innocence and not have them approached by a stranger offering money? I wanted to scream, "I'm a physician, and we just came off a week-long ski vacation for five. We don't need your charity for fortune cookies—which are free!" But I just turned away with a lump in my chest. While this could have simply been an altruistic act ignorant to the implications, I was nonetheless infuriated and offended.

Dr. Walker is an Ivy League graduate and physician. Why was the woman's initial reaction upon seeing this Black woman and children the assumption that she must need money? While well-intended, the example illustrates that our society has a long way to go in terms of bias.

Hopefully, these stories make you uncomfortable or angry. Maybe you are wondering how these stereotypes impact medicine. Bias, racism, and stereotypes impact the entire system, including the admissions process, residency selection, hiring, wages, and academic advancement. What are you going to do as a leader to be part of the change? You are either actively working to fix the injustices and racism that exist or you are part of the problem. Dr. Chuck Callahan gives a useful analogy. He talks about an old house he currently owns. He did not build the house, similar to how all of us did not create the systemic racism that exists. However, he is now responsible for and the caretaker of this house, just like we are responsible for fixing and taking care of the injustices that exist in our world. I know not everyone is going to agree with me—some of you may even want to stop reading. That's your decision, but I would argue that if you care about all people, you will keep reading and trying to learn and understand.

It's hard for me, as a cisgender white man, to write about diversity. I still do not fully understand and recognize the scope of my privilege. When writing about these topics, my goal is to help. I suspect many of you leaders, like me, feel uncomfortable when talking or writing about these potentially sensitive topics. I get the discomfort, but let's just step back and think about the discomfort, pain, and suffering some of our colleagues and patients have lived with their entire lives. We need to embrace our discomfort because we care about them and want to be part of the solution. As Chelsea Hayes pointed out to me, "It is critically important for people like me, who belong to dominant groups, to speak up and take action." So true! We have a voice and need to make a difference!

One final point on this that Chelsea emphasized—we need to think broadly about diversity and privilege:

> When people think about diversity, most people automatically think about race. That is important, but they're missing a lot. This is really about privilege. This is about how all of us experience privilege on a daily basis and we use that privilege to make our lives better. That's what people have to get comfortable understanding and talking about.

For this chapter, I reached out to a couple of colleagues and friends to help me say what is important. Each of them has provided me with some guidance on the different points that we make in this chapter. The goal of the chapter is fourfold. I like to think of it in terms of the diversity pyramid. First, the hope is that you are uncomfortable with the stories that are shared and it will make you want to learn more. We will make this easy, as we provide suggested resources. With that learning, the hope is that you will develop a new understanding. As you learn and understand, we want you to act and apply what you are learning, individually and as a leader. The change you want to see in your organization can start with you.

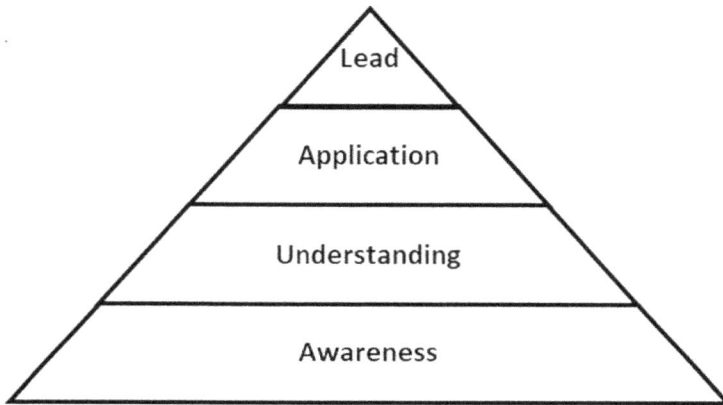

Figure: Diversity Pyramid for Leaders

I want to take a brief pause to explain an important concept of being allies versus accomplices that I think is critical for us to consider.[2] Frederick Joseph wrote a book called *The Black Friend: On Being a Better White Person*.[3] This should be on your reading list. It has multiple stories and lessons that will challenge some of your assumptions and ways of thinking. In particular, he offers an encyclopedia of racism that defines terms we often hear.[4] He ends his book talking about the need to be accomplices instead of allies. The difference is "someone who is hoping for change and someone who is trying to make change."[5] My hope is that after reading this chapter, you will be an accomplice—and maybe, even more importantly, you will work to change the system and develop more accomplices.

What can we do as leaders to support diversity, equity, and inclusion? There are books and courses leaders can read and take on this topic. We don't have time to cover this topic in the detail that it deserves, but I want to highlight a few things that I hope will inspire you and point you in the right direction to help be a force of change.

The first responsibility we have as leaders, and as humans, is to learn. What have you done to learn about issues that underrepresented groups face? What can you do to learn in the future? Sometimes this is as simple as asking them about the challenges they may face, the concerns they have about their professional development, or personal issues they may be having.

Laurie Baedke described this in her interview when talking about the importance of diversity on our teams:

> We demonstrate care for them in terms of asking questions to get to know them better, to understand what motivates them, to ask about what things might be barriers to them right now, [which] allows them to feel included and to have a sense of belonging on our team. It fosters and nurtures trust or psychological safety, which are necessary in team interactions. It's vital for leadership. You can't measure it on a financial statement...but it is absolutely the grease that leads to a more frictionless interaction or execution of any task or process.

For those who want to learn more about the data and learn from thought leaders, seek them out on social media and watch them speak online or in person. Dr. Quinn Capers (interventional cardiologist and Chair of Medicine at Howard University College of Medicine, former Associate Dean for Faculty Diversity, Vice Chair for Diversity and Inclusion, and the Rody P. Cox Professor in Internal Medicine at UT Southwestern in Dallas) has called these issues a national emergency.[6] He has spoken and written widely on these topics—if you get the chance to listen to him, you will be educated and inspired. At the 2022 National American College of Physicians Meeting, he talked about the need to increase the diversity and number of Black physicians. This statement in particular should be a call to action for all of us: "But I'm here to say the most powerful anti-racist statement that we can make is to diversify our ranks ."[7]

A few books that are challenging to read because they will likely make you uncomfortable are *Caste: The Origins of Our Discontents* by Isabel Wilkerson,[8] *How to Be an Antiracist* by Ibram X. Kendi,[9] and *The Sum of Us: What Racism Costs Everyone and How We Can Prosper Together* by Heather McGhee.[10] Being uncomfortable is exactly what we need to be—it is in the discomfort that we learn. My hope is that you seek this discomfort. As Dr. Hutchinson pointed out, "Seeking discomfort requires a clear benefit at the end of the process, like with exercise or learning a language. We chose to do the uncomfortable things for the end results. Uncomfortable things, like hunger, make us move to relieve the discomfort."

Make learning about racism and bias a priority for you and for your organization. Through learning, we will develop understanding, creating the impetus to apply what we learned and lead thusly. We can make an individual difference by supporting and advocating for people. Look at the chapter we have on "Care Enough to Invest in Those You Lead" and think about who you coach, mentor, and sponsor. Do they all look like you? We can amplify voices during meetings. We can highlight and magnify excellent performances by simply talking about others or by nominating and recognizing them more formally with awards.

Laurie Baedke models this for us:

> The best way that I love to care for others is to advocate for them and to sponsor them—especially because I'm particularly passionate about women and individuals from other underrepresented or minoritized or historically

excluded groups. I think one of the best ways that I can care for people and demonstrate love and compassion to others is to advocate for them.

At any level of leadership, we have the ability to invest in someone else's personal and professional development. Never underestimate how even these sometimes small acts can make a huge difference over time. If you care about these issues, you will invest in people and take a more diverse approach to who you invest in.

The final thing we can and should do as leaders, if we care about this issue, is to work for systematic change. This is going to look different within each of our work environments and includes some of the items we talked about above. As Dr. Jeff Hutchinson says, this is a "convoluted problem with no simple solutions." However, as he points out in the quote at the beginning of this chapter, we have spent too long just talking about the issues. It is time for action. It's time for leadership.

We need to hold leaders accountable for DEI efforts within their institutions. If we think this is important, we need to measure our DEI efforts and examine our processes through a DEI lens. Dr. Hutchinson said, "We can't change what we don't measure." Dr. Quinn Capers suggested in a Perspective in *The New England Journal of Medicine* that "institutions add 'enhancing diversity' to the list of metrics for reappointment as a leader in academic medicine."[11] We need leaders at all levels to be considering these issues and then to be held accountable for making progress. Here is a list of a few things you could measure:

1. Number of underrepresented employees, including by ethnicity, LGBTQIA+, people with disabilities, and others

2. Number of underrepresented employees who are interviewed for positions

3. Retention of underrepresented employees

4. Number of underrepresented people in leadership positions

5. Salary comparisons

6. Workplace satisfaction related to DEI—can include other metrics here as well, such as well-being

7. Number of invited speakers from underrepresented groups

8. Breakdown of those winning awards or receiving bonuses

9. How, specifically, your organization is investing in developing the workforce. Think about who you send to what conferences, who gets selected for leadership development programs, and who is on each committee that may be a stepping stone to future leadership positions.

While more challenging to measure, each organization should examine bias in all stages of work, including interviewing, hiring, and promotion processes. For those unsure how to do this, there are a plethora of other resources available to help organizations navigate through these areas. The first step is caring enough as a leader to act.

Once you have the data, you should ask these questions that executive coach and leadership consultant Chelsea Hayes asks organizations. These are powerful questions that should motivate all of us:

"What story is our data telling?"

"Is this a story we are proud of?"

"What are we willing to do to create a story we are proud of?"

My friends, I will leave these questions for you to ponder for your organization. We all have room to improve. Think about your stories and where you can make changes to better support those you lead and be able to share positive stories that you are proud of with others.

Be a leader who has the desire to make real and substantive change!

Prescription for Caring in Leadership

1. Speak to a colleague or someone you lead to better understand their perspectives about bias and racism in medicine.

2. Mentor, coach, or sponsor someone who is underrepresented in medicine.

3. Invite and pay someone to speak to your team or organization about DEI issues in medicine.

4. Establish mechanisms to track and measure metrics related to DEI.

5. Implement ways for people to provide ongoing anonymous feedback (positive and constructive) related to DEI and determine how and if the culture supports belonging and inclusion.

6. Develop a strategic plan related to DEI for you and your organization.

7. If you are in a leadership position, support those who lead DEI efforts with time and money. Do not make positions related to DEI and then not give them the support to be successful.

8. Read *Athena Rising*,[12] *The Black Friend*,[13] *How to Be an Antiracist*,[14] *Legacy: A Black Physician Reckons with Racism in Medicine*,[15] or *Caste: The Origin of Our Discontents*.[16]

CHAPTER 21

Care Enough to Be a
Positive Force of Energy

"Positive leaders care about the people they lead.
They care about their team and organization.
They care about changing the world because
they know the world needs changing."[1]
—Jon Gordon
The Power of Positive Leadership

THINK OF THE BEST experience you have ever had working in medicine. Was it helping a patient or a patient's family? Was it teaching or mentoring? Was it successfully leading your department or division? How does it make you feel to reflect on that experience? I suspect you are smiling. Some of you may even be tearing up a little. We need to focus on these positive events and help people feel this way more often as leaders.

Medicine is a serious business, but we should not take ourselves too seriously. The past several years, I have greatly come to appreciate just how important it is to work with people who are positive. Work can be demanding and even depressing, so having a team that makes it fun is important. Martin Rooney, in the book

High Ten: An Inspiring Story About Building Great Team Culture, reminds us not to be afraid of the "F-word" (fun) at work![2] In fact, come up with ways to ensure those you work with are having fun. As an aside, the first time I made a slide entitled "Use the 'F-word' more often," my public affairs team said I could not say "the F-word" in a talk. I asked why saying "FUN" in a talk was not allowed and ultimately won them over.

As leaders, we need to foster a positive work environment. Chelsea Hayes talked about how she welcomes new employees in a fun way to connect with them:

> When we have people join our team, whether they're contractors or employees, we ask them some really specific questions. If they were going on a road trip, what are the five snacks that they could not live without? Then they answer the question. We keep that information in a database, and then at some point throughout their first year with the company, we send them all five of those things. We send them an obnoxious amount. If they say, like, dark chocolate–covered pretzels, then we'll get like six bags from Costco and send it to them. And that's just so that they know that we're in this virtual working world together. It's hard for us to support each other, but maybe they had a tough meeting or something was challenging with a client, so it's a fun pick-me-up. It's also something that's very cost-effective. How much are chocolate-covered pretzels? Twenty bucks, right? I found that to be a very fun way to keep in touch, and snail mail is always fun to receive.

(I like wasabi almonds, just in case you were curious.)

Everyone has an internal energy battery. We are either recharging someone or draining them. We all need more chargers in our lives. Be an energy booster! And as my good friend Lauren Weber, MD reminded me, "Don't forget to charge yourself." What would our work and home environments look like if we all charged each other's energy batteries and ensured that we took care of our own?

What, exactly, is positivity? Researcher and author of *Positivity: Discover the Upward Spiral That Will Change Your Life*, Barbara Fredrickson, PhD, defines positivity as feeling ten positive emotions: joy, gratitude, serenity, interest, hope, pride, amusement, inspiration, awe, and love.[3] Describing the importance of positivity, she writes, "We turn toward positivity, stretching our minds open to take in as much as we can."[4] This leads to us building well-being and new connections or relationships, and, as she states, "With positivity, you go from classifying people as separate 'me' and 'you' to seeing more interconnection, as in 'we' and 'us.'"[5] Conversely, negative emotions limit our creativity, thinking, and connection with others: "Threatened with negativity, our minds constrict."[6]

One can see positivity is not just about feeling good but about improving performance and, ultimately, lives.

The idea of positivity is supported by evidence, including a meta-analysis by Lyubomirsky, King, and Diener of 225 studies of over 275,000 people, as Fredrickson highlighted.[7] One of her conclusions, and something we should all consider, was "the shift that I needed to make—and that you may need to make—is to view positivity as a wise and healthy investment in ourselves and in the world around us."[8]

Are you willing to invest in creating positivity to make your life and the lives of those around you better? The question you should ask yourself is, "How can I foster positivity for myself and in the lives of others in our work environment?"

The good news (and something I appreciate as an infectious diseases doctor) is that positivity, according to Fredrickson, is "remarkably contagious."[9] She is not alone. Dr. Julia DiGangi, author of *Energy Rising: The Neuroscience of Leading with Emotional Power,* was interviewed on the *Lead From The Heart* podcast by Mark Crowley. She stated, "Emotions are a contagion. We catch them just like a cold from others."[10,11]

Great news! Every action you take as a leader to foster positivity results in others taking similar actions.

How important is it for us to be a source of positivity? We set the tone as leaders, and we have large spheres of influence. If we are not serving as catalysts for positivity, our organizations are going to be running low. Consider how many people you interact with each day. When you walk into the room, do you want the energy of the room to increase, or do you want everyone to find a corner to hide in?

Dr. Chuck Callahan actually counted the number of interactions with people he had during a sample day. It was 283. He had 283 chances a day to positively impact and energize someone else at work. The more interactions we have and create for ourselves, the more we can impact others—and the more they can impact us. This can be as simple as a smile and hello. Dr. Callahan emphasized this point, stating, "People talk about how the leader creates the mood of an organization. The neurophysiology of that is with mirror neurons. You walk down the hallway, you greet somebody by name, or you smile at them. You create resonance for that moment, and like an oscillating tuning fork, that resonance carries for some distance."

Let's talk about smiling for a second. Specifically, a happy-to-see-you smile. Smiles are cues of belonging and caring for those with whom we work. How much does it cost to smile? Seems like you will get a great return on your investment for this action as a leader. Angela Costa, the chief nurse executive for Allegheny Health Network, talked about the power of a smile and the potential impact of not smiling or greeting people:

> Everyone deserves to be smiled at and deserves to receive a hello. I used to tell new managers and staff that everyone deserves to receive a "good morning." If I have five people and only say hello to three of them, then the other two may be worried all day about why I didn't say hi to them, wondering if I may be mad at them. So, I always walk into a room conscious of making sure I acknowledge everyone, because you might disrupt their day if you don't.

Treating people with kindness, dignity, and respect should be an expectation, but we sometimes fall short in our organizations. Leaders can set this expectation and then reinforce it through thanking people when it occurs and holding people accountable when it doesn't.

Anne Thompson, PT, EdD shared that we should "build a culture that empowers kindness and productivity and professionalism, and [in which] people feel that [they] can learn here. [They] can do some good here." Be intentional about building positive connections at work so people feel inspired to work.

Angela Costa gave a great example about infusing positive energy in the workplace by getting people to say nice things about each other:

> Some days, when we were having rough days, I would tell people during a staff meeting, "We're going to go around

the room and you're going to say something nice about the person next to you—and it can't be what they're wearing." It really opened up conversations. I'm sure they were making fun of me and laughing at me, but the rest of the day, they would be saying nice things. It got them talking and had them saying nice things. It started to build some friendships with people, because they would say, "I noticed when Fred [walks] in the room, the first thing he does is acknowledge the patient." It was picking up positive traits that people probably didn't even know they had. I just love to showcase people and get them talking about being kind and how they can make a difference in someone's life—a positive difference in someone's life.

This is a great example of how we can cue people to focus on the positive and make people feel valued and proud about when they do—as their colleagues point out—Caring Acts of Leadership.

Beyond generating feelings of pride, kindness, and being valued, this can have a profound impact because we never know when someone may need it most. Make a habit of encouraging others. Encouraging others is free. As Angela Costa said, "I'm just kind to people, because you never know what that person's experiencing that day." Your kindness and encouragement can change their day—change their life.

There are countless ways to be kind. You can check out "100 Random Acts of Kindness Ideas" by Jennifer Taylor on the SignUpGenius website.[12] Be kind to each other. We can build people up or tear them down. Just as important, when someone smiles at you, treats you with kindness, or thanks you for a job well done, you are likely to pass that on to one of the next people you interact with. Never forget the ripple of leadership on positivity.

300 smiles x 300 people in your day x 300 people they interact with = EXPONENTIAL POSITIVITY

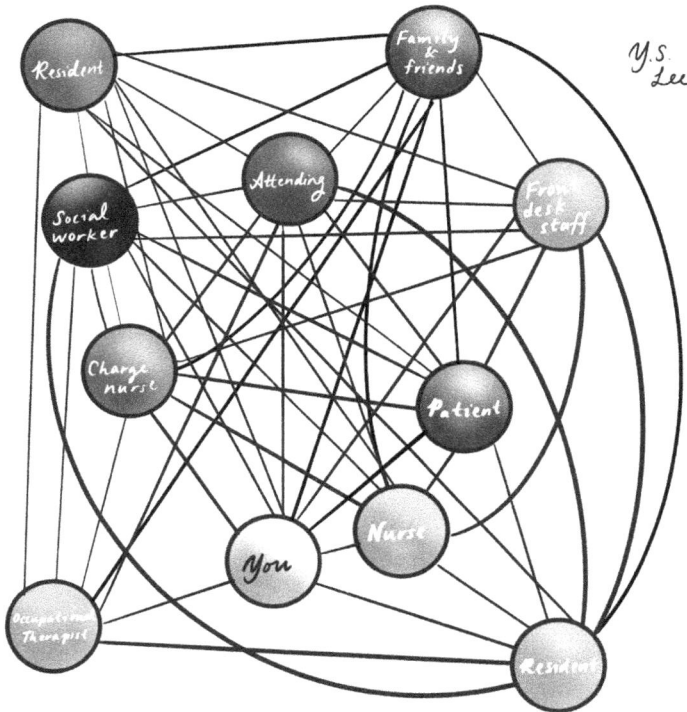

Figure: Ripple Effect of Leadership. Every interaction we have extends to the people that person subsequently interacts with.

What is the right amount of positivity? Some people will say you can overdo it and have toxic positivity, but I think that is a misconception. You obviously cannot ignore the issues you are facing as an organization, but honestly, it is hard to overdo being positive. Plus, I would make a wager that many of us would rather have a work environment that is overly positive than one that is toxic and filled with negativity.

3:1 Positivity Ratio

Going back to the work of Fredrickson, she may be most famous for her positivity ratio. Her research has led to the conclusion that people need a ratio of three positive emotions for every negative one in order to flourish and not languish.[13] Dr. Alex Niven highlighted this in his interview, stating, "I was once taught that to maintain a positive work environment, you have to say three positive things for every constructive thing that you say. I'm not sure if I'm as good at that as I would like to be, especially at home. But I think that awards and recognition are really important, and all of those things translate into that umbrella of caring."

This is an important reminder as a leader, son, father, and husband that I need to focus on positive things in order to help those in my life flourish. This is why the next chapter on gratitude is so important. It is also why the chapters on feedback, mentoring, coaching, and sponsorship are important. In fact, the other chapters in this book can all serve as catalysts for creating positivity. If we invest in others and help them see their value, purpose, and impact, they will feel pride, gratitude, and joy.

So, we are surrounded by opportunities for positivity. The key is to be intentional about bringing these opportunities to life. It's good for the people you lead, and it's good for you! The Five Actions for Positivity listed below offer ways to inject positivity into your life, the lives of others, and your organizations.

Five Caring Acts of Leadership to Catalyze Positivity

1. Battle for positivity.

We are prone to negative thoughts. Let's face it: we could have delivered a powerful presentation or done great on a test, but we often remember and focus on what didn't go as well as we would have liked or the questions we missed. We might say things like "I never get anything done," or "I am failing at work." In fact, you had a lot of patients today and helped a number of families. Consider journaling each day about the good things you get done—you might be surprised and feel better about what is left on your to-do list. Remember, your to-do list will never be empty, so give yourself credit with your "I'm Done List." Make it a point to focus on the positive. Fight the urge to focus on the negative, and tell yourself about great things you are doing. This is important for those you lead as well.

When I am coaching leaders, they tend to bring problems and issues. They don't often appreciate the amazing work they do, so I try to remind them of the many things they are doing well.

With one person I was coaching recently, we developed her leadership superpower list—her most important strengths. When we meet, I ask her about her superpowers to reinforce the great things she is doing as a leader. That acknowledgment of positivity allows her to work on other areas. Consider making your own list or having those you lead make a list of what they are already doing well.

As a leader, help those you lead fight the negativity bias and win the battle in their minds. Your job is to help them recognize the positive things they do. As leaders and people, we ultimately get to decide what story we are telling ourselves and allowing ourselves to believe. We need to win the mental battle for positivity so we can translate that into our actions and spread positivity to others.

2. Find and highlight meaning.

Spend time reflecting on the meaning in your work, and point out the meaningful work of others. Don't take for granted the amazing stuff you and your coworkers do each day. Give yourself credit. This creates positivity through the pride that people feel! Consider putting your personal purpose or vision statement on a wall in your office or in a notebook. At the end of each day, list two or three actions that support your purpose. What you will see each day is the value that you generate and how you support others to fulfill their purposes. These acts are building blocks of personal and organizational success. They may not seem like that big of a deal to you, but these acts can have huge impacts on others. End the day recognizing your impact on others! Make it a leadership habit to remind others of the impact they have as well. Let me give you an example:

> Team,
>
> Thank you! We are so busy that sometimes we forget that every interaction we have with a patient and their family is potentially one of the most important events in their life. Your devotion to patient care not only impacts them, but it impacts their families and everyone else they interact with. I just want you to know how much I appreciate the difference you are making in their lives. Don't take for granted what is routine for us. It is life-changing for them. THANK YOU for all that you do.

3. Count your blessings (at least three of them).

We have so many amazing things in our lives, yet we often focus on what we don't have. The idea behind this activity is to put the spotlight on the positive things in our lives. One activity that has gained popularity and has been studied in medicine is the "Three Good Things" exercise.[14-17] There are multiple ways to do this. It can be done online, or you could simply use a journal or cell phone to keep track. You identify three good things each day and write out what makes you feel good about each of those.

Challenge your team to identify the positive things as well. At the start of meetings, ask one of the following questions. These can be during individual or group meetings. Rather than just the perfunctory "How are you doing?" dig a little deeper with these questions. These questions also emphasize what you think is important for those you lead:

    a.   "Tell me something you are thankful for."

    b.   "Tell me something you are most proud of from this past week."

    c.   "Tell a story about a colleague in the room and how they helped you or how you saw them helping someone else."

    d.   "Tell me about a patient that you helped this week."

    e.   "Tell me how you helped a colleague this week."

    f.   "Tell me about someone you taught or mentored this week."

4. Be kind.

Recognizing your own kind acts, the kindness of others, and the power of being kind to others generates positivity. We can be intentional about building positive connections at work. Never miss an opportunity to be kind to someone. We never know when someone is really struggling and just needs someone to be kind to them. This could be holding a door for an elderly patient coming into the clinic or stopping to help someone who looks like they are lost in the hospital. It could be spending five minutes extra to give feedback to an employee or student on their performance. It could be taking time to thank someone for a job well done. It could be as simple as smiling at someone or saying hello to someone in the hall.

Consider making a kindness bingo card for your favorite acts of kindness, then crossing them off each week or month. Be creative with your list. Here are a couple of acts of kindness that I like to do: I try to ask my front desk staff how they are doing and thank them for helping me and our patients. I take the time to acknowledge and thank the cashiers in our cafeteria. I once gave a residency coin to recognize one of the food service workers and thank him for always being so upbeat and kind to people. I loved seeing him each day because he brightened my day, and I wanted him to know it. Buy a gift card when checking out at the grocery store and give it to the cashier to thank them for their work. Give a large tip (you can decide what counts as "large") to your server or delivery driver.

Imagine how much more kindness there will be in the world if each person who reads this book takes on such a challenge. (I am hoping that is a lot, because it means people are reading the book!)

5. Get outside.

My colleague and fellow infectious diseases physician Dr. Carlie Cerne did a Medicine Grand Rounds on the importance of being out in nature as a source of positive emotion:

Being outside in nature makes me feel connected to the earth that we all belong to. Recognizing one belongs to something greater than oneself can be a powerful tool in wellness. Nature has long been recognized for its healing properties, evidenced by restorative gardens being established in infirmaries during the Middle Ages and industrial city parks being constructed in the 1800s to reduce disease. Aristotle used to hold meetings in nature so he could be present with a clear head. When I feel connected to nature, my stress melts away. I feel healthier, happier, more relaxed, more mindful, and I always try to encourage my patients and peers to get outside more to reap these benefits.

Are we busy? Yes. Do I have time to go outside? Yes; at a minimum, we have to go outside to go to work. According to Fredrickson, as little as twenty minutes outside each day can increase positivity and allow one to have more open thinking.[18] The next time you decide to read this book, sit outside to do it. Park farther from your office and get a short walk in. Make it a habit to walk outside while talking to friends or family on the phone. Consider holding meetings outside or even holding a meeting while walking outside. Sit outside and think about what acts of kindness you have seen, what you are grateful for, and the purpose and value of your work. If nothing else, being outside will give you a boost in your vitamin D levels!

Energy Killers

As mentioned earlier, you can be someone who energizes a room or someone who sucks the energy from it. Author Jon Gordon, in the book *The Energy Bus,* calls these people "Energy Vampires."[19] He recommends posting a sign in your workspaces that says, "No Energy Vampires Allowed."[20]

I had a chief resident, Dr. Melanie Wiseman, who had the ability to bring energy to every situation. She was passionate about patient care and teaching—and it showed—but she was perhaps even more enthusiastic about helping trainees grow as physicians and leaders. She was the type of person who always made people feel excited. Hopefully, you know a few of these people. You probably also know a few people who when you see them, you suddenly find yourself bracing for their negativity.

The good news is that we get to choose the type of energy we bring to work and to home each day. This is not always easy, but recognizing the importance of being positive because of its impact on others has changed my perspective on more than one occasion. Whenever I feel myself starting to lean toward cynicism or start to complain, I try to remember that others are feeding off of my energy and watching my behavior closely. I attempt to transition to a more positive outlook. I want to be that person whom people see as a positive force of energy.

In his book *The Power of Positive Leadership,* Gordon provides a compelling argument for being a caring, positive leader.[21] He writes, "Positivity leads to winning."[22] How do leaders play a role? According to Gordon, "Positive leaders care about the people they lead...Because they care, they do more, give more, encourage more, help more, guide more, mentor more, develop more, build more, and ultimately accomplish more."[23] This takes time, as Gordon points out: "Unity, relationships, and teamwork are developed slowly, one day; one interaction; one moment; one loving, serving, and caring act at a time."[24]

Since you are reading this book, presumably you want to be this type of caring leader. Start with simple Caring Acts of Leadership in every interaction.

Obstacles or Opportunities

The benefits of positivity extend to the organizational level. In medicine and life, we don't get to choose the challenges we face, but we can always choose how we respond. We can look at them as obstacles, or we can see them as opportunities for success and for learning. One of the things I must remind myself of when leading is that every challenge I am facing is preparing me for future challenges. Sometimes I need this reminder because the current situation stinks.

Our job as leaders is to help people see challenges as opportunities and paint a picture of a brighter future. Often, the biggest barriers or challenges present us with our most unique and rewarding opportunities. One of my favorite quotes is "Never let a good crisis go to waste," which is attributed to Winston Churchill.[25] More recently, President Obama's Chief of Staff and later Chicago Mayor, Rahm Emanuel, used the quote: "You never want a serious crisis to go to waste. What I mean by that, it's an opportunity to do things you could not do before."[26] When something bad happens, there is opportunity in that situation to improve, innovate, and learn.

Let me give you an example that will resonate with many of you. Suppose you are in a residency training program and you have a shortage of support staff to schedule appointments. Consequently, that task has fallen on residents. You have brought this up to hospital leadership to no avail. When your program receives a citation from the Accreditation Council for Graduate Medical Education, all of a sudden you have a crisis, and the hospital is willing to put the resources into fixing the problem. It would be nice if it did not require a duty-hours violation to get needed resources, but the crisis provides the opportunity. Need resources that have not been given to your nurses? An imminent Joint Commission visit is an opportune time to ask for them again.

One method of seeing challenges as opportunities is to reframe the situation. A valuable exercise to do with people is reframing leadership challenges. I learned this from Page Morahan, PhD, who was the founding director of the Executive Leadership in Academic Medicine (ELAM) program. This is a terrific exercise to do with your team to help them practice seeing opportunities and not obstacles. The exercise is done by having each person identify one challenge they are facing. The challenge is then given to another person, who must reframe it into an opportunity.

Here are two examples:

Example 1

Person A: We lost our front desk staff for the clinic and must hire someone else.

Person B: We get to hire new front desk staff and can use their orientation to teach them about our values, culture, and best practices for managing the front desk.

Example 2

Person A: One of our employees is really struggling with time management.

Person B: We have a great opportunity to help this employee with time management skills that will benefit them for the rest of their career.

When I teach reframing, I pair it with the Stockdale Paradox, made famous by Jim Collins in the book *Good to Great*.[27] Admiral James Stockdale was one of the longest-held prisoners of the Vietnam War in the infamous "Hanoi Hilton." He always believed he would "get out...and prevail in the end"; it just may not be today.[28] He described how other prisoners would get their hopes up about being set free on holidays—and when they were not, some lost hope and died. The Stockdale Paradox, as described by Collins, was to have unwavering optimism for the future while confronting the brutal facts of today.[29] Being transparent about problems and not sugarcoating the real issues builds trust with those you lead. You can be positive in the face of uncomfortable facts.

The Hittable Problem

How do we approach the obstacles that life sends our way? One of my favorite quotes is by Stoic author Ryan Holiday, who said, "Leaders are dealers in hope."[30] Our job as leaders is to help people see a bright and possible future. We must help them see what they can't see so that we can get them there. Dr. Wiley Souba writes about this in an article titled "Hittability: The Leader's Edge."[31] He had the chance to talk to baseball legend Ted Williams—who was the last Major League Baseball player to have a 0.400 average, back in 1941! Souba asked Williams what his key to success was, and Williams replied, "I don't know. The ball just shows up as hittable."[32] I wish I could bottle that skill for my baseball-player son. Souba's lesson was that as leaders, we need to frame problems as hittable. Many times, the people we work with are so focused on the problem that they cannot see the way to success. They may not believe it is possible. Your job as the leader is to help them reframe that belief and give them the confidence needed to move forward.

Major General Jeff Clark, former chief of the Army Medical Corps, was a master at this. He used to say that "leaders lead through change. It's going to be okay." In fact, he said it so often at times that at one point, I started to think he had dementia. What I found, though, was that I was repeating these phrases to those I was leading myself. It dawned on me that his overcommunicating the message had its intended impact, which was to get all of us to buy into the message and have faith that things were going to be okay. Leaders have to show to those we lead a brighter future and communicate that the problem we are facing is hittable. Never underestimate the power of a leader's positive outlook.

Major General Jeffrey Clark shared this lesson, which nicely summarizes this chapter: "If you are the leader, you set the tone—whether you're intending to or not. You just do."

Prescription for Caring in Leadership

1. Take five minutes now and think about everything positive you have at work and at home. Reflect on these things at least once a week, but ideally daily. Add to the list as things evolve.

2. Encourage someone on your team this week—pick someone who you think might least expect it.

3. Take the Positivity Test by Dr. Barbara Fredrickson at https://www.positivityratio.com/single.php and think about how you can be more positive.[33]

4. Commit to implementing one or more of the Five Actions for Positivity.

5. Practice reframing problems/challenges as opportunities. Do this exercise with your team or direct report.

6. Post a "No Energy Vampires Allowed"[34] sign on or near your desk to remind you and others in your workspace of the impact of negativity.

7. Pause when problems arise and ask yourself and your team what new opportunities there may be because of the challenge.

8. Read one of the books mentioned above or the article by Dr. Wiley Souba on hittability[35] to learn more about how to battle for positivity.

CHAPTER 22

Care Enough to Say Thank You

"Appreciation can make a day—even
change a life. Your willingness to put it
into words is all that is necessary."
—Margaret Cousins

MEDICINE AND SOCIETY ARE facing an ever-growing pandemic. The issue is resulting in burnout and many people in medicine feeling devalued. The diagnosis is "gratitudopenia." Data suggests that up to "65% of Americans received no recognition in the workplace last year."[1] Many healthcare providers do amazing, life-changing, and lifesaving work, yet are never thanked. I have seen this numerous times.

A colleague told me that despite working for a hospital for several years, no one there had ever thanked her for the work she did. Imagine taking care of hundreds, even thousands, of patients and never having someone from the leadership team give you a personal thank-you. Imagine teaching countless students and never being thanked. Imagine cleaning hundreds of patient rooms or delivering innumerable patient meals thanklessly. Unfortunately, many of you may not just be imagining this. A recent poll by Gallup reported that "only 23% of employees strongly agree that they get the right amount of recognition for the work they do."[2]

We need to make gratitude a priority to be leaders who care. I would encourage you to watch the TED Talk "Everyday Leadership" by Drew Dudley, which currently has over six million views.[3] At least 100 are by me, because it's worth watching multiple times. It was life-changing. The video recounts how when he worked at a small college, he had an interaction with a student during the orientation period.[4] Years later, she found him to thank him for it. She had decided she was not going to go to college, but then he did something the morning of their interaction to change her entire perspective on the school, and it had resulted in her deciding to stay. The event also resulted in her meeting her future husband.[5] Profound! As he tells the story, he does not even remember the event. The lesson is that every day, we have interactions that can alter someone's life forever, but we don't recognize them. Dudley calls these "lollipop moments."[6]

As leaders and humans, we need to be better about helping others know the value and meaning they have had in our lives. If someone has done something that you are eternally grateful for, don't you want them to know that? If they cared about you and you care about them, shouldn't the expectation be that you let them know? Watch the video, and then make a list of everyone you need to go back and thank. Then, make thanking people a habit moving forward.

A few of my colleagues and I have spoken on this topic before, and it is always amazing to hear these lollipop moment stories. I want to highlight one, because I think it emphasizes the lesson and demonstrates that you don't have to be in a position of power to make a life-changing difference. At one meeting, we asked for "lollipop moment" examples. A fourth-year medical student said that the year prior, she had spent a ton of time with one particular patient. The patient had obesity and was in an abusive relationship. The patient worked at a fast food restaurant and was eating two burgers an hour while on shift. The student, because she had time and cared about her, spent time talking to the patient. She told her that she should consider finding a new job and get out of the relationship because neither were good for her. About a year later, the student was in line at Subway, and the cashier said, "You don't remember me?" The student was puzzled and said no. The cashier at Subway then recounted how the student had taken so much time with her when she was admitted and had given her advice. The patient had taken the advice: she changed her job to Subway, changed her eating habits, and got out of her relationship. The patient had lost a significant amount of weight and was feeling much better about herself. The student had made an enormous impact on this patient's life, and she would never have known had she not happened to go to Subway that day.

We cannot change the fact that we will not know the impact we have on everyone we meet and every interaction. Yet, we can be intentional about thanking as many people as possible for the ways they impact our lives and the lives of others. Major General Jeffrey Clark pointed this out:

> *"Actively look for opportunities to say thank you," and "Never pass up an opportunity to say thank you."— Retired Major General Jeffrey Clark*

He added, "Saying thank you is especially important for our unsung heroes—those who work at our front desks, lab, pharmacy,

X-ray, housekeeping, patient records, and admin sections. I never walked by a front desk without stopping to speak and say thank you."

The Value of Gratitude

There shouldn't need to be a monetary reason to thank people, but for those who think this will take too much time and question the return on investment, the data is clear that gratitude has a positive impact on the workplace environment. In their book, *Nine Lies About Work: A Freethinking Leader's Guide to the Real World*, Marcus Buckingham and Ashley Goodall argue that "positive attention is 30 times more powerful than negative attention in creating high performance on a team."[7-9]

Not only does gratitude increase morale and performance, it can also lead to less employee turnover and decrease the rate of burnout. In their book *Encouraging the Heart*, Kouzes and Posner highlight some of the data that support these claims.[10] A survey they did reported that a simple thank-you "was the most important non-financial award someone can get at work."[11] More recent work by Adam Grant and Francesca Gino demonstrated that a simple thank-you can increase effort at work by 50 percent.[12] In the book *How Full Is Your Bucket?*, Rath and Clifton report that in a survey of over 15 million employees, they found "regular recognition and praise" led to increased productivity, increased engagement, increased job retention, increased customer satisfaction, and improved job safety.[13]

Maybe you think this data does not apply to medicine. Well, the work by Stanford Chief Wellness Officer Dr. Tait Shanafelt suggests otherwise. His research on the impact of leadership demonstrated that the simple act of recognizing others for a job well done decreases burnout by 17 percent and improves job satisfaction by 39 percent.[14] That is an impressive return on investment for showing how much you care about someone and the work that they do. Saying thank you is a spark that ignites good performance.

The other important point about thanking people is that you are emphasizing what is important to you and your culture. A thank-you reinforces your organizational values and the behaviors you desire. Saying thank you is positive feedback and not just an act of gratitude. When you see someone doing something that is a core value, thank them for it. Point it out. By doing this repeatedly, it makes it obvious what is valued and what the culture should be. Creating culture is not magic but intentionally working at it. In the book *The Culture Code*, Daniel Coyle writes that we should "overdo thank-yous."[15] He states, "This is because thank-yous aren't only expressions of gratitude; they're crucial belonging cues that generate a contagious sense of safety, connection, and motivation."[16] Saying thank you is a building block to the culture you want in your organization.

> *Saying thank you is a spark that ignites good performance.*

Ways to Thank People

Hopefully, you are convinced that thanking people needs to become one of your core activities. This goes for work and home! But if thanking people is important, then how do we do this effectively? In Appendix D, I have put a Gratitude Prescription for you to use. I will also review a few specific examples below. Post it somewhere and track what you are doing. This needs to become an intentional daily habit—just like taking other prescriptions.

Have you ever gotten a handwritten thank-you card? I have every single card someone has written for me in a file in my desk drawer. There are some days when I pull them out just to read them. On rough days, those notes of encouragement are like a jolt of energy. A reminder of why we do what we do. Dr. Chuck Callahan said, "Become a writer of notes." He recounted a story of when he was a junior officer in the military and had published a paper in a leading pediatrics journal. He got a letter in the mail from General Scottie, the Medical Corps Commander at the time. He was blown away that a general officer would take the time to recognize his article and write him a brief note. He still has that letter, and it resulted in him writing hundreds—if not thousands—of thank-you notes over the course of his career.

Writing thank-you cards is an easy way to make a huge impact on those you lead. I would encourage you to have some in your desk at all times, so when you want to thank someone, the barrier of getting a card is not an issue. I buy them in boxes of 50 or 100. Another thing we have done is put them in places at work so that anyone can grab one. Put them in your main administrative office, front desk, break room, or team rooms so that, as needed, people can pick one up and write. Imagine: at the end of shift, the floor nurse takes the time to write a thank-you card to a custodial staff member for the work he or she did in quickly cleaning a room. Maybe you see a note passed on from a busy resident thanking a nurse for correcting a mistake on an order the resident made, teaching him or her a lesson and doing it in a kind way. The moments are there for capturing, highlighting, and thanking!

What do these thank-you cards mean to people? There was a nurse practitioner who worked near my old office. We were in completely different departments, so I only knew her because our offices were close to each other. She worked hard, often staying late into the evening. (We both obviously need better work-life balance, but that is not the point of this story.) Recognizing how hard she worked, I wrote her a thank-you card. The card was short, and the message was simple. I told her that I noticed how hard she worked and that I appreciated what she did for her patients and our organization. I gave her the card and walked back to my office. A short while later, she appeared at my door with tears in her eyes. She was so grateful and wanted me to know how much she appreciated me thanking her and noticing her efforts. It took me less than ten minutes to completely change her day, maybe her week, maybe her life. She seems to smile more every time I see her now. No one in healthcare should not feel valued for the work they do. Every one of us has the ability to change this paradigm.

Texts or Emails of Gratitude

Not only can you write thank-you cards, but you can send text messages or emails. Personal thank-you cards seem to carry more meaning, but that does not mean we should not use multiple different methods of communicating gratitude. The goal is to catch people doing great things and recognize those things. Make them personal and specific—remember, this is *positive* feedback. Emails and texts tend to be a little less personal, given they take less time to write than a thank-you card. I like to use these to give almost immediate feedback when I see something or to randomly surprise someone with gratitude. The beauty of a text in particular is you can send it and the person will get it immediately. An example might be that you watch someone give a presentation and you text them to say, "Wow! You totally crushed that presentation. It was so valuable to me. I learned several new things and wanted you to know what a great teacher and facilitator you are! Thanks for making us all better!"

A colleague, Dr. Joe Maciuba, is an internal medicine residency program director. He developed a "Reasons to Celebrate" email that he sends out each month. The email tries to capture all the great things that residents and faculty do. It highlights academic accomplishments as well as those related to leadership, service to the community, and well-being. These are things he sees as important parts of the residency culture. It shines a spotlight of gratitude on the impact of the residents and faculty.

I had an intern, Ruth Reese, who was working incredibly long hours, but she was able to spend her spare time volunteering at her church and handing out COVID supplies to inner-city Baltimore. I sent her an email thanking her for modeling leadership and serving others. As a program, our vision was "Developing Military Medical Corps Officers to Transform American Medicine." These acts were helping to transform her community, so I wanted her to know how much I appreciated it. I am sure she did these things without the need for any additional motivation, but I think all of us appreciate feeling valued.

Gifts of Gratitude

Generally, gifts are reserved for special occasions; however, giving a gift can turn any time into a special occasion, so be creative when being grateful. There are so many different gifts and tokens of appreciation that can be given. One important point highlighted in two of my favorite books, *Encourage the Heart*[17] and *How Full Is Your Bucket?*,[18] is that gifts should be personalized. Think beyond plaques, although these can be nice as well. Make the gift special and unique to what the individual values. (Honestly, you just need to read those two books, as both will change your life and the lives of those you lead.)

A few years ago, I worked with a chief resident, Dr. Melanie Wiseman. Chief residents work incredibly hard and long hours. She was a huge fan of Kim Scott, the author of *Radical Candor*.[19] I reached out to Kim, and she was incredibly gracious and inscribed a book directly to Melanie. The gift meant a lot to her, and she was honored that we made an effort to do something to personally recognize her. When I retired from the Army, a group of graduating residents and the incoming chief residents gifted me with a Terrible Towel sign by retired Steelers quarterback Ben Roethlisberger that included a note from the Roethlisberger family thanking me for my service. They also gave me a leather journal with notes from all the people I had led and what that leadership had meant in their careers. These gifts were incredibly thoughtful and meant so much to me, because they showed that my investment in those I led had made a difference.

Awards of Gratitude

Some organizations may have recurring awards that they give on a similar time frame (monthly, yearly, etc). These awards emphasize what you value within your organization. I would encourage you to think about ways to increase the number and frequency of awards. There is a gap in recognition, and our job as leaders is to fill that gap and help people feel valued.

> *There is a gap in recognition, and our job as leaders is to fill that gap and help people feel valued.*

One tradition in the military is giving out Commander's Coins. These are special coins designed by the commander and given to people for excellence. Receiving a coin is considered a tremendous honor. Dr. Greg Argyros, president of

MedStar Washington Hospital Center, and Dr. Charles Callahan, vice president at University of Maryland, have carried this tradition to their organizations after leaving the Army.

Dr. Callahan and retired Colonel Dr. Jim Ficke, the chair of orthopedics at Johns Hopkins, were chosen by their institutions to lead the state's "Baltimore Convention Center Field Hospital" for COVID treatment, testing, and vaccination. Dr. Ficke designed a coin that the two directors funded, which became a treasured symbol of excellence for those who received it from the thousands employed by the hospital during the pandemic.

Dr. Argyros and his team at Washington Hospital Center (WHC) have created a multitude of innovative ways of recognizing excellence as well. They have shout-out awards that go to teams for great saves or teams that demonstrate exceptional teamwork. They have SPIRIT awards for individuals who exemplify the values of WHC: "Spirit is the acronym for the fundamental elements of performance at MedStar: Service, Patient First, Innovation, Respect, and Trust." Dr. Argyros said the majority of these go to non-clinicians. He provided the following example of someone given an award based on a nomination from the Chief of Vascular Surgery:

> A patient came in for her post-op visit. She didn't want to talk about her care. She wanted to talk about someone she had an interaction with. She had surgery, and there was some reason she was going to need to stay a couple of days beyond what was expected. She was very sad. The environmental services employee who had cleaned her room heard her crying. He didn't ignore that person crying. He went in and said, "What's going on?" She explained she was sad because she was having to stay a few more days, and he said, "What can I do?" She said, "I'd love a chocolate cupcake." He went and got a chocolate cupcake and brought it to her. For the rest of her hospitalization, he brought her a chocolate cupcake every day. That's what she wanted to tell the vascular surgeon. She wanted this guy to be recognized. So, I did. We did it in front of his department. The people are so humble, and they're wowed by this.

Continually looking for ways to recognize people and make it a part of their culture, Washington Hospital Center started using an app called Wambi.[20] According to the company, the word means "to express gratitude for a special moment shared between people."[21] The app allows clinicians, non-clinicians, and even patients and family members to message someone to say thank you for a job well done. The app also filters out negative comments so it cannot be used to send negative messages. It has been really effective, according to Dr. Argyros:

> Wambi is a way to recognize people for small acts that they've done. It's quick, as it is an app on your phone. You can say, "Josh, I just saw you with a patient. You were wonderful, great job." It comes to you immediately. It's a way to give instant recognition every day, multiple times a day, to people. You know there is the need for positive reinforcement all the time, and those are just ways in which you can do it. The coin is the

highest level, but all these other ones are critically important. We get to recognize people formally hundreds of times a year. Wambi, we just started in June, and it's going like wildfire. Patients can give it. Teammates can send them to each other. It's just a way to meet that need for positive reinforcement.

Whether it is a coin, a pin, or some other symbol of excellence, be creative and work toward intentional methods of supporting your culture and recognizing your people. Use multiple methods and consider different tiers for impact. The simple act of thanking people is one of the most underused yet most powerful leadership tools.

Nominating for Awards

One of my all-time favorite quotes from Mrs. Stephanie Colón, who works for the Office of the Surgeon General as the Deputy G-1/4/6 (personnel, logistics, and strategy), is "I have award-winning people who work for me. Do you know why? Because I take the time to write them up for awards when they deserve them."[22]

This was part of the U.S. Army Junior Officer Leader Course that Dr. John Blickle, a former chief resident of mine, took. It is so true.

I am a little hesitant to write this next part, because I don't want to give away this secret, but it's worth sharing: there are often few nominations for awards, at every level. I have been part of committees for local-, regional-, and national-level awards, and there are many times when fewer than five people are nominated. Imagine working in a hospital with hundreds of faculty, and only a couple of people are nominated—or being part of a national organization with thousands, maybe hundreds of thousands, of members and only a few people being nominated. Three important points to take away from this: First, win or lose, who does not feel incredibly proud and valued to be nominated by peers, superiors, or subordinates for an award? For this reason, I have tried to make it a habit of giving the nomination letter to the person we nominated, whether they win or lose—that way, they can see how much we value their efforts. Second, the person may win, which of course is wonderful. Finally, you are emphasizing how important these behaviors are to the individual and others in the organization.

If you are nominating someone for an award, it is because you care about them and want to recognize them. Please do not ask them to write the nomination. This might just be me, but this says, "I care about you, but not enough to take the time to write your award." You can ask for their input and what to highlight, but *you* should write the nomination. Awards take time, so as a leader, you may want to work with your team to split up who writes nominations. Ideally, the award nomination comes from the person who will have the most impact with the awards selection committee. You might ghostwrite an award and have your program director, department chair, chief nursing officer, or hospital CEO submit the nomination. This is a good way to get people's names and accomplishments in front of senior leadership. As a senior leader, make it a point to not only recognize your people but let those who you lead know that you are willing to help nominate more junior people in your organization. This connects you with the front lines.

Create Awards as a Leader

From an organizational standpoint, leaders should take an inventory of the awards they have and think about how they could expand their awards and recognition programs. If you are in a position of leadership, you have the ability to create new awards. If you are not, then you can suggest this to those in leadership. While only one or a few may be able to be recognized each year, this adds up over time—and nominating someone helps them feel valued.

What awards does your organization currently have? What are you specifically recognizing? Remember, part of the purpose of awards—and saying thank you—is to emphasize and encourage the behaviors that you want to see more of. Having a dedicated award for a specific behavior or action demonstrates that that behavior or action is important to the organization. You are emphasizing what you want the culture of your organization to be like.

It is important to think about who receives awards at your institution. The data is clear that in most institutions, awards go to white men more often than any other groups. I am not going to go through all the data, but it is consistent across almost every specialty in medicine. Check out the work of Dr. Julie Silver from Harvard, if you want to see the data.[23] Examine who wins awards, and think about diversity when nominating—potentially, create awards to recognize diversity. For example, I know of groups that have created specific awards for Women Leaders in Medicine or Best Faculty for Diversity, Equity, and Inclusion. The answer is not just to give those specific awards to underrepresented individuals but rather to think more broadly about equity in all awards processes.

If you have teaching awards, could you have more? Instead of just the top teacher, what about the best inpatient teacher, the best outpatient teacher, best overall teacher, best junior faculty, best senior faculty, or most impactful lecture of the year? What about instead of just one awardee, you have the Top Five or Ten Teachers? You could have the same level of awards for mentoring. What about taking the time to recognize individuals in your organization who sponsor others? I have yet to see a specific award dedicated to being a sponsor, but it is on my list to create. (Please let us know if you are doing this and how!)

What awards do you have for your trainees? What is important to you as a program and as a hospital? You should have an award for each individual thing: clinical care, bedside manner, teaching, leadership, research, quality improvement, advocacy, volunteerism, and diversity, equity, and inclusion.

Think about unique awards given from each department as well. This includes things like the Brown Finger Award given by the Gastroenterology Service (you can guess why it is called "Brown Finger"—this is why a good bowel prep is important) or the Golden Sputum Award given by the Pulmonary Department. My wife won the Golden Calipers Award for electrocardiogram reading when she was a resident—twenty years later, she is still proud of that accomplishment. While giving a presentation at the International Conference on Resident Education, a participant said their residency program gives out the Sunshine Award to the resident who always brightens the room and lives of others. I want this person to work with me! These awards are fun and meaningful to those who receive them.

Some individuals are so good that they could win these awards every year. While we want to continue to encourage them and support the amazing work they do, we should share the wealth. Awards should have a lockout period so you cannot win it more than once every three to five years, or maybe after you have won it twice, you are ineligible to win it again. For some awards, you can only win it once. For these folks, think about nominating them for regional or national awards. If someone is really a standout and legend at your institution, you could consider naming an award after them. It is a way to recognize them for a lifetime of work, and then to recognize others.

How are nurses recognized within your institution? Is a nurse from each floor recognized each month? How are nominations received, and are they given to the nurses to let them know how appreciated they are, win or lose?

To support teamwork and interprofessional relationships, consider having awards given to those outside your group. For example, a residency program may recognize a clinic and inpatient nurse each month who supports residents the most. Nurses may pick a resident physician who best supports and communicates most effectively with nursing staff.

Let's think broadly. How are our pharmacists, physical therapists, radiation oncology technicians, front desk staff, etc., recognized? How do you help the cleaning staff and garage attendants feel valued for the important role they play?

What am I missing? Make a list of all the awards you have, then review them and consider what gaps you might have for different people, professions, and behaviors.

In this chapter, we have talked about the issue of gratitudopenia. We have highlighted numerous ways to demonstrate gratitude as ways to thank people for their impactful work and to reinforce the behaviors we want in our organizations.

My challenge to you: make gratitude your leadership superpower!

Prescription for Caring in Leadership

1. Reflect on what you are grateful for and who you are grateful for.

2. Send a thank-you card to someone who has done something meaningful for you in your life.

3. Send a random text message to someone to thank them. Now, before you continue reading!

4. Show up unannounced to a team meeting and thank the team.

5. Send an email to an unexpecting person and thank them for their role in the organization.

6. Nominate someone for an award.

7. Create a new award for your organization.

8. Develop ways to recognize people for daily actions of excellence and actions that are important to your organization.
   a. Coins
   b. Pins
   c. Wambi

CHAPTER 23

Care About Your Legacy

"Memories of our lives, of our works, and
our deeds will continue in others."
—Rosa Parks

HOW DO YOU WANT to be remembered? Take a moment and seriously think about what you want people to say about you at the end of your career. What about at your funeral? In the book *Road to Character*, David Brooks talks about whether you are working for your CV or your eulogy.[1] Many of us in healthcare have been with people at the end of their lives. Many of us have been with family members or patients who have died. The main focus at these times is not about the amount of money made or individual accomplishments—at the end of our careers and life, it is always about the impact we had on others.

If you care as a leader, then it's ultimately not about you but about those you lead. Major General Clark emphasized this point: "It's not about you...it's about mission and people. I was given the privilege of serving in leadership positions to care about the mission and people."

How will your leadership and life look through those two lenses? Did you care for your people? Did you care about and accomplish the mission?

Our work in medicine and our mission are of incredible importance. They have lifesaving and life-altering value. We should be proud of our accomplishments and the amazing work we do, whether that is in patient care, teaching, or research. Strive to be remembered for how your work served the greater good and how, through your work, you made the lives of patients, trainees, and those you worked with better. Every day in healthcare, we have the unique opportunity to add value to the lives of others.

Our legacies as leaders extend beyond our patient care and other accomplishments to the impact on those that we led. There is a ripple effect, as every person we have led impacts others, creating an enormous impact and legacy. For many, this means thousands over the course of their career. The return on investment from caring as a leader is a legacy of future caring leaders. For example, if you are a charge nurse and you teach a new nurse how to more effectively communicate with a physician, that nurse will use those skills thousands of times in their career.

Dr. Chuck Callahan talked about how we are ultimately a "tapestry of the stories of people we have been leading...we become a thread of their tapestry." There is a story written about one of the most successful college football coaches of all time, Nick Saban, in which the author talks about his recruiting poster.[2] Coach Saban's success is not about the championships won but the lives changed among all the individuals he coached over the years. What an honor to be part of the lives of those we lead. Care about and invest in those you lead, and your tapestry and recruiting poster will shine brightly for eternity!

One of the reasons I wanted to be a program director and train young physicians was because I loved the idea of impacting the way they would care for patients, teach, and lead throughout their careers. When we as leaders teach one person, those lessons impact not just them but the exponential number of people they interact with in the future. Our investment in leading is one of the most impactful things we can do as humans. I hope this makes you excited about the impact of your legacy as a leader.

Dr. Caroline Blackie talked about the importance of caring as a leader when thinking about her legacy. She described the importance of developing caring leaders as part of how she wants to be remembered:

> I can tell you some of the things that I consider a measure of success. I would like for every individual that I have had the opportunity to lead to have comprehensively incorporated that the essence of what it means to lead is to care for those for whom you are responsible. Caring is not lip service. It means touching their lives in a positive way that can be articulated and that is meaningful to them—not to me, to them...Compassion, caring, open-hearted communication, and decision-making. These are the essence of what it means to lead. There is a dearth of resources on this. Over the course of my career, if my people can incorporate caring-inspired leadership and make it their own, they will all be outstanding leaders in life. Being cared for changes who you are, at the cellular level, and it changes you for good. It's magic! It would be thrilling for me if my people all knew that they were cared for, seen, appreciated, valued for everything they brought to the table. I would love for this to be my legacy.

What would medicine look like if we all worked to develop other caring leaders? This is not magic. This is about the hard and intentional work of being a caring leader. If we care about the people we lead and our legacies as leaders, we cannot leave our leadership up to chance. We have to invest in becoming the most effective leaders we can be. This means being students of leadership and taking advantage of the lessons in this book to care about those we lead. If you do that, people may describe your leadership as magical.

In the previous chapters, we talked about tactical steps you can take as a leader to demonstrate caring for those you lead. If you follow the prescriptions for caring in leadership, you will be investing in those you lead and your organizations. Over time, those investments will build influence for you as a leader, and people will look to you as someone who made them better. Someone who helped shape their life. There is no greater investment you can make as a leader and person than in someone else. Each of them then goes on to impact countless others at work and at home.

Brigadier General Clint Murray and Dr. Darilyn Moyer have both had tremendously successful careers. They highlight the fact that investing in those you lead will define part of your legacy. Dr. Moyer has led over 170,000 physicians and shaped the way internal medicine is delivered, nationally and globally. Yet, when asked about her legacy, she said without hesitation that it was about building up and investing in those she led. Her answer is a model of the legacy of a caring leader:

> *"The hallmark of a good leader? You have to care more about the people that you're shepherding than about yourself. It's not what's on my CV but what is on the CVs of the folks whom I've coached, mentored, and sponsored along the way... Leave the place better than you found it. That's what legacy is."— Dr. Darilyn Moyer*

While talking about career success in military medicine, BG Murray similarly stated, "Your legacy through mentoring likely has a more lasting impact on military medicine than anything else you do."

This speaks volumes about the impact of caring about the careers of those you lead, given the fact that BG Murray has risen to the rank of general officer, become a full professor, and published over 300 papers in his illustrious career. The impact on those you lead and how you invest in them lasts well beyond your other achievements.

I will end this chapter on a personal note. I have thought a lot about how I want to be remembered. I hope those I have worked with and touched throughout my life will say that I cared about them and that I helped them get better as a teacher, leader, and person. If I positively impacted their lives and they remember me for that, then I will feel like I accomplished my mission. When I retired from the Army in 2023, my internal medicine residents bought a commemorative stone that was placed in the courtyard at my medical school, the Uniformed Services University. The stone had my name and said, "Coach, Mentor, and Caring Leader." I feel blessed to think I am on the right track, but I know there is still much work to be done investing in others. What do you want your commemorative stone to say?

Hopefully, this book will have a positive impact on those of you who read it and on the hundreds or thousands of people who you will lead throughout your lives. May my legacy be that of a Caring Leader.

Prescription for Caring in Leadership

1. Write your retirement speech or eulogy. Think about what you would want people to say about you at the end of your career. Reflect on where you are at achieving this and what actions it would take to get closer to meeting that goal.

2. Make up an award in your honor. What would it be about?

3. Read *The Last Lecture* by Randy Pausch.[3]

4. Watch the TED Talk or read the book or *Harvard Business Review* article "How Will You Measure Your Life?" by Clayton Christensen.[4]

Epilogue

"We all have that moment where we need to connect with another person. As a leader and as a follower, everybody needs that, and I think that we have lost that around me. We have lost that in healthcare. I'm hopeful that my n-of-one, a small drop in the ocean, can fix that."
—Suzanna Fitzpatrick, DNP, CRNP

M Y HOPE IS THAT everyone reading this book will feel as though they can and will make a difference. A generation of caring leaders can transform healthcare and medical education. Imagine the impact of thousands—if not hundreds of thousands—of caring leaders.

Let's not imagine it. Let's make it reality.

I began this book talking about the need for effective leaders. General Omar Bradley, famous World War II military commander, was talking to a group of military leaders and told them, "Leadership is intangible," and nothing can take its place.[1] My friend and colleague Dr. Jessica Servey always says that at the heart of most problems in medicine is "a leadership issue." Without hesitation, I agree with both.

In all arenas of life, we need effective leaders. We need leaders who care deeply about those they lead and their organizations. Knowing you finished this book, I can confidently say that you are one of those leaders. The ideas in this book—the prescriptions for caring in leadership —provide a way ahead to be a caring leader. Every day, you get the opportunity to make a difference in someone's life. If you care, you know what you have to do. Follow these prescriptions to build compassion and excellence within medicine.

It's your move.

Lead with caring—someone's life depends on it.

Acknowledgments

WRITING A BOOK HAS been an incredible journey—one that is accomplished not just by me as the author but by everyone who has supported me or inspired me during this journey. I want to first thank my Lord and Savior Jesus Christ. My foundation of caring is based on my faith and serving others. Thank you to my family for always loving me and supporting my dreams. Suzette, thank you for letting me hole up in the basement for almost two years and believing in me! Thank you for being an example of a caring leader. Dad, we have come a long way from where it all started in rural Pennsylvania. Jer, keep being a model caring leader in your arena. Grandma Pat, thank you for inspiring me, keeping my mom's legacy alive, and reminding me of how proud she would be. My mom was a caring leader, and the lessons she taught continue to guide me.

I will forever be grateful to those who allowed me to interview them for this book. Each of them shared their valuable time and wisdom. Many of them I did not know, and they were so gracious and willing to help. What I shared from the interviews in the book is only a small portion of what I learned from them. I want you to know I will forever hold each of you in a special place in my heart. You are all exemplary caring leaders!

I would love to thank all the caring leaders whom I have had the opportunity to know and work with in my life. So many of them invested in me and their leadership and legacy in part of this book. My American Legion baseball coach, Darryl Jones, taught me more than he will ever know. I have already highlighted Greg Argyros in this book, but it is worth repeating: he is a tremendous caring leader and had a profound impact on my life. Brian Cuneo demonstrated to me how taking care of your people is always the priority. Glenn Wortmann taught me about infectious diseases and showed me how to develop and sponsor others. Louis Pangaro led by example—I learned many lessons from him, including those in the book. Jessica Servey has taught me so many things about leading and just how important leadership is within healthcare. She helped me think in new ways and think about strategic ways to invest in those we lead. Lisa Moores taught me how to care about people and invest in them. Steve Durning shows me almost daily how to lead and invest in others. Lieutenant General Eric Schoomaker and former USU Dean Art Kellermann invested in me early in my career and showed me the power of mentoring and sponsorship. Both senior leaders spent hours with me talking about leadership. I am forever grateful. They helped change the trajectory of my career. Lauren Weber was one of the first people I shared the idea of this book with and was a constant source of inspiration and feedback during the process. Lauren is an inspiring leader, asks great questions, and challenges assumptions and beliefs.

I need to thank my chief residents from when I was the internal medicine program director. They were all caring leaders, and each of them made me a better leader. They include Joe Maciuba, Paul Happel, Jeff Gray, Kim Fabyan, Andrew Mertz, Guen Hunt, John Blickle, Melanie Wiseman, Rainey Johnson, Samara Lieberman, Kathryn Driggers, and Mike Orrick.

Many people contributed to the book with ideas and editing of chapters or segments. I greatly appreciate everyone who took the time to give me feedback along the way. If I forgot someone, I am sorry! The following people all provided input or advice: Jess Bunin, Carlie Cerne, Brian Clyne, Jess Edison, Cristin Mount, and Pat Young. John Blickle shares my passion for leadership, and he provided some excellent ideas and resources. He knows military leadership as well as anyone I have met.

Scott Allan has been my writing coach for over a year, thanks to selfpublishing.com. I appreciate his wisdom and keeping me accountable to the process. Each month, he provided me with sound advice, and knowing that a call was coming was motivating to keep writing.

Yeonsoo Sara Lee agreed to be the illustrator for the images in the book. Her amazing work speaks for itself, and I am so glad that she was willing to be part of this process. Her star is going to shine brightly for years to come!

Adam Barelski and Richele Corrado have been the most amazing colleagues and friends for the past several years. They have been constant encouragers and have been with me through the best and worst of times. Your friendship and support mean the world to me.

Finally, I want to thank everyone in healthcare. As the ideas for this book became clear, I recognized how so many of you are caring leaders. We lead like we care for our patients. I am inspired by your work, and I hope that this book helps us all to be more effective for our patients and for us to take care of each other.

Lead with caring, my friends!

Building Caring-Inspired Leaders

Are you excited about being a leader who leads from a place of caring after reading this book? Are you ready to build your legacy as a caring-inspired leader?

I would love to partner with you or your organization.

- Keynotes and workshops to fuel leadership growth
- Leadership coaching
- Building leadership programs
- Leadership retreats

Are you interested in creating leaders who care?

Check out my website or follow me on social media for more information.

Website: www.joshuahartzellMD.com

Email: info@joshuahartzellMD.com

X: @joshuadhartzell

LinkedIn: https://www.linkedin.com/in/JoshHartzellMD/

APPENDIX A

Prescription for Caring in Healthcare Leadership Reading List

Here is a list of leadership books that I have found helpful. The first three are directly related to caring as leaders. The rest are organized into personal, interpersonal/team, and organization to help you decide what to read based on your desired area of growth. The final section is books on diversity, equity, and inclusion. This is not an exhaustive list but is meant to help you get started. My top four books would be *The Culture Code, Radical Candor, The Five Dysfunctions of a Team,* and *Good to Great.* The other books are listed in no particular order.

Role of Caring in Leadership: Specific Books

Lead From The Heart: Transformational Leadership for the 21st Century – Mark Crowley

Encouraging the Heart: A Leader's Guide to Rewarding and Recognizing Others – James Kouzes and Barry Posner

The Art of Caring Leadership®: How Leading with Heart Uplifts Teams and Organizations – Heather Younger

Compassionate Leadership: Sustaining Wisdom, Humanity and Presence in Health and Social Care - Michael A. West

Personal

Dare to Lead: Brave Work. Tough Conversations. Whole Hearts. - Brené Brown

Extreme Ownership: How U.S. Navy SEALs Lead and Win - Jocko Willink and Leif Babin

Turn the Ship Around! A True Story of Turning Followers into Leaders - David Marquet

Flying in the Face of Fear: A Fighter Pilot's Lessons on Leading with Courage - Kim Campbell

It Worked for Me: In Life and Leadership - Colin Powell

The Leadership Challenge: How to Make Extraordinary Things Happen in Organizations (7th Edition) - James Kouzes and Barry Posner

The last two books in this section are related to personal development and career planning. The lessons are applicable for personal growth and leading organizations.

Essentialism: The Disciplined Pursuit of Less - Greg McKeown

Atomic Habits: An Easy & Proven Way to Build Good Habits & Break Bad Ones - James Clear

Interpersonal / Team

Radical Candor: Be a Kick-Ass Boss Without Losing Your Humanity – Kim Scott

The Five Dysfunctions of a Team: A Leadership Fable – Pat Lencioni

How Full Is Your Bucket? – Tom Rath and Don Clifton

Theodore Roosevelt on Leadership: Executive Lessons from the Bully Pulpit – James Strock

Athena Rising: How and Why Men Should Mentor Women – David Smith and Brad Johnson

Organizational

The Culture Code: The Secrets of Highly Successful Groups – Daniel Coyle

Good to Great: Why Some Companies Make the Leap…And Others Don't – Jim Collins

Drive: The Surprising Truth About What Motivates Us – Daniel Pink

Diversity, Equity, and Inclusion

Legacy: A Black Physician Reckons with Racism in Medicine – Uché Blackstock

How to Be an Inclusive Leader, Second Edition: Your Role in Creating Cultures of Belonging Where Everyone Can Thrive – Jennifer Brown

JOSHUA D. HARTZELL, MD

The Sum of Us: What Racism Costs Everyone and How We Can Prosper Together – Heather McGhee

Black Man in a White Coat: A Doctor's Reflections on Race and Medicine – Damon Tweedy

Leadership Philosophy Template

There are many ways to develop a leadership philosophy. Use a model or template that feels authentic to you. The questions below will help you identify key elements of a leadership philosophy. You can write one or two statements or short paragraphs per question, and the total philosophy should be about a page. Being clear and brief facilitates easier communication of your philosophy to others.

1. Who are you personally and professionally? Where are you from? Think about what influenced you as a leader—this helps connect you with those you lead. Consider talking about other leaders that you admire and who have inspired you.

2. What are your core values as a leader?

3. Define or emphasize the actions that bring these values to life.

4. Talk about your expectations for the team. Consider not just the goals for the organization but how important it is to you that while achieving organizational goals, you care about the personal and professional development of each member of your team. You expect each person to be committed to the betterment of each other and the organization.

5. What is not tolerated? Be clear about zero tolerance for sexual harassment, bullying, and dishonesty. Add others you see as important.

6. What is your communication style? Make it a point that you want and expect to get feedback. Make it clear you value their input and that everyone should value feedback from each other so you can grow individually and as an organization.

7. Define your priorities. I would consider emphasizing well-being and diversity, equity, and inclusion.

Communicating the Philosophy

1. Send a document in letter form to those you lead.

2. Talk about it in a meeting and go back to it at times when decisions are made based on its contents.

3. Create a presentation with it.

4. Deliver it via a podcast or video message to your team.

References:

https://extension.psu.edu/tips-for-developing-a-personal-leadership-philosophy – accessed on 13 April 2024

References: Deierlein, T. (2015). Why you should have a written leadership philosophy. *Leader to Leader, 2015*(77), 13-18. The article was posted on LinkedIn and is available at https://www.linkedin.com/pulse/why-you-should-have-written-leadership-philosophy-tom-deierlein/ – accessed on 13 April 2024

APPENDIX C

Sponsorship Scorecard

THERE ARE NUMEROUS WAYS to sponsor people to help advance their careers. Be intentional about investing in others, and make it a habit to intentionally create opportunities for those you lead. Consider making it a goal to do all of these in a year or to pick three and do them in a year.

1. Sponsor someone for a local or national committee that will advance their career.

2. Invite someone to coauthor a paper and have them be the first or senior author.

3. When invited to give a talk or write a paper, decline and recommend a more junior colleague for the opportunity. You can also do the talk or paper with them.

4. Invite someone to give a talk or grand rounds at your institution to help advance their career.

5. Connect a colleague to networks outside your institution to help the people you work with get invited to give talks.

6. Recommend someone to moderate a panel for a conference.

7. Suggest someone to be an abstract reviewer for a national meeting.

8. Help someone find influential research collaborators.

9. Nominate someone for an award.

10. Create the opportunity for someone to attend a professional development course that will advance their skills and career.

11. Advocate for someone to get hired. Call someone you know and put in a good word to help them get an interview for the position.

12. Host a sponsorship party where you bring together more senior and junior people with the goal that the connections will lead to sponsorship. Check out the article by Dr. Julie Silver below for more on this.

13. Give presentations about sponsorship at your institution to teach people about the concept and how to do it.

14. Encourage those you lead to bring sponsorship opportunities to you.

15. Make sponsorship an expectation of those you lead.

References:

Check out this blog post written by Dr. Jessica Servey and me for more. Dr. Servey helped develop this scorecard years ago and wrote about it in this blog post. https://www.wimedicine.org/blog/superhero-sponsorship

Silver JK. "Six Practical Strategies to Mentor and Sponsor Women in Academic Medicine." J Med Internet Res. 2023 May 25;25:e47799.

Gratitude Prescription

Here is a list of ways to think about and express gratitude. Make these a habit as a caring leader. Post this list somewhere as a reminder and consider doing at least one every day.

Practicing personal gratitude:

1. Reflect on one thing you are grateful for every morning and at the end of the day.

2. Keep a journal of things and people you are grateful for.

Expressing gratitude to those you are privileged to lead:

3. Thank someone in person today.

4. Stop by a team that you lead and thank people individually or as a group.

5. Give handwritten thank-you cards to people at least once a month.

6. Gift a book and write an inscription in it about how much the person means to you and your organization.

7. Text or email someone a note of thanks or to recognize important behaviors you want to see repeated by them or others.

8. Place a whiteboard in your workspace for people to leave encouraging notes of gratitude for others.

9. Send out a Reason 2 Celebrate (R2C) email once a week or month highlighting the great things your team has done. What you put in the email matters. Focus on the things you want to see more of and that are important to you and your organization.

10. Nominate someone for an award.

11. Review the awards you have at your institution and create new awards for your organization based on gaps for what you recognize or want to recognize more. Maybe you have a Nurse of the Year—why not have a Nurse of the Month? Maybe you already have Teacher of the Year—consider having a Teaching Top Ten or an All-Star Teacher Team. You don't have to self-impose limits on the number of people you recognize.

12. Create a coin to give out as recognition for your organization.

13. Recognize great performance by sponsoring and paying for someone to attend a professional development course. Thank them by investing in them.

14. Bring breakfast, lunch, or dinner to thank your team for a job well done.

A Prescription for Caring in Healthcare Leadership Notes Page and References

Introduction

1. The Case for Leadership Training with Dr. Josh Hartzell. Leading the Rounds Podcast, October 25, 2021.https://podcasts.apple.com/us/podcast/the-case-for-leadership-training-with-dr-josh-hartzell/id1516013076?i=1000539594458

2. General James McConville. *"People First: Insights from the Army's Chief of Staff."* February 16, 2012, https://www.army.mil/article/243026/people_first_insights_from_the_armys_chief_of_staff

3. Ibid.

Section 1:
Caring in Leadership and Why It Matters

Chapter 1: The Link Between Caring and Leadership

1. Hippocrates is frequently referenced as having given this quote: "Cure sometimes, treat often, comfort always." Finding the origins of some quotes and aphorisms can be challenging. I did my best throughout this book to give

credit to the originator of quotes or stories. Shaw Q. On aphorisms. Br J Gen Pract. 2009 Dec 1;59(569):954–5.

2. This quote is attributed to Plato: "Caring about the happiness of others, we find our own."

3. Robert Greenleaf, *Servant Leadership: A Journey into the Nature of Legitimate Power and Greatness* (New York/ Mahwah, NJ: Paulist Press, 2002).

4. Greenleaf, *Servant Leadership*, 62, 142, 255-56.

5. Greenleaf, *Servant Leadership*, 62.

6. Greenleaf, *Servant Leadership*, 142

7. Dr. Lauren Weber is a cardiologist, leadership consultant, and certified executive coach. She cofounded a business called All Levels Leadership. This podcast captures some of her ideas on leadership: https://podcasts.apple.com/us/podcast/ want-to-be-a-good-leader-be-a-good-follower-with/ id1516013076?i=1000546756576

8. Personal conversation with Dr. Lauren Weber

9. Ibid.

10. Ibid.

11. James Kouzes and Barry Posner, *The Leadership Challenge* (5th ed.) (San Francisco: John Wiley & Sons, 2012).

12. Kouzes and Posner, *The Leadership Challenge*, 276. The ideas cited are discussed multiple times throughout the book.

13. James Kouzes and Barry Posner, *Encouraging the Heart: A Leader's Guide to Rewarding and Recognizing Others* (San Francisco: Jossey-Bass, 2003), xiv.

14. Kouzes and Posner, *Encouraging the Heart*.

15. Kouzes and Posner, *Encouraging the Heart*, xvii.

16. Kouzes and Posner, *Encouraging the Heart*, 15.

17. Mark Crowley, *Lead From The Heart: Transformational Leadership For The 21st Century* (Carlsbad, CA: Hay House, Inc, 2011, 2022).

18. Crowley, *Lead From The Heart*, xix.

19. Crowley, *Lead From The Heart*, xx.

20. Heather Younger, *The Art of Caring Leadership: How Leading with Heart Uplifts Teams and Organizations* (Oakland: Berrett-Koehler Publishers, Inc, 2021).

21. Younger, *The Art of Caring Leadership*, xvii.

22. Younger, *The Art of Caring Leadership*. Each chapter has action steps that leaders can take.

23. Michael West, *Compassionate Leadership: Sustaining Wisdom, Humanity and Presence in Health and Social Care* (United Kingdom: The Swirling Leaf Press, 2021).

24. West, *Compassionate Leadership*, 4.

25. West, *Compassionate Leadership*, 6.

26. This article provides an excellent overview of leadership theory and recommends a new model called Wellness-Centered Leadership. Table 2 should be printed out and kept handy as it has over 40 behaviors that I would call Caring Acts of Leadership. Shanafelt T, Trockel M, Rodriguez A, Logan D. Wellness-Centered Leadership: Equipping Health Care Leaders to Cultivate Physician Well-Being and Professional Fulfillment. Acad Med. 2021 May 1;96(5):641-651.

27. Ibid.

28. Ibid.

29. Ibid.

30. Crowley, *Lead From The Heart*.

31. Younger, *The Art of Caring Leadership*.

32. Kouzes and Posner, *Encouraging the Heart*.

33. West, *Compassionate Leadership*.

34. Shanafelt T, Trockel M, Rodriguez A, Logan D. Wellness-Centered Leadership: Equipping Health Care Leaders to Cultivate Physician Well-Being and Professional Fulfillment. Acad Med. 2021;96(5):641-651.

Chapter 2: Dismantling the Myth of Caring Being Soft

1. This quote is found in many places. I believe the original source was an 8 September 2018 New York Times Opinion article: "Lady of the Rings: Jacinda Rules" by Maureen Dowd. Available at https://www.nytimes.com/2018/09/08/opinion/sunday/jacinda-ardern-new-zealand-prime-minister.html.

2. Amy Vertrees, *Become the Boss MD* (Lioncrest Publishing, 2023).

3. Michael West, *Compassionate Leadership: Sustaining Wisdom, Humanity and Presence in Health and Social Care* (United Kingdom: The Swirling Leaf Press, 2021), 1.

4. Michael West and Suzie Bailey. Five Myths of Compassionate Leadership. 28 May 2019. Available at https://www.kingsfund.org.uk/blog/2019/05/five-myths-compassionate-leadership.

5. West, *Compassionate Leadership*, 4.

6. Ruth Gotian, *The Success Factor: Developing the Mindset and Skillset for Peak Business Performance* (London: Kogan Page, 2022).

7. Groover S, Gotian R. Five 'power skills' for becoming a team leader. Nature. 2020 Jan;577(7792):721-722.

8. Ibid.

9. Ibid.

10. Ibid.

11. Jocko Willink and Leif Babin, *Extreme Ownership* (New York: St Martin's Press, 2015).

12. Jocko Willink, *Leadership Strategy and Tactics: FM-02* (New York: St. Martin's Press, 2019), 135-137.

13. Willink, *Leadership Strategy and Tactics.*

14. Willink, *Leadership Strategy and Tactic,* 135-137.

15. Willink, *Leadership Strategy and Tactics,* 135.

16. Willink, *Leadership Strategy and Tactic,* 136.

17. Ibid.

18. Mark Hertling, *Growing Physician Leaders: Empowering Doctors to Improve Our Healthcare* (New York: Florida Hospital, Rosetta Books, 2016).

19. Hertling, *Growing Physician Leaders*, 21.

20. Michael West, *Compassionate Leadership: Sustaining Wisdom, Humanity and Presence in Health and Social Care* (United Kingdom: The Swirling Leaf Press, 2021).

21. Michael West and Suzie Bailey. Five Myths of Compassionate Leadership. 28 May 2019. Available at https://www.kingsfund. org.uk/blog/2019/05/five-myths-compassionate-leadership.

Chapter 3: The Business Case for Caring as a Leader

1. The quote to begin the chapter is from the interview and subsequent discussion with Laurie Baedke.

2. Jon Gordon Weekly Newsletter. ROIP vs ROI. https://jongordon.com/positivetip/roip.html. I would recommend following Jon's newsletter and reading his books and blog posts.

3. Heather Younger, *The Art of Caring Leadership: How Leading with Heart Uplifts Teams and Organizations* (Oakland: Berrett-Koehler Publishers, Inc, 2021), 139-146.

4. Younger, *The Art of Caring Leadership,* 140.

5. Ibid.

6. Younger, *The Art of Caring Leadership,* 144-145.

7. Link to the Heather Younger podcast with Garry Ridge. He is an amazing leader, has been on multiple podcasts, and has written his own book. He is a caring leader who we can learn from and model our leadership after. https://heatheryounger.com/73-leaders-with-heart-help-their-people-step-into-the-best-versions-of-themselves/. For bonus listening, you can check him out on the *Lead From The Heart* podcast as well: https://markccrowley.com/garry-ridge-the-ceo-most-of-us-wish-we-had/

8. Younger, *The Art of Caring Leadership,* 141-142.

9. Ibid.

10. Mark Crowley, *Lead From The Heart: Transformational Leadership For The 21st Century* (Carlsbad, CA: Hay House, Inc, 2011, 2022).

11. Crowley, *Lead From The Heart,* 57.

12. Crowley, *Lead From The Heart,* 67.

13. Jim Clifton and Jim Harter, *Culture Shock: An unstoppable force is changing how we work and live. Gallup's solution to the biggest leadership issue of our time.* (Washington D.C.: Gallup Press, 2023).

14. Clifton and Harter, *Culture Shock,* 14.

15. Clifton and Harter, *Culture Shock,* 137.

16. Crowley, *Lead From The Heart,* 42.

17. Michael West, *Compassionate Leadership: Sustaining Wisdom, Humanity and Presence in Health and Social Care* (United Kingdom: The Swirling Leaf Press, 2021).

18. West, *Compassionate Leadership*, 47-62.

19. West, *Compassionate Leadership*, 58.

20. MedStar Washington Hospital Center recognition for Most Socially Responsible Hospital in Washington DC: https://www.medstarhealth.org/news-and-publications/news/medstar-washington-hospital-center-named-the-most-socially-and-racially-responsible-hospital

21. MedStar Washington Hospital Center recognition for being in top 100 hospitals for customer loyalty: https://nrchealth.com/wp-content/uploads/2022/08/CLA_2022_Winners.pdf

22. MedStar Washington Hospital Center US News and World Report Rankings. Available at https://health.usnews.com/best-hospitals/area/washington-dc

23. West M, Eckert R, Collins B, Chowla R (2017). Caring to change: how compassionate leadership can stimulate innovation in health care. London: The King's Fund. Available at www.kingsfund.org.uk/publications/caring-change. The table from this article highlights some ways leaders can foster innovation. The article has numerous other valuable insights for caring leaders as well. If you are not going to read West's book, then check out this article. The table was used with permission from The King's Fund.

24. West, *Compassionate Leadership*, 47-62.

25. West M, Eckert R, Collins B, Chowla R (2017). Caring to change: how compassionate leadership can stimulate innovation in health care. London: The King's Fund. Available at www.kingsfund.org.uk/publications/caring-change, page 5.

26. Ibid. Table used with permission from The King's Fund.

27. Ibid.

28. Medscape does surveys on physicians and nursing well-being. They are worth reading, and the titles speak for themselves in terms of the problems. I find it sad that we have a paper titled this about the status of physicians in healthcare. Medscape US Physician Burnout and Depression Report titled "'I Cry but No One Cares': Physician Burnout & Depression Report 2023," available at https://www.medscape.com/slideshow/2023-lifestyle-burnout-6016058?faf=1#1.

29. Nursing report. "Fulfillment and Frustration: Medscape Nurse Career Satisfaction Report 2023," available at https://www.medscape.com/slideshow/2023-nurse-career-satisfaction-6016810?icd=login_success_email_match_norm#1. Accessed on 16 December 2023.

30. Rodrigues H, Cobucci R, Oliveira A, Cabral JV, Medeiros L, Gurgel K, Souza T, Gonçalves AK. Burnout syndrome among medical residents: A systematic review and meta-analysis. PLoS One. 2018 Nov 12;13(11):e0206840.

31. This paper reports that maybe as many as 1/5 of physicians drink to hazardous levels. Halsall L, Irizar P, Burton S, Waring S, Giles S, Goodwin L, Jones A. Hazardous, harmful, and dependent alcohol use in healthcare professionals: a systematic review and meta-analysis. Front Public Health. 2023 Nov 28;11:1304468.

32. Dewa CS, Loong D, Bonato S, Trojanowski L. The relationship between physician burnout and quality of healthcare in terms of safety and acceptability: a systematic review. BMJ Open. 2017;7(6):e015141.

33. Medscape US Physician Burnout and Depression Report titled "'I Cry but No One Cares': Physician Burnout & Depression

Report 2023," available at https://www.medscape.com/slideshow/2023-lifestyle-burnout-6016058?faf=1#1.

34. Ibid.

35. Ibid.

36. Ibid.

37. Ibid.

38. Nursing report. "Fulfillment and Frustration: Medscape Nurse Career Satisfaction Report 2023," available at https://www.medscape.com/slideshow/2023-nurse-career-satisfaction-6016810?icd=login success email match norm#1.

39. Ligibel JA, Goularte N, Berliner JI, Bird SB, Brazeau CMLR, Rowe SG, Stewart MT, Trockel MT. Well-Being Parameters and Intention to Leave Current Institution Among Academic Physicians. JAMA Netw Open. 2023 Dec 1;6(12):e2347894.

40. Ibid.

41. Dewa CS, Loong D, Bonato S, Trojanowski L. The relationship between physician burnout and quality of healthcare in terms of safety and acceptability: a systematic review. BMJ Open. 2017 Jun 21;7(6):e015141.

42. Dewa CS, Loong D, Bonato S, Trojanowski L, Rea M. The relationship between resident burnout and safety-related and acceptability-related quality of healthcare: a systematic literature review. BMC Med Educ. 2017 Nov 9;17(1):195.

43. Jun J, Ojemeni MM, Kalamani R, Tong J, Crecelius ML. Relationship between nurse burnout, patient and organizational outcomes: Systematic review. Int J Nurs Stud. 2021 Jul;119:103933.

44. Aiken LH, Lasater KB, Sloane DM, et al. Physician and Nurse Well-Being and Preferred Interventions to Address Burnout in Hospital Practice: Factors Associated With

Turnover, Outcomes, and Patient Safety. *JAMA Health Forum.* 2023;4(7):e231809.

45. Shanafelt T and Kuriakose C. Widespread Clinician Shortages Create a Crisis that Will Take Years to Resolve. NEJM Catal Innov Care Deliv. 2023;4(3).

46. Aiken LH, Lasater KB, Sloane DM, et al. Physician and Nurse Well-Being and Preferred Interventions to Address Burnout in Hospital Practice: Factors Associated With Turnover, Outcomes, and Patient Safety. *JAMA Health Forum.* 2023;4(7):e231809.

47. Ibid.

48. Shanafelt T and Kuriakose C. Widespread Clinician Shortages Create a Crisis that Will Take Years to Resolve. NEJM Catal Innov Care Deliv. 2023;4(3).

49. Ibid.

50. Navinés R, et al. Burnout in residents during the first wave of the COVID-19 pandemic: a systematic review and meta-analysis. Front Psychiatry. 2024;14:1286101.

51. Nicki Brown. Resident physicians go on strike at hospital once called 'the epicenter of the epicenter' of the country's coronavirus pandemic. 22 May 2023. Available at https://www.cnn.com/2023/05/22/us/new-york-city-hospital-residents-strike/index.html.

52. Shanafelt T, Goh J, Sinsky C. The Business Case for Investing in Physician Well-Being. JAMA Intern Med. 2017 Dec 1;177(12):1826-1832.

53. Ibid.

54. Jennifer Peltz. Nurses go on strike at 2 big New York City hospitals. 9 January 2023. Available at https://apnews.com/article/nyc-nurses-strike-d81f32cb7ac709404eb795a6d8822b34.

55. Relias 2022 Nurse Salary Research Report: Trends and Insights for Leaders and Recruiters. Available at https://www.relias.com/resource/2022-nurse-salary-research-report. Accessed on 19 June 2024.

56. Gone for now, or gone for good? How to play the talent game and win back workers. McKinsey Quarterly. 9 March 2022. Available at https://www.mckinsey.com/capabilities/people-and-organizational-performance/our-insights/gone-for-now-or-gone-for-good-how-to-play-the-new-talent-game-and-win-back-workers.

57. Boulay RM. Looking After Our Own. N Engl J Med. 2023 Feb 16;388(7):581-583.

58. Ibid.

59. Crowley, *Lead From The Heart.*

60. Younger, *The Art of Caring Leadership.*

Section 2:
Being a Caring-Inspired Leader Starts with You

Chapter 4: Care Enough to Take Care of Yourself

1. The quote "In no relationship is the physician more often derelict than in his [or her] duty to himself [or herself]" by Dr. Johnston, As a Physician, Washington Med Ann 1902; 1:158-61 was one that I learned from friend and colleague Dr. Rohul Amin.

2. The idea that self-care is not selfish has been in many blogs and resources. Many of us still struggle with taking care of ourselves, thinking we need to prioritize others. Available at https://www.emblemhealth.com/blog/health/self-care-is-not-selfish.

3. Shanafelt T and Kuriakose C. Widespread Clinician Shortages Create a Crisis that Will Take Years to Resolve. NEJM Catal Innov Care Deliv. 2023;4(3).

4. Shanafelt TD, Gorringe G, Menaker R, Storz KA, Reeves D, Buskirk SJ, Sloan JA, Swensen SJ. Impact of organizational leadership on physician burnout and satisfaction. Mayo Clin Proc. 2015;90(4):432-40.

5. Ibid.

6. Ligibel JA, Goularte N, Berliner JI, Bird SB, Brazeau CMLR, Rowe SG, Stewart MT, Trockel MT. Well-Being Parameters and Intention to Leave Current Institution Among Academic Physicians. JAMA Netw Open. 2023 Dec 1;6(12):e2347894.

7. Robert Gabsa And Shruti Rastogi published a blog post on 23 June 2020 titled "Take Care of Your People, and They'll Take Care of Business." I love the title! Available at https://www.gallup.com/workplace/312824/care-people-care-business.aspx.

8. Ibid.

9. Ibid.

10. There are numerous accounts of General Stanley McChrystal only sleeping four hours a night. This is not something we should aspire to do, and most, if not all, of us will be less effective if we sleep this little. Available at https://en.wikipedia.org/wiki/Stanley_A._McChrystal.

11. Jade Scipioni. White House advisor Dr. Fauci works 20-hour days and his wife reminds him to eat, sleep and drink water. 2 April 2020. Available at White House advisor Anthony Fauci's wife on his hectic schedule (cnbc.com).

12. Greg McKeown, *Essentialism: The Disciplined Pursuit of Less* (New York: Currency, an imprint of Random House, 2014, 2020), 94.

13. McKeown, *Essentialism*, 91-102. Chapter 8 is all about how sleep is essential. He highlights data on its importance and anecdotes of leaders' relationship to sleep.

14. Petrofsky LA, Heffernan CM, Gregg BT, Smith-Forbes EV, Sturdivant RX. Sleep and Military Leaders: Examining the Values, Beliefs, and Quality of Sleep and the Impact on Occupational Performance. Mil Med. 2024;189(5-6):1023-1031.

15. Ibid.

16. Ibid.

17. Ibid.

18. Sleep is a force multiplier! The quote was taken from this paper: Teyhen DS, Capaldi VF 2nd, Drummond SPA, Rhon DI, Barrett AS, Silvernail JL, Boland DM. How sleep can help maximize human potential: The role of leaders. J Sci Med Sport. 2021 Oct;24(10):988-994.

19. This study demonstrated that training leaders could possibly result in sleep improvement for an entire Army unit: Adler AB, Bliese PD, LoPresti ML, McDonald JL, Merrill JC. Sleep leadership in the army: A group randomized trial. Sleep Health. 2021 Feb;7(1):24-30.

20. I first heard the line about a strategic plan for life on the Jocko Podcast on 31 December 2021. Available at https://youtu.be/7uk981NZkLg.

21. Ibid.

22. James Clear, *Atomic Habits: An Easy & Proven Way to Build Good Habits & Break Bad Ones* (New York: Avery, an imprint of Random House, 2018).

23. Clear, *Atomic Habits*, 16.

24. Ibid.

25. McKeown, *Essentialism*.

26. McKeown, *Essentialism*, 19.

27. McKeown, *Essentialism*, 131.

28. McKeown, *Essentialism*, 109.

29. Schrager S, Sadowski E. Getting More Done: Strategies to Increase Scholarly Productivity. J Grad Med Educ. 2016 Feb;8(1):10-3.

30. Ibid.

31. I have seen this article about Colonel Mark Blum numerous times. It is a powerful piece about prioritizing our time and not having regrets about what we missed out on. Available at https://www.linkedin.com/pulse/important-vs-urgent-col-mark-blum-commander-212th-field-brian-lilly/

32. Ibid.

33. Ibid.

34. Ibid.

35. McKeown, *Essentialism*.

Chapter 5: Care Enough to Prepare

1. The quote by Sir William Osler is famous. I initially found it on https://en.wikiquote.org/wiki/William_Osler, accessed on 22 December 2023. The following text was referenced: Braude, J. M. (1962). *Lifetime speaker's encyclopedia*. Prentice-Hall.

2. Dr. Ramey Wilson podcast. Available at https://www.wardocspodcast.com/post/col-ramey-wilson-md-mph-special-operations-command-surgeon-understanding-the-big-picture.

3. Ibid.

4. https://www.aamc.org/data-reports/curriculum-reports/data/curriculum-topics-required-and-elective-courses-medical-school-programs

5. https://www.acgme.org/programs-and-institutions/programs/common-program-requirements/

6. The CanMEDS 2015 Framework included the role of leadership for physician trainees. Available at https://canmeds.royalcollege.ca/en/framework, accessed on 22 December 2023.

7. The nursing accreditation standards were taken from the NLL Commission for Nursing Education Accreditation. They are available at https://cnea.nln.org/standards-of-accreditation under the 2021 accreditation standards tab.

8. National Academies of Sciences, Engineering, and Medicine; National Academy of Medicine; Committee on the Future of Nursing 2020–2030. The Future of Nursing 2020-2030: Charting a Path to Achieve Health Equity. Flaubert JL, Le Menestrel S, Williams DR, Wakefield MK, editors. Washington (DC): National Academies Press (US); 2021 May 11. PMID: 34524769.

9. Brunt BA, Bogdan BA. Nursing Professional Development Leadership. 2023 Apr 23. In: StatPearls [Internet]. Treasure Island (FL): StatPearls Publishing; 2023 Jan–. PMID: 30085606.

10. Ibid.

11. Ibid.

12. The Pharmacy accreditation standards were taken from https://www.acpe-accredit.org/pdf/Standards2016FINAL2022.pdf.

13. The Physical Therapy accreditation standards were taken from https://www.capteonline.org/about-capte/resource_documents/accreditation-handbook.

14. James Clear, *Atomic Habits: An Easy & Proven Way to Build Good Habits & Break Bad Ones* (New York: Avery, an imprint of Random House, 2018).

15. Jim Mattis and Bing West, *Call Sign Chaos: Learning to Lead* (Random House, 2019), 42.

16. Daniel Coyle, *The Culture Code: The Secrets of Highly Successful Groups* (New York, Bantam Books, 2018).

17. The quote by retired Army Major General Patrick Donahoe was seen on X: @PatDonahoeArmy 5:18 AM 1/20/19.

18. Nancy Koehn, *Forged in Crisis: The Making of Five Courageous Leaders* (New York: Scribner Book Company, 2017).

19. Koehn, *Forged in Crisis*, 3.

20. Koehn, *Forged in Crisis*, 7.

Chapter 6: Care About Your Values and Purpose

1. The Leadership Challenge is now in its 7th edition. I have and used a copy of the 5th edition for this book. I consider it one of the foundational leadership texts for teaching and learning about leadership. James Kouzes and Barry Posner, *The Leadership Challenge* (5th ed.) (San Francisco: John Wiley & Sons, 2012).

2. Bill George and Zach Clayton, *True North: Leading Authentically in Today's Workplace* (Hoboken, NJ: John Wiley & Sons, Inc, 2022).

3. Brené Brown, *Dare to Lead: Brave Work, Tough Conversations, Whole Hearts* (New York: Random House, 2018).

4. Souba WW. The Inward Journey of Leadership. J Surg Res. 2006 Apr;131(2):159-67.

5. Ibid.

6. George and Clayton, *True North*, 15-36.

7. George and Clayton, *True North*, 15.

8. George and Clayton, *True North*, 37-58. The term "crucible" is often talked about in leadership. I first heard it from

Warren Bennis, but it is also used by Bill George in his book, where he quotes Bennis. As an aside, *On Becoming a Leader* was one of the first books I read on leadership.

9. Warren Bennis. *On Becoming a Leader* (New York: Basic Books, 2009), xxiv.

10. Souba WW. The Inward Journey of Leadership. J Surg Res. 2006 Apr;131(2):159-67.

11. Ibid.

12. George and Clayton, *True North*, 19.

13. George and Clayton, *True North*, 177.

14. Prasad Kaipa. What Wise Leaders Always Follow. HBR Insight Center. The article highlights the life of Dr. Govindappa Venkataswamy and the importance of having a North Star. It is available at https://hbr.org/2012/01/what-wise-leaders-always-follo.

15. Ibid.

16. Ibid.

17. Ibid.

18. Kouzes and Posner, *The Leadership Challenge*, 34.

19. Brown, *Dare to Lead*, 188.

20. This is probably one of my favorite all-time Brené Brown quotes. It is such a terrific piece of advice and also spoken in her authentic voice. Brown, *Dare to Lead*, 190.

21. Leonard Berry and Kent Seltman, *Management Lessons From Mayo Clinic: Inside One of the*

World's Most Admired Service Organizations (New York: McGraw-Hill, 2008), 20.

22. Kouzes and Posner, *The Leadership Challenge*, 45.

23. Ed Ruggero and Dennis Haley, *The Leader's Compass: A Personal Leadership Philosophy Is Your Key to Success* (Academy Leadership Publishing, 2013).

24. Kouzes and Posner, *The Leadership Challenge*, 47.

25. This is an outstanding article to help guide the development of a personal leadership philosophy. It covers why a leadership philosophy is important and elements that should be included. Deierlein, T. (2015). Why You Should Have A Written Personal Leadership Philosophy. *Leader to Leader, 2015*(77), 13-18. You can access a free version on his LinkedIn page: https://www.linkedin.com/pulse/why-you-should-have-written-leadership-philosophy-tom-deierlein/.

26. Ibid.

Section 3:
Caring Acts of Leadership

Chapter 7: Care Enough to Take Care of Those You Lead

1. Heather Dockray. Definition of community care and interview with Nakita Valerio, who had the viral tweet quoting her by Stephanie Tait (@StephTaitWrites), about community care. https://mashable.com/article/community-care-versus-self-care

2. Ibid.

3. Ibid.

4. Ibid.

5. Daniel Pink, *Drive: The Surprising Truth About What Motivates Us* (New York: Riverhead Books, 2009).

6. Pink, *Drive*, 1-33, 77-81.

7. Pink, *Drive*, 85-146.

8. Pink, *Drive*, 85-108.

9. Pink, *Drive*, 131-146.

10. McKinlee Covey. "People Don't Burn Out Because They're Working Too Hard, They Burn Out Because They're Having Too Little Impact"—Liz Wiseman and Doug Conant on Leading in Ambiguous Times. ConantLeadership. This blog post by McKinlee Covey talks about Liz Wiseman and Doug Conant and the value of recognizing the impact people have at work. Available at https://conantleadership.com/liz-wiseman-doug-conant/.

11. Jon Gordon, *The Power of Positive Leadership* (Hoboken, NJ: John Wiley & Sons Inc, 2017), 149.

12. I wrote this blog post based on an experience I had one day when I basically wanted to give a resident physician no credit for saving a patient's life. It was a huge lesson for me. https://www.kevinmd.com/2019/03/how-physicians-can-find-meaning-in-their-work.html, published on 29 March 2019.

13. Stanley ML, Neck CP, Neck CB. The dark side of generosity: Employees with a reputation for giving are selectively targeted for exploitation. Journal of Experimental Social Psychology. Volume 108, 2023.

14. Ibid.

15. I saw this "Lamps Out Time" by Lieutenant General Beagle in several places. He has set the expectations for boundaries on the time of the people he's led. He published the whole memo on X, and that is where the quotes are from. https://twitter.com/Beags_Beagle/status/1628393534234525700?cxt=HHwWiIC8qdbSm5ktA-AAA, accessed on 24 December 2023.

16. Steve Beynon. Military.com, 9 June 2022. https://www.military.com/daily-news/2022/06/09/10th-mountain-

commander-says-leaders-need-leave-soldiers-alone-after-hours.html.

17. "Lamps Out Time" by Lieutenant General Beagle.

18. Ibid.

19. Lieutenant General Beagle mentioned that taking care of people does not always mean giving people time off in this LinkedIn post: https://www.linkedin.com/posts/milford-beagle-jr-beags-47934b24_lampsout-activity-7034159391121555456-NIZK/.

20. Shanafelt TD, Gorringe G, Menaker R, Storz KA, Reeves D, Buskirk SJ, Sloan JA, Swensen SJ. Impact of organizational leadership on physician burnout and satisfaction. Mayo Clin Proc. 2015 Apr;90(4):432-40.

21. Ibid.

22. Ibid.

23. Ibid.

24. Ibid.

25. Pink, *Drive*, 85-146.

26. Shanafelt TD, Gorringe G, Menaker R, Storz KA, Reeves D, Buskirk SJ, Sloan JA, Swensen SJ. Impact of organizational leadership on physician burnout and satisfaction. Mayo Clin Proc. 2015 Apr;90(4):432-40.

27. Ibid.

28. Pink, *Drive*.

29. Shanafelt TD, Gorringe G, Menaker R, Storz KA, Reeves D, Buskirk SJ, Sloan JA, Swensen SJ. Impact of organizational leadership on physician burnout and satisfaction. Mayo Clin Proc. 2015 Apr;90(4):432-40.

Chapter 8: Care Enough to Get to Know Your People

1. Mark Crowley, *Lead From The Heart: Transformational Leadership For The 21st Century* (Carlsbad, CA: Hay House, Inc, 2011, 2022), 129.

2. Heather Younger, *The Art of Caring Leadership: How Leading with Heart Uplifts Teams and Organizations* (Oakland: Berrett-Koehler Publishers, Inc, 2021), 75.

3. Younger, *The Art of Caring Leadership*, xii.

4. Jim Harter. A Great Manager's Most Important Habit. 30 March 2023, Gallup Workplace Blog. Available at https://www.gallup.com/workplace/505370/great-manager-important-habit.aspx.

Chapter 9: Care Enough to Be Present

1. The opening quote is from Admiral McRaven. The term "troop the line" is a military phrase that means getting out and walking among the troops to ensure that the orders are being carried out and troops are meeting standards. It is also about being present, seeing those you lead and them seeing you. William McRaven, *The Wisdom of the Bullfrog: Leadership Made Simple (But Not Easy)* (New York: Grand Central Publishing, Inc, 2023)

2. Retired Colonel Ramey Wilson and I had a discussion about leadership, and this quote really stood out.

3. Bill George and Zach Clayton, *True North: Leading Authentically in Today's Workplace* (Hoboken, NJ: John Wiley & Sons, Inc, 2022), 207.

4. James Kouzes and Barry Posner, *Encouraging the Heart: A Leader's Guide to Rewarding and Recognizing Others* (San Francisco: Jossey-Bass, 2003), 22.

5. Ibid.

6. The General McChrystal quote was taken from an interview with National Public Radio by Rachel Martin. Available at https://www.npr.org/2020/04/01/825056988/how-to-take-a-leadership-role-during-a-crisis. Accessed on 31 December 2023.

7. Stanley McChrystal and Chris Fussell. What 9/11 Taught Us About Leadership in a Crisis: Sept. 11 changed how U.S. Special Forces operated — and offers lessons for today's leaders. New York Times, 23 March 2020. Available at https://www.nytimes.com/2020/03/23/opinion/coronavirus-mcchrystal-leadership.html. Accessed on 31 December 2023.

8. President Obama called the Monrovia Medical Unit. Available at https://obamawhitehouse.archives.gov/the-press-office/2014/11/05/readout-president-s-call-monrovia-medical-unit.

9. A documentary has been made about the U.S. Public Health Service (PHS) that has audio recordings of part of this call to the PHS team in Monrovia: https://www.youtube.com/watch?v=sDmcBbowV30.

Chapter 10: Care Enough to Set High Expectations

1. Daniel Coyle, *The Culture Code: The Secrets of Highly Successful Groups* (New York: Bantam Books, 2018), 56.

2. Coyle, *The Culture Code*, 56-57.

3. Coyle, *The Culture Code*. Coyle mentions Pixar, the Navy SEALs, and the San Antonio Spurs throughout this book in relation to the culture of their organizations.

4. The Vince Lombardi quote is found in multiple locations. I first saw it while visiting the NFL Hall

of Fame in Canton, Ohio. Many websites quoting Lombardi have it as well: https://www.goalcast.com/vince-lombardi-quotes-appreciate-excellence/.

5. Dr. Julie Silver is a leading figure in gender equity in medicine and leadership development. You can learn more about her from her website: https://juliesilvermd.com/. Accessed on 1 January 2024.

6. Laurie Baedke quoted Brené Brown in her interview. The original quote is from Brené Brown's books. Brené Brown, *Dare to Lead: Brave Work, Tough Conversations, Whole Hearts* (New York: Random House, 2018).

7. The idea about cheering for people you work with more than you cheer for your sports team was introduced to me by Kouzes and Posner. They also made the "First Essential" to encourage the heart by setting high standards. James Kouzes and Barry Posner, *Encouraging the Heart: A Leader's Guide to Rewarding and Recognizing Others* (San Francisco: Jossey-Bass, 2003), xi.

Chapter 11: Care Enough to Hold People Accountable

1. The quote from Kobe Bryant that opens the chapter is from this blog post by Jessica Sager: https://parade.com/1234641/jessicasager/kobe-bryant-quotes/.

2. This is one of my all-time favorite leadership books. I recommend you read it and give it to others all the time. It should be mandatory reading for leaders and teams. Patrick Lencioni, *The Five Dysfunctions of a Team: A Leadership Fable* (San Francisco: Jossey-Bass, 2002).

3. Nate Regier, *Compassionate Accountability: How Leaders Build Connection and Get Results* (Oakland: Berrett-Koehler Publishers, 2023).

4. Nate Regier, Why compassionate accountability is the next leadership superpower. SmartBrief. Published 11 July 2023 at https://www.smartbrief.com/original/why-compassionate-accountability-is-the-next-leadership-superpower.

5. Ellie Lindhjem wrote this blog post, published on 9 February 2023: https://www.aaoe.net/news/631425/How-to-be-a-Leader-with-an-Accountability-Mindset.htm.

6. Ibid.

7. General Colin Powell is famous for many reasons and has numerous leadership quotes and lessons. I am not sure of the exact source of this quote, as it is often shared as one of his leadership lessons. General and former Secretary of State Colin Powell famously said, "The most important thing I learned is that soldiers watch what their leaders do. You can give them classes and lecture them forever, but it is your personal example that they follow."

8. Jocko Willink and Leif Babin, *Extreme Ownership* (New York: St Martin's Press, 2015), 17-13.

9. Jocko Willink. Extreme Ownership. TEDxUniversityofNevada. Inspiring talk about leadership and accountability. Available at https://www.youtube.com/watch?v=ljqra3BcqWM.

10. Discussed in both the book and TEDx talk referenced as 8 and 9, respectively. The TEDx Talk is more powerful, as it has Jocko's emotion tied to it.

11. Willink and Babin, *Extreme Ownership*, 27.

12. Willink and Babin, *Extreme Ownership*. This is the idea and message of the book.

13. Jocko Willink. Extreme Ownership. TEDxUniversityofNevada.

14. The work by Amy Edmondson on psychological safety and failure is some of the most impactful research on leadership. This book is a must-read for healthcare leaders. Amy Edmondson, *The Fearless Organization: Creating Psychological Safety in the Workplace for Learning, Innovation, and Growth* (Hoboken, NJ: John Wiley & Sons, Inc, 2019), 3-24.

15. Edmondson, *The Fearless Organization*, 77-102.

16. Edmondson, *The Fearless Organization*, 159.

17. Edmondson, *The Fearless Organization*, 15.

18. Lencioni, *The Five Dysfunctions of a Team*.

19. Willink and Babin, *Extreme Ownership*.

20. Edmondson, *The Fearless Organization*.

21. Regier, *Compassionate Accountability*.

Chapter 12: Care Enough to Give Feedback

1. Laurie Baedke, *Mentor, Coach, Lead to Peak Professional Performance* (Chicago, IL: Health Administration Press, 2023), 117.

2. Mark Crowley, *Lead From The Heart: Transformational Leadership For The 21st Century* (Carlsbad, CA: Hay House, Inc, 2011, 2022), 71.

3. Ibid.

4. Sue Tetzlaff. A Healthcare Organization's 3-Point Pathway to Normalizing Feedback as an Act of Caring. Available at https://www.radicalcandor.com/feedback-in-healthcare/.

5. Ibid.

6. Kim Scott, *Radical Candor: Be a Kick-Ass Boss Without Losing Your Humanity* (New York: St. Martin's Press, 2019).

7. Scott, *Radical Candor*, 9.

8. Scott, *Radical Candor*, xii and 30. Scott uses the idea throughout the book, and the four quadrants of radical candor are on the cover of the book. Keep it on your desk as a reminder.

9. Ken Blanchard and Spencer Johnson, *The New One Minute Manager* (London: Thorsons, 2015), 37-29.

10. Blanchard and Johnson, *The New One Minute Manager*, 49.

11. I was fortunate to spend a month at Stanford learning how to teach from Kelley Skeff, MD, PhD and Georgette Stratos, PhD. They are amazing educators who changed my life. Much of what I learned about teaching, including feedback, was from them. Their information is on this website: https://med.stanford.edu/sfdc/clinical_teaching.html?tab=proxy.

12. Holmboe ES, Yepes M, Williams F, Huot SJ. Feedback and the mini clinical evaluation exercise. J Gen Intern Med. 2004 May;19(5 Pt 2):558-61.

13. Scott, *Radical Candor*.

14. Blanchard and Johnson, *The New One Minute Manager*.

15. Ende J. Feedback in clinical medical education. JAMA. 1983 Aug 12;250(6):777-81.

Chapter 13: Care Enough to Receive Feedback

1. The quote at the beginning of the chapter is from Ann Marie Houghtailing. This quote is commonly seen but originally from her book. Ann Marie Houghtailing, *How I Created a Dollar Out of Thin Air* (The Houghtailing Group, 2013).

2. Atul Gawande, Personal Best: Top athletes and singers have coaches. Should you? The New Yorker, 26 September

2011. Available at https://www.newyorker.com/magazine/2011/10/03/personal-best.

3. Ibid.

4. Ibid.

5. Ibid.

6. Ibid.

7. Algiraigri AH. Ten tips for receiving feedback effectively in clinical practice. Med Educ Online. 2014 Jul 28;19:25141. This article is open access and available for free at https://www.ncbi.nlm.nih.gov/pmc/articles/PMC4116619/pdf/MEO-19-25141.pdf.

8. Table 1 is reproduced here from this open access article by Algiraigri: https://www.tandfonline.com/doi/figure/10.3402/meo.v19.25141?scroll=top&needAccess=true.

9. Sheila Heen and Douglas Stone. Finding the Coaching in Criticism. Harvard Business Review, January–February 2014. Available at https://hbr.org/2014/01/find-the-coaching-in-criticism. Of note, Sheila Heen's TEDx Talk, "How to use others' feedback to learn and grow," is outstanding. It is available at https://www.youtube.com/watch?v=FQNbaKkYk_Q.

10. Ibid.

11. The term "growth mindset" was coined by Carol Dweck in her book. Carol Dweck, *Growth Mindset: The New Psychology of Success* (New York: Ballantine Books, 2006, 2016).

12. Sheila Heen and Douglas Stone. Finding the Coaching in Criticism. Harvard Business Review, January–February 2014. Available at https://hbr.org/2014/01/find-the-coaching-in-criticism.

13. Ibid.

14. Ibid.

15. Ibid.

16. Ibid.

17. Sheila Heen and Douglas Stone, *Thanks for the Feedback: The Science and Art of Receiving Feedback Well* (New York: Penguin Books, 2015).

Chapter 14: Care Enough to Seek and Value Feedback from the Team

1. Omar N. Bradley. On Leadership. The U.S. Army War College Quarterly: Parameters. 1981;11(1):1-7.

2. Bill Taylor. True Leaders Believe Dissent Is an Obligation. Harvard Business Review, 12 January 2017. Available at https://hbr.org/2017/01/true-leaders-believe-dissent-is-an-obligation?ab=at_art_art_1x4_s03.

3. The quote is from Dr. Louis Pangaro, former Chair of Medicine at the Uniformed Services University.

4. This Colin Powell quote is found everywhere, often without a citation. I believe it is originally from his book. Colin Powell and Joseph Persico, *My American Journey* (New York: Random House, 1995).

5. Patrick Lencioni, *The Five Dysfunctions of a Team: A Leadership Fable* (San Francisco: Jossey-Bass, 2002).

Chapter 15: Care Enough to Be Humble

1. The opening quote is from Mother Teresa.

2. Humility definition taken from the online Oxford Learner's Dictionaries at https://www.oxfordlearnersdictionaries.com/us/definition/english/humility.

3. Flood-Stith C. It's Not Hard to Be Humble: The Role of Humility in Leadership. Fam Pract Manag. 2018 May/Jun;25(3):25-27.

4. Atul Gawande, "Cowboys and Pit Crews." The New Yorker, 26 May 2011. Available at https://www.newyorker.com/news/news-desk/cowboys-and-pit-crews.

5. Ibid.

6. Brené Brown has written multiple books and delivered innumerable talks on vulnerability. *Dare to Lead* is one that resonated with me. Brené Brown, *Dare to Lead: Brave Work, Tough Conversations, Whole Hearts* (New York: Random House, 2018).

7. Amy Edmondson, *The Fearless Organization: Creating Psychological Safety in the Workplace for Learning, Innovation, and Growth* (Hoboken, NJ: John Wiley & Sons, Inc, 2019), xvi.

8. Edmondson, *The Fearless Organization*, 159.

9. Ruberton PM, Huynh HP, Miller TA, Kruse E, Chancellor J, Lyubomirsky S. The relationship between physician humility, physician-patient communication, and patient health. Patient Educ Couns. 2016;99(7):1138-1145.

10. Edmondson, *The Fearless Organization*.

11. Edmondson, *The Fearless Organization*, 46.

12. Edmondson, *The Fearless Organization*, 153-183.

13. Ou, A. Y., Waldman, D. A., & Peterson, S. J. (2018). Do Humble CEOs Matter? An Examination of CEO Humility and Firm Outcomes. *Journal of Management*, 44(3), 1147–1173.

14. Ibid.

15. Ibid.

16. Brunzel, J., Ebsen, D. The Role of Humility in Chief Executive Officers: a Review. *Rev Manag Sci* 17, 1487–1532 (2023).

17. Ibid.

18. Ibid.

19. Jim Collins wrote about the importance of humility as a Level 5 Leader. Jim Collins, *Good to Great: Why Some Companies Make the Leap...and Others Don't* (New York: HarperCollins Publishers, Inc., 2001).

20. Collins, *Good to Great*, 20.

21. Ibid.

22. Collins, *Good to Great*, 21.

23. Collins, *Good to Great*, 38.

24. The survey by McKinsey & Company was published as part of an article on their website: https://www.mckinsey.com/capabilities/people-and-organizational-performance/our-insights/psychological-safety-and-the-critical-role-of-leadership-development.

25. Dr. Oxentenko mentioned Dr. Sasha Shillcutt, who is a practicing anesthesiologist, author, and speaker. She has published two books and has a consulting company focused on women in medicine called Brave Enough: https://www.becomebraveenough.com/.

26. W. Brad Johnson and David Smith, *Athena Rising: How and Why Men Should Mentor Women* (New York: Bibliomotion, Inc., 2016).

27. David Smith and Brad Johnson, *Good Guys: How Men Can Be Better Allies for Women in*

the *Workplace* (Boston: Harvard Business Review Press, 2020).

28. An interesting study that showed saying "us" and "we" improves chances of being elected in Australia. Steffens

NK, Haslam SA. Power through 'Us': Leaders' Use of We-Referencing Language Predicts Election Victory. PLoS One. 2013 Oct 23;8(10):e77952.

29. Edgar Schein, *Humble Inquiry: The Gentle Art of Asking Instead of Telling* (San Francisco: Berrett-Koehler Publishers, Inc., 2013)

Chapter 16: Care Enough to Listen

1. The quote is from Larry King. The original source is uncertain. Taken from "The Best Quotes by Larry King: 'I Never Learned Anything While I Was Talking,'" published by Newsweek, 23 January 2021. Available at https://www.newsweek.com/best-quotes-larry-king-i-never-learned-anything-while-i-was-talking-1563928.

2. D. Michael Abrashoff, *It's Your Ship: Management Techniques from the Best Damn Ship in the Navy* (New York: Grand Central Publishing, 2002, 2012), 55.

3. Ibid.

4. Ibid.

5. Abrashoff, *It's Your Ship*, 54.

6. Ibid.

7. Abrashoff, *It's Your Ship*, 55.

8. Ibid.

9. Ibid.

10. Abrashoff, *It's Your Ship*, 2.

11. W. Brad Johnson and David Smith, *Athena Rising: How and Why Men Should Mentor Women* (New York: Bibliomotion, Inc., 2016).

12. David Smith and Brad Johnson, *Good Guys: How Men Can Be Better Allies for Women in the Workplace* (Boston: Harvard Business Review Press, 2020).

13. Abrashoff, *It's Your Ship,* 54-59.

14. Amy Edmondson, *The Fearless Organization: Creating Psychological Safety in the Workplace for Learning, Innovation, and Growth* (Hoboken, NJ: John Wiley & Sons, Inc, 2019), 159.

15. The quote about listening is by Professor Deborah Tannen in the Department of Linguistics at Georgetown University.

16. Many people talk about listening to learn. Stephen Covey coined the idea about "seeking first to understand" in his book. Stephen Covey, *The 7 Habits of Highly Effective People: Powerful Lessons in Personal Change* (New York: Free Press, 1989), 235-260.

17. Dan Lyons, *STFU: The Power of Keeping Your Mouth Shut in an Endlessly Noisy World* (New York: Henry Holt and Company, 2023), 15.

18. Ibid.

19. Ibid.

20. Lyons, *STFU,* 1.

21. Liz Wiseman, *Impact Players: How to Take the Lead, Play Bigger, and Multiply Your Impact* (New York: HarperCollins Publishers), 181, 197.

22. Wiseman, *Impact Players,* 197.

23. Lyons, *STFU.*

Chapter 17: Care Enough to Delegate

1. This is one of the most read *Harvard Business Review* articles of all time and a must-read for leaders. William

Oncken and Donald Wass. "Management Time: Who's Got the Monkey?" Harvard Business Review. November–December 1999.

2. The quote by General Patton is found broadly, but the original source is unclear. This is the reference I used. Team Mighty. "11 Gen. George Patton Quotes That Show His Strategic Awesomeness." Military.com. Available at https://www.military.com/history/2021/08/05/11-general-george-patton-quotes-show-his-strategic-awesomeness.html.

3. L. David Marquet, *Turn the Ship Around! A True Story of Turning Followers into Leaders* (New York: Penguin Group, 2012).

4. Ibid.

5. Ibid.

6. Marquet, *Turn the Ship Around!*, xxiii.

7. The concept of Mission Command is outlined in Army Doctrine, ADP 6-0: Mission Command, Command and Control of Army Forces. Available at https://armypubs.army.mil/epubs/DR_pubs/DR_a/ARN34403-ADP_6-0-000-WEB-3.pdf.

8. Ibid.

9. Ibid.

10. Ibid.

11. Ibid.

12. The quote by Dr. Kasi Chu was posted on LinkedIn at https://www.linkedin.com/posts/activity-7117006983311826946-uq8x?utm_source=share&utm_medium=member_ios.

13. Ibid.

14. Jocko Willink, *Leadership Strategy and Tactics: FM-02* (New York: St. Martin's Press, 2020), 13-19 and 128-129.

15. Ronald A. Heifetz and Marty Linsky, *Leadership on the Line: Staying Alive through the Dangers of Leading* (Boston: Harvard Business Review Press), 51-74.

16. Willink, *Leadership Strategy and Tactics*, 13-19.

17. William Oncken and Donald Wass. "Management Time: Who's Got the Monkey?" Harvard Business Review. November–December 1999.

Chapter 18: Care Enough to Invest in Those You Lead: Mentoring, Coaching, and Sponsorship

1. The story by Dr. Niven was published on the CHEST website as "A Collection of Leadership Stories for Chest Clinicians." Available at https://www.chestnet. org/-/media/chesnetorg/Get-Involved/Documents/ MentoringCompilationFINAL.ashx.

2. W. Brad Johnson and David Smith, *Athena Rising: How and Why Men Should Mentor Women* (New York: Bibliomotion, Inc., 2016).

3. Laurie Baedke, *Mentor, Coach, Lead to Peak Professional Performance* (Chicago, IL: Health Administration Press, 2023), 58.

4. Baedke, *Mentor, Coach, Lead*, 56.

5. Sarah Grimstead. The Power of Reverse Mentoring: The transfer of workplace knowledge is no longer a one-way street. Fast Company, 30 November 2022. Available at https://www.fastcompany.com/90806803/ the-power-of-reverse-mentoring.

6. Atul Gawande, "Personal Best." The New Yorker, 26 September 2011. Available at https://www.newyorker.com/magazine/2011/10/03/personal-best.

7. Table used with Laurie Baedke's permission: *Mentor, Coach, Lead*, 87-88. She cited "How to Be an Effective Sponsor" by Elizabeth McDaid, published in The Council of Insurance Agents & Brokers and Leaders' Edge, available at https://www.leadersedge.com/brokerage-ops/how-to-be-an-effective-sponsor. The original work appears to have come from a 7 August 2019 *Harvard Business Review* article by Rania Anderson and David Smith, available at https://hbr.org/2019/08/what-men-can-do-to-be-better-mentors-and-sponsors-to-women.

8. The term #spentor is attributed to Dr. Julie Silver, who has been a leading researcher in inequity in awards and advancement of women in medicine. She writes and speaks broadly on the topic of women in medicine: https://www.wimedicine.org/blog/on-spentorship, accessed on 19 January 2024. Read this article for some great advice on mentoring and sponsoring. Silver J. Six Practical Strategies to Mentor and Sponsor Women in Academic Medicine. J Med Internet Res 2023;25:e47799. Available at https://www.jmir.org/2023/1/e47799/PDF.

9. Ibid.

10. The quote "what gets measured gets managed" or "what we measure matters" has often been ascribed to Peter Drucker, but when you look for sources, there are variations of what he actually said. Available at https://www.growthink.com/content/two-most-important-quotes-business.

11. Baedke, *Mentor, Coach, Lead*.

12. Sally Helgesen and Marshall Goldsmith, *How Women Rise: Break the 12 Habits Holding You Back from Your Next Raise,*

Promotion, or Job (New York: Hachette Book Group, Inc., 2018).

13. Johnson and Smith, *Athena Rising.*

Chapter 19: Care Enough to Advocate

1. The quote to begin the chapter is from Dr. Vineet Arora, MD, MAPP, MACP, who is the Dean for Medical Education at the University of Chicago Pritzker School of Medicine. Available at https://www.healio.com/news/primary-care/20230428/acp-keynote-speaker-this-is-the-way.

2. Katie McHugh, Gabriel Bosslet, Caroline Rouse, and Tracey Wilkinson. "Doctors think 'advocate' is a dirty word. But it's our ethical responsibility." Available at https://www.statnews.com/2023/06/01/caitlin-bernard-indiana-abortion-10-year-old-advocacy/.

3. Ibid.

4. Terry Gross. "A Trauma Surgeon Who Survived Gun Violence Is Taking On The NRA." Heard on Fresh Air or available at https://www.npr.org/sections/health-shots/2018/11/28/671519701/this-trauma-surgeon-survived-gun-violence-now-hes-taking-on-the-nra.

5. Saralyn Cruickshank. "Using His Story to Change the Narrative on Gun Violence." Available at https://hub.jhu.edu/2022/05/25/joseph-sakran-gun-violence-this-is-our-lane/.

6. Ibid.

7. Ibid.

8. Ibid.

9. Tracy Kidder, *Mountains Beyond Mountains: The Quest of Dr. Paul Farmer, a Man Who Would Cure the World* (Random House Trade Paperbacks, 2009).

10. Michael Useem, *Leading Up: How to Lead Your Boss So You Both Win* (New York: Crown Business, 2001).

Chapter 20: Care About Diversity, Equity, and Inclusion

1. Chelsea Hayes shared this data with me and it helped add more meaning to the story that Isaiah told me. These are not just perceptions but reality. Available at https://www.hsph.harvard.edu/news/hsph-in-the-news/blacks-whites-police-deaths-disparity/. Accessed on 13 January 2024. Original study cited in this article: Schwartz GL, Jahn JL (2020). Mapping fatal police violence across U.S. metropolitan areas: Overall rates and racial/ethnic inequities, 2013-2017. PLoS ONE 15(6): e0229686.

2. Joseph Frederick, *The Black Friend: On Being a Better White Person* (Somerville, IL: Candlewick Press, 2020).

3. Ibid.

4. Ibid.

5. Ibid.

6. Dr. Quinn Capers is a nationally recognized leader in medicine with a focus on diversity, equity, and inclusion. He is a phenomenal speaker, and you can find many of his talks online. He has published widely on bias and the issues of race in medicine. The title of his talk at Oregon Health and Science University on 10 October 2019 is "The Lack of Diversity in Medicine is a National Emergency: The Way Forward." Available at https://www.ohsu.edu/school-of-medicine/lack-diversity-medicine-national-emergency.

7. His quote is from this article: "Promoting Diversity in Medicine" by Mollie Frost. Available at https://immattersacp.org/archives/2022/07/promoting-diversity-in-medicine.htm. Accessed on 15 January 2024.

8. Isabel Wilkerson, *Caste: The Origins of Our Discontents* (New York: Random House, 2020).

9. Ibram X. Kendi, *How to Be an Antiracist* (New York: One World, 2019).

10. Heather McGhee, *The Sum of Us: What Racism Costs Everyone and How We Can Prosper Together* (New York: One World, 2021).

11. Capers Q 4th. Diversifying the Physician Workforce – From Rhetoric to Positive Action. N Engl J Med. 2023;388(10):865-867.

12. W. Brad Johnson and David Smith, *Athena Rising: How and Why Men Should Mentor Women* (New York: Bibliomotion, Inc., 2016).

13. Frederick, *The Black Friend.*

14. Kendi, *How to Be an Antiracist.*

15. Uché Blackstock, *Legacy: A Black Physician Reckons with Racism in Medicine* (New York: Viking, 2024).

16. Wilkerson, *Caste: The Origins of Our Discontents.*

Chapter 21: Care Enough to Be a Positive Force of Energy

1. The quote to begin the chapter comes from Jon Gordon's book. I definitely recommend this book, as it has tactical strategies to be a more effective leader and create a positive culture. Jon Gordon, *The Power of Positive Leadership* (Hoboken, NJ: John Wiley & Sons Inc., 2017), 128.

2. Martin Rooney, *High Ten: An Inspiring Story About Building Great Team Culture* (Hoboken, NJ: John Wiley & Sons, Inc., 2021), 235.

3.   Barbara Fredrickson, *Positivity: Discover the Upward Spiral That Will Change Your Life* (New York: Harmony Books, 2009), 8-9, 39.

4.   Fredrickson, *Positivity*, 55.

5.   Fredrickson, *Positivity*, 64.

6.   Fredrickson, *Positivity*, 55.

7.   Lyubomirsky S, King L, Diener E. The benefits of frequent positive affect: Does happiness lead to success? Psychol Bull. 2005 Nov;131(6):803-55.

8.   Fredrickson, *Positivity*, 29.

9.   Fredrickson, *Positivity*, 69.

10. I first heard about the work of Dr. Julia DiGangi on the *Lead From The Heart* podcast. Available at https://markccrowley. com/julia-digangi-harnessing-emotional-energy-for-personal-leadership-success/.

11. Julia DiGangi, *Energy Rising: The Neuroscience of Leading with Emotional Power* (Boston: Harvard Business Review Press, 2023).

12. I loved this list of ways to be kind: "100 Random Acts of Kindness Ideas" by Jennifer Taylor. Available at https:// www.signupgenius.com/groups/random-acts-of-kindness-ideas.cfm. Accessed on 19 January 2024.

13. Fredrickson, *Positivity*, 32, 120-138.

14. More information about Three Good Things can be found at https://the3goodthings.org/about.

15. Cline M, Roberts P, Werlau T, Hauser P, Smith-Miller C. Three good things: Promote work-life balance, reduce burnout, enhance reflection among newly licensed RNs. Nurs Forum. 2022;57(6):1390-1398.

16. Gold KJ, Dobson ML, Sen A. "Three Good Things" Digital Intervention Among Health Care Workers: A Randomized Controlled Trial. Ann Fam Med. 2023 May-Jun;21(3):220-226.

17. Rippstein-Leuenberger K, Mauthner O, Bryan Sexton J, Schwendimann R. A qualitative analysis of the Three Good Things intervention in healthcare workers. BMJ Open. 2017 Jun 13;7(5):e015826.

18. Fredrickson, *Positivity*, 193.

19. Jon Gordon, *The Energy Bus: 10 Rules to Fuel Your Life, Work, and Team with Positive Energy* (Hoboken, NJ: John Wiley & Sons, Inc.), 73.

20. Gordon, *The Energy Bus*, 74.

21. Gordon, *The Power of Positive Leadership*.

22. Gordon, *The Power of Positive Leadership*, 135.

23. Gordon, *The Power of Positive Leadership*, 128.

24. Gordon, *The Power of Positive Leadership*, 134.

25. The origin of the quote about never wasting a crisis is hard to pin down. It appears to have been said by many people over time with slightly different versions. Here are two references about it: Nancy Kirsner. Never Let a Good Crisis Go to Waste: 10 Golden Nuggets Mined from the Pandemic. Wholebeing Institute. Available at https://wholebeinginstitute.com/crisis-10-nuggets-pandemic/.

26. John Mutter. Opportunity From Crisis: Who Really Benefits from Post-Disaster Rebuilding Efforts. Foreign Affairs, 18 April 2016. Available at https://www.foreignaffairs.com/world/opportunity-crisis.

27. Jim Collins, *Good to Great: Why Some Companies Make the Leap...and Others Don't* (New York: HarperCollins Publishers, Inc., 2001), 83-87.

28. Collins, *Good to Great*, 83.

29. Collins, *Good to Great*, 85.

30. Ryan Holiday, *Courage Is Calling: Fortune Favors the Brave* (New York: Portfolio/Penguin, 2021), 17.

31. Souba W. Hittability: The Leader's Edge. Acad Med. 2017;92(4):444-447.

32. Ibid.

33. The positivity test created by. Dr. Barbara Fredrickson is available at https://www.positivityratio.com/single.php.

34. Gordon, *The Power of Positive Leadership*, 134.

35. Souba W. Hittability: The Leader's Edge. Acad Med. 2017;92(4):444-447.

Chapter 22: Care Enough to Say Thank You

1. Tom Rath and Donald Clifton, *How Full Is Your Bucket? Positive Strategies for Work and Life* (New York: Gallup Press 2004, 2009), 26.

2. Ben Wigert, 6 Workplace Trends Leaders Should Watch in 2024. Available at https://www.gallup.com/workplace/547283/workplace-trends-leaders-watch-2024.aspx.

3. The TED Talk by Drew Dudley is one of my all-time favorites. It is inspirational. Available at https://www.ted.com/talks/drew_dudley_everyday_leadership?language=en. Accessed on 19 January 2024.

4. Ibid.

5. Ibid.

6. Ibid.

7. I originally saw this data in *Harvard Business Review* by David DeSteno, https://hbr.org/2018/02/how-to-cultivate-gratitude-compassion-and-pride-on-your-team, and then looked at the blog post by Christine Kininmonth cited below.

8. Christine Kininmonth, Top Quotes from Marcus Buckingham's New Book "Nine Lies About Work." Growth Faculty, 11 May 2019. Available at https://www.thegrowthfaculty.com/blog/TopquotesfromMarcusBuckinghamsnewbook NineLiesAboutWork.

9. Marcus Buckingham and Ashley Goodall, *Nine Lies About Work: A Freethinking Leader's Guide to the Real World* (Boston: Harvard Business Review Press, 2019).

10. James Kouzes and Barry Posner, *Encouraging the Heart: A Leader's Guide to Rewarding and Recognizing Others* (San Francisco: Jossey-Bass, 2003), xiv, 4-5, 13.

11. Kouzes and Posner, *Encouraging the Heart*, 14.

12. Adam Grant and Francesca Gino on this *Harvard Business Review* podcast. Available at https://hbr.org/podcast/2013/11/the-big-benefits-of-a-little-t.

13. Rath and Clifton, *How Full Is Your Bucket?*, 17.

14. Shanafelt TD, Gorringe G, Menaker R, Storz KA, Reeves D, Buskirk SJ, Sloan JA, Swensen SJ. Impact of organizational leadership on physician burnout and satisfaction. Mayo Clin Proc. 2015;90(4):432-40.

15. Daniel Coyle, *The Culture Code: The Secrets of Highly Successful Groups* (New York: Bantam Books, 2018), 78.

16. Coyle, *The Culture Code*, 80.

17. Kouzes and Posner, *Encouraging the Heart*, 89-98.

18. Rath and Clifton, *How Full Is Your Bucket?*, 61-66.

19. Kim Scott, *Radical Candor: Be a Kick-Ass Boss Without Losing Your Humanity* (New York: St. Martin's Press, 2019).

20. Wambi is a company that started an app to allow people to message each other notes of gratitude. Available at https://wambi.org.

21. Ibid.

22. The quote was originally told to me by my chief resident when he attended a Junior Officer Leadership Development course held by Army Medicine. The quote was from a senior leader, Mrs. Stephanie Colón, who works in the Office of the Army Surgeon General.

23. Dr. Julie Silver has numerous papers related to awards and equity. This is one example: Silver JK, et al. Where Are the Women? The Underrepresentation of Women Physicians Among Recognition Award Recipients From Medical Specialty Societies. PM R. 2017 Aug;9(8):804-815.

Chapter 23: Care About Your Legacy

1. David Brooks, *The Road to Character* (New York: Random House, 2015), xi.

2. Joe Byerly. A Leader's Legacy: What Does Your Recruiting Poster Look Like? Available at https://fromthegreennotebook.com/2013/09/06/what-does-your-recruiting-poster-look-like/.

3. Randy Pausch, *The Last Lecture* (New York: Hyperion, 2008).

4. Clayton Christensen has given a TEDxBoston Talk, written a book, and published in *Harvard Business Review* about the importance of how you live your life. This is a powerful lesson. Available at https://hbr.org/2010/07/how-will-

you-measure-your-life   or   https://www.youtube.com/
watch?v=NW3_a9hWBo0.

Epilogue

1. The original quote by General Omar Bradley is "Leadership
   is an intangible. No weapon, no impersonal piece of
   machinery ever designed can take its place." Bradley, Omar
   N. On Leadership. The U.S. Army War College Quarterly:
   Parameters 11, 1 (1981). Available at https://press.
   armywarcollege.edu/parameters/vol11/iss1/5.